Ecologies of Theater

Also by Bonnie Marranca

Theatrewritings
American Playwrights: A Critical Survey (with Gautam Dasgupta)

As Editor

The Theatre of Images
American Dreams: The Imagination of Sam Shepard
Hudson Valley Lives
American Garden Writing

(with Gautam Dasgupta)

Interculturalism and Performance: Writings from PAJ
The Theatre of the Ridiculous
Animations: A Trilogy for Mabou Mines

PAJ BOOKS

Bonnie Marranca and Gautam Dasgupta,
Series Editors

Ecologies of Theater

Essays at the Century Turning

Bonnie Marranca

The Johns Hopkins University Press ||||||| *Baltimore and London*

© 1996 The Johns Hopkins University Press
All rights reserved. Published 1996
Printed in the United States of America on acid-free paper
05 04 03 02 01 00 99 98 97 96   5 4 3 2 1

The Johns Hopkins University Press
2715 North Charles Street
Baltimore, Maryland 21218-4319
The Johns Hopkins Press Ltd., London

Library of Congress Cataloging-in-Publication Data will be found
at the end of this book.
A catalog record for this book is available from the British Library.
ISBN 0-8018-5272-2
ISBN 0-8018-5273-0 (pbk.)

for Herbert Blau

Men follow manifold paths. Whoever traces them and com-
pares them will see wonderful figures arise; figures that seem
to belong to that great secret writing that one perceives everywhere, upon wings, egg shells, in clouds, in snow, crystals and
the structure of stones, on water when it freezes, on the inside
and the outside of mountains, of plants, of animals, of human
beings, in the constellations of the sky, on pieces of pitch or
glass when touched or rubbed, in iron filings grouped about a
magnet, and in the strange conjunctures of chance.   *Novalis*

Nothing conveys more vividly and compellingly the notion of
a destiny shaping human ends than do the great styles, whose
evolutions and transformations seem like long scars that Fate
has left, in passing, on the face of the earth.   *André Malraux*

One's mind and the earth are in a constant state of erosion, mental rivers wear away abstract banks, brain waves undermine cliffs
of thought, ideas decompose into stones of unknowing, and
conceptual crystallizations break apart into deposits of gritty
reason. Vast moving faculties occur in this geological miasma,
and they move in the most physical way. This movement seems
motionless, yet it crushes the landscape of logic under glacial
reveries. This slow flowage makes one conscious of the turbidity
of thinking. Slump, debris slides, avalanches all take place
within the cracking limits of the brain. The entire body is pulled
into the cerebral sediment, where particles and fragments make
themselves known as solid consciousness. A bleached and fractured world surrounds the artist. To organize this mess of corro-
sion into patterns, grids, and subdivisions is an esthetic process
that has scarcely been touched.   *Robert Smithson*

Contents

Acknowledgments, xi

Introduction
Species of Thought: Ecology and the Theater, xiii

Ecologies of Theater I
Gertrude Stein, John Cage, Robert Wilson:
The Play of Landscape

Presence of Mind, 3

The Mus/ecology of John Cage, 25

Robert Wilson and the Idea of the Archive:
Dramaturgy as an Ecology, 34

St. Gertrude, 49

Natural Histories of the Drama

A Cosmography of Herself:
The Autobiology of Rachel Rosenthal, 59

Despoiled Shores:
Heiner Müller's Natural History Lessons, 71

The State of Grace: Maria Irene Fornes at Sixty-two, 80

Performance World, Performance Culture, 87

All the Football Field's a Stage, 96

New England Still Life: Fornes's *Evelyn Brown*, 101

Self-portrait in Gray, 103

PAJ, A Personal History, 105

The Controversial 1985–1986 Theater Season:
A Politics of Reception, 127

Theater and the University at the End
of the Twentieth Century, 157

Private Landscapes

Garden/Theater, 181

A Hudson Valley Life, 185

**Ecologies of Theater II
Continental Drift**

The Century Turning (International Events), 197

Thinking about Interculturalism, 207

Meredith Monk's Atlas of Sound: New Opera
and the American Performance Tradition, 224

The Forest: Robert Wilson and Interculturalism, 233

The Culture of *Perestroika*, 242

Berlin Theatertreffen, 1984, 254

Isak Dinesen in Three Parts, 258

The Virtual Theater of Herbert Blau, 277

Acts of Criticism, 286

Acknowledgments

The writings and talks in this volume have appeared previously in *Performing Arts Journal*, *Kenyon Review*, *Village Voice*, *Soho Weekly News*, LIVE, *Performance Art*, and *Hudson Valley Regional Review*, and abroad in *ArtInternational* (Paris), *Dialog* (Warsaw), SPAN (New Delhi), *Theatruliu National* (Bucharest), *MASKA* (Slovenia), *Prima fila* (Florence), and *Theater Heute* (Berlin).

With the exception of a few selections that were originally published in the mid-seventies, these pieces have been written since the 1984 publication of my book *Theatrewritings*. The date at the end of each selection indicates its year of publication. The section entitled "Private Landscapes" features the prefaces to two books that in the last decade I edited and introduced with extensive literary, historical, and biographical essays, *American Garden Writing* (PAJ Publications, 1988; Penguin Books, 1989) and *Hudson Valley Lives* (Overlook Press, 1991). I include them here because they are conceptually linked to my writings on theater and culture and have been essential in contributing to the development of my thinking about ecology.

Over the years I have enjoyed the friendship and conversation of many friends whom I would like to thank for their exchange of ideas and support of my writing: Herbert Blau, Mac Wellman, Frederick Turner, Marc Robinson, Maria Irene Fornes, Carolee Schneemann, Andrzej Wirth, Antonio Attisani, Ulla Ryum, Hanne Jorna, Johannes Birringer, Alessandro Fersen, Daryl Chin, Larry Qualls, Hanne Tierney, Shelley Berc, Frantisek Deak, James Flannery, Philip Blumberg,

Michal Kobialka, Stanley Kauffmann, and Gregory Whitehead. I am especially grateful to my husband, Gautam Dasgupta, my constant companion in intellectual life.

The organization of this volume and some of the recent writing took shape at the Rockefeller Study and Conference Center in Bellagio, Italy, on Lake Como, where I was fortunate to be in residence in August–September 1994. It is impossible to envision a more glorious world in which to contemplate the ecologies of art and landscape.

Introduction

Species of Thought

Ecology and the Theater

IIIIIIII   I have always wondered what Gertrude Stein meant when she
called a play a landscape. The marvel of her image revealed itself decade by decade as I observed how essential landscape, field, and geography are in the conceptual vocabulary of American performance and
the extent to which the idea of nature (or the real) was transposed into a
description of performance space by avant-garde artists. That this space
would also be a spiritual space accounts for the emphasis on mind and
perception in American performance, whose subject has always been
vision, or revelation. In this sense, the American avant-garde is tied historically to the spiritual dimension of European modernism in the beginnings of abstraction at the turn of the century and its early decades,
and to Buddhism in the postwar years. It was important to inquire into
the relationship of mind, space, and spirit as a formal issue before I
could find the way to an ecology.

As an approach to writing about theater, the notion of ecology has
been in my thoughts for a very long time, and though it surfaced in
earlier work, the decisive shift in this direction was prompted by my research for the two nontheater books I completed in recent years, *American Garden Writing* (1988) and *Hudson Valley Lives* (1991), which drew
upon natural and cultural histories of the last several centuries. Two important themes emerged in these collections, whose prefaces are published here as "Private Landscapes," to serve as a point of departure for
the larger issues explored in *Ecologies of Theater*: the recognition of an

ecosystem as part of a cultural system and of natural history as inseparable from the history of the world.

Reading the narratives of cultures and landscapes, I began to ask
whether there wasn't a more worldly way of experiencing theater. How
do geography and climate influence a work? What are the ways in
which plant and animal life, animate and inanimate entities, the natural and the artificial interact? How do biology and the body determine
the human drama? Frequent travels abroad influenced this line of inquiry as I followed the expression of culture in different kinds of landscapes, the quality of air and light and water and wind; the design of
doors, windows, parks, and textures of stone and wood. What effect do
they have on the performing body, the perception of objects in space?
And what of the diverse species of birds and plants and the spectacle of
contemporary life in the new ecologies of cities? *Ecologies of Theater* is
the beginning of my search for a "theaterwriting" more conscious of the
magnitude of performance worlds where landscape, myth, and cultural
memory create and bear witness to all histories of life.

The word *ecology*, which derives from the Greek *oikos*, meaning
"home" or "place to live," was used by the nineteenth-century German
zoologist Ernst Haeckel to describe the relationship of organisms to
their organic and inorganic environment. I have enlarged this definition
to contemplate the world of a work as an environment linked to a cultural (aesthetic) system. Texts themselves are always alive in the world,
finding new life in the way they are absorbed into the works of artists
through the ages and in the subjectivity of each reader/spectator. A text,
then, can be considered as an organism, and a collective of texts, images,
or sounds an ecosystem. The interaction of this ecosystem and its cultural system elaborates an ethics of performance I want to acknowledge.
Moreover, there is a second frame at work in this process: the created
work as an ecosystem/cultural system that includes its manner of production, reception, and funding, as well as institutions and interacting
artistic communities. Another kind of ecology might analyze the flow
of energy and production between these systems as a mode of cultural
politics. The essays "*PAJ*, A Personal History" and "Theater and the University at the End of the Twentieth Century" move in that direction.

But this volume is not concerned with sociological analysis or political economies. Nor does it offer a method or paradigm or unified theory

of theater. I write against the hazy pollution of theory that threatens increasingly to make art an endangered species in our time. I am more sympathetic to a lyrical, philosophical, and experimental approach to art practice and the writing about it. Here I am simply following traces of my current thinking in works of art that I admire. Although not every essay in this book directly takes up the ecology question, which only came to the foreground of my work in recent years, my intention is to let this theme run through and around the writings on art and artists, on important events and issues, on publishing, editing, writing, and teaching, to form its own currents of thought. In their attention to the ecology of the image, the essays printed here are an extension of my early work in *The Theatre of Images* (1977), but now turned to a history of imagery in the theater, and contemporary theater iconography. From time to time I have experimented with what I think of as an "image essay," commentary based on photographs, an example of which is the selection titled "*The Forest*: Robert Wilson and Interculturalism."

"Ecologies of theater" became a kind of trope around which to organize thoughts of a speculative nature, as I note in "Acts of Criticism." It offered a conceptual means to illuminate the utopian, visionary strain in late-twentieth-century performance, embodied in the works of Robert Wilson, Meredith Monk, and Rachel Rosenthal, as well as a frame of reference for complex political imagery, especially in Heiner Müller's merging of the human figure and the landscape. Finally, it evoked alternative ways of thinking about the making of texts and the commentary on them, reflected in my characterization of Wilson's dramaturgy as an ecology and Rosenthal's performance as autobiology.

The ecology perspective I propose is not that of traditional literary studies organized primarily around the rhetoric of writings on nature or metamorphosis, or genres, like the eclogue and pastoral, or the nature/culture argument and existential crisis. Such points of departure are anthropocentric. Nor do I have any affinity for the apocalyptic end-of-nature school of thought or the frequently anti-technology, anti-modern aspects of the "deep ecology" philosophy of New Age thinking. Furthermore, I am opposed to turning this commentary into a branch of cultural studies, with all its political set pieces on the "social construction" of the individual. What I have looked to for inspiration is the philosophical tradition that began early in the century with Kandinsky's passionate writings on art, mind, and spirit and continues into our own time in the exquisite though more secular thought of John Cage. My linkage of ecology and aesthetics in the search for newer and deeper kinds of knowledge outlines the biocentric worldview in certain works, a nonhierarchical embrace of the multiplicity of species and languages in a work, in the world, that can address the issue of rights in nonsentient beings—provocatively, sounds in the case of Cage, whose mus/ecology I celebrate here.

From the point of view both of theater and of science, my orientation is non-Aristotelian, as are the works I choose to write about. They do not imitate nature but create alternative worlds in which the different species lead autonomous lives, and there is writing to be read in rocks and trees and mountains and sand. What I am drawn to most are the concepts of field, space, landscape, especially as they contribute to a theatrical and critical vocabulary that opens itself up to an ethical and spiritual vision.

Attention to dramatic field, landscape, space, and then, specifically, to the ecological theme begins in my essays of the early eighties, such as "Alphabetical Shepard," "The Real Life of Maria Irene Fornes," "Nuclear Theater," and, more expansively, in "Reading Chekhov," which includes a section entitled "Ecologies of Theater." I wrote about Chekhov as a gardener, citing his attachment to the earth and to the future as an aspect of his dramatic and metaphysical ethos. His *Uncle Vanya* contrasts the subtle difference in the words *landscape* and *scenery* and elsewhere links the rights of nature and the rights of women. Later Chekhov would refer to *The Seagull* as "four acts and a landscape." Any modern ecology must take into account his breakthrough in conceiving dramatic space as landscape and bringing a new sense of nature into the drama. In a more developed symbolist dramaturgy, his contemporary Maeterlinck pushed theater further in this direction by uncovering the semantic powers of space. Symbolist aesthetics ushered in the new world of theater that transformed setting into performance space, and Maeterlinck was fully to bring together natural history and human history as the subject of drama.

Moving from modern drama to contemporary avant-garde performance, more than three decades ago Allan Kaprow, clarifying his own happenings and other performance activities, defined the new performance spaces as "environments," an idea that Richard Schechner extended into a theory of environmental theater, whose attention to levels of feedback offered a view of what today might be considered community ecology. This direction in performance thinking signaled an essential recognition of the organic, living relationship between the body and its experience of space or environment, moving performance from the confines of a theater into the world. In the fifties and sixties, many different theaters and artists reconceived the interaction of performance space and spectator, among them The Living Theatre, Peter Brook, The Polish Theatre Laboratory, Théâtre du Soleil, The Bread and Puppet Theatre, Anna Halprin, Meredith Monk, and The Performance Group. Similarly, in the visual arts, site-specific pieces and installations (the direct descendant of happenings), whose subject is the sense of place of a work, reflect an evolving awareness of ecology, space, and spectatorship. History has shown that each new vision of art reconfigures human life in the natural world, and surely any elucidation of a theater ecology begins in the understanding of performance space.

I refer to an ecology of theater rather than, say, an ecology of performance because I wish to preserve the historical concept of *theatrum mundi*, which has always linked the theatrical world, the world of society, and the natural world in the history of ideas. The feeling that all the world's a stage is a familiar one, and performance in everyday life a contemporary way of being in the world, but scholars once wrote of the theater of plants and the theater of insects. I prefer to work toward situating my discoveries within the classical perspective, which encompasses philosophy, history, geography, aesthetics, religion, economy, and myth in its discourse on human affairs and artifacts, even though in contemporary thought the ecocentric worldview challenges the anthropocentrism of humanism.

Parts of this essay were conceived at the Rockefeller Study and Conference Center in Bellagio, Italy, which rests on the promontory where Pliny the Younger is thought to have built his villa. Already in the second century he envisioned the ecology of place in the Roman manner of unifying culture and horticulture. His adoptive father, the elder Pliny, gave the world the magnificent *Natural History* before becoming asphyxiated by the fumes of Vesuvius, which turned so many bodies into landscapes. No matter that much of its science is no longer tenable. There is Calvino's imaginative writing through Pliny to remind us moderns of what is noble in his great effort to know all that there was in the world he made his home. If now at the end of the twentieth century many assumptions of classical science have been disproved, other ways of comprehending the physical world can still join contemporary beliefs to the classical heritage. Science and visionary art have always led parallel lives at the frontiers of human consciousness.

In terms of a psychology that any attention to ecology entails, I have found highly evocative the writings of Gregory Bateson, who considered the nature of psychic integration in art within the context of an "ecology of mind." The mental processes responsible for the organization of ideas in such an ecology he regarded as *aesthetic sensibility*, and the desire for consolidation in art as a quest for grace. The visual artist Robert Smithson held a similar view of aesthetic process working through the sedimentations of the mind, and in theater the meditations of Richard Foreman and Herbert Blau map a labyrinthine ontological territory. It is this valiant search by artists, their inner struggle with faith, process, and values, or the spiritual dimension of art as a realm of absolute thought and primacy of vision, that engages me now. Here again Bateson proves a valuable guide in situating epistemology as a branch of natural history, thus joining mind and ecology. So, for example, an essay that identifies "spiritual style" in the learning plays of Maria Irene Fornes, though it may not address ecology by name, refers to it by highlighting the expression of grace in her work and the quality of her life in the theater in relation to its institutions. From another perspective, the legacy of Joseph Beuys points the way to linking conceptual art, ecology, and philosophy in a framework that draws its strength from combining rigorous social research and spiritual awareness.

In the last decade, the materialist turn in criticism and art-making and the hyperpoliticization of culture have failed to acknowledge the extraordinary range of human subjectivity, especially the spiritual energy that constitutes an individual life and its creative acts. The vocabulary of new schools of criticism disregards qualities of imagination, intuition, the spirit, the poetic self—everything that cannot be explained by social and political factuality. Likewise, the debased rhetoric of certain conservative factions, in its anti-modernism mingled with the shallow talk of religious values, has also failed to bring any organizing intelligence to issues of a spiritual and philosophical nature, which now need desperately to be articulated in public discourse. The new philistinism, of whatever political inclination, has distorted the role of art in a life, in a society, to suit its utilitarian goals. Engagement with art for its own intrinsic sensual value and creation of other worlds has once again become taboo.

Even as we approach the second millennium, the words to render the world of the spirit and the desire for its expression in life and art remain elusive and imprecise, making extraordinary demands on contemporary language, thought, and emotion. But it is of the utmost importance to create a climate in which this theme and impulse can return in a progressive, radical inquiry to art and criticism, where it has always had a place, either as religious expression or as the secularization of the spiritual. In its very essence, the subject of ecology embraces spiritual and ethical concerns as it organizes the union of subjectivity and belief systems in artistic forms.

The history of modernism and the avant-garde is rooted in this striving toward the transformation of human thought and society that led artists to reimagine the possibilities of art, opening it up to abstraction, conceptual performance and revolutionary perceptions of time and space, new experiments in sound and language, and the unceasing pursuit of knowledge. Modernism and all that it embraces in its complexity, range of feeling and form, and restless desire for experience still shapes the artistic-political-cultural vocabulary of contemporary discussion. The writings collected here were conceived with this modernist heritage in mind, as they discover at the century turning its many forms, strategies, and spiritual ideals, which appear transvalued in contemporary settings to herald the directions of future artistic practice. The ecstatic union of art and science and spirit will create the art of the new century, just as it did one hundred years ago, and what we can discern already are the traces of a new vision of art, which is always a new ecology.

(1995)

Ecologies of Theater I

Gertrude Stein,
John Cage,
Robert Wilson:
The Play of Landscape

Presence of Mind

A few years ago, in the newly redesigned Bryant Park, adjacent to the New York Public Library in midtown Manhattan, a statue of Gertrude Stein was set in place. The *New York Times* account of the event, not without a humorous aside, noted that except for the monument to St. Joan of Arc farther uptown at Riverside Park this was the only sculpture of a woman in a New York City park, not counting Alice in Wonderland and Mother Goose. The bronze statue of Stein, seated in one of her long skirts, probably brown corduroy, legs wide apart, shoulders slightly hunched over, was made in 1923 by her friend Jo Davidson, who admitted that he had made her into a modern Buddha. Perhaps such female companions are not so extraordinary for a woman who loved saints and, well, lived in a kind of wonderland with her own Alice. Besides, as the "Mother Goose of Montparnasse," she never hesitated to sprinkle a few nursery rhymes into her writing.

If city parks tend to be peopled with statues of the great men of history, literary biographies are filled with the great men of letters. Still, when one looks out over the vast field of twentieth-century literature, Gertrude Stein inhabits a landscape all her own. Provocation and confidence claim equal measure in her declaration that "the most serious thinking about writing in the twentieth century has been done by a woman." Herself.

Gertrude Stein had come to Paris to live in the early years of the new century and never stopped writing, completing her masterwork of almost one thousand pages, *The Making of Americans*, by 1911, though it

3

was not published until the mid-twenties. By that time she had already written *Three Lives*, *Tender Buttons*, and *A Long Gay Book*, and many, many portraits, plays, and stories. Since major publishers for the work were in short supply, and she suffered frequent rejection throughout her career, Stein published several books in her own Plain Edition, set up with proceeds from her sale of Picasso's *Girl with a Fan*, and elsewhere when she could find the support in independent literary magazines and presses in America, England, and France.

It was in 1913, in Mallorca, where Stein and her beloved Alice B. Toklas would later return to escape World War I, that she began to write plays. *What Happened* was the first of a long list that would number perhaps eighty (the exact figure is yet to be determined) by the time she completed *The Mother of Us All* in 1946, the year she died. Only a small selection of her plays have ever been produced, and Stein had to wait twenty years before she saw one of them on the stage, the now legendary production of *Four Saints in Three Acts*. She was sixty years old.

Stein's first triumph in the theater coincided with her return to America in 1934 after an absence of three decades. By now she was a well-known figure in progressive artistic and intellectual circles, her reputation enhanced by the best-selling *Autobiography of Alice B. Toklas*, published in America the year before her arrival. *Four Saints* had its premiere at the Wadsworth Athenaeum in Hartford, Connecticut, before moving on to Broadway and then Chicago, where she saw it. She and Toklas were met at the dock by scores of reporters who had come to cover the event for the New York dailies. The famous Gimbel's department store featured a window display of "Four Suits in Two Acts." Stein herself marveled that cab drivers and shopkeepers recognized her on the street. The *New Yorker*, among several newspapers and magazines, featured a cartoon of the opera, and the New York Times building announced "Gertrude Stein has arrived in New York" in revolving lights.

Four Saints, which was to become a starting point for the American art theater tradition, brought together the ingenuity of Virgil Thomson, who composed the music, the producer-director John Houseman, Stein's painter friend Florine Stettheimer, who designed the sets and costumes, and the young choreographer Frederick Ashton. Thomson chose an all-black cast to sing the opera, for which Maurice Grosser had written a libretto based on the Stein original. Stark Young, one of

America's most sensitive theater critics, was moved to write of the production: "But only now and then in the theatre can we hope for something of the quality of a thing in nature (a tree, a melon, a sheet of water, a flight of birds). The point in such a case is not that it is beautiful or not beautiful, but that it lives in itself."

In her joyful miracle play Stein brings together the writer's life and the saintly life as illuminated texts, her own and St. Therese of Avila's, synchronizing modern Paris and baroque Spain. For Stein genius is a form of sainthood, and the contemplative or spiritual life of writer and saint a state of grace. In a fabulous subversion of plot *Four Saints* incorporates the process of writing as part of the opera itself, moving between the documentation of Stein's attempt to shape the work and the composition that is the result of that process. Real time is integrated into dramatic time. "How many saints are there in it," St. Therese asks. More and more saints are added, until there are over two dozen. "A great many saints can sit around with one standing." Stein continually interrupts the narrative with new ideas for the play on weather, birds, flowers, objects, or stage directions. As the "plot" of a play unfolds, it becomes clear that the plot of a garden, St. Therese's *hortus conclusus*, is also being elaborated. The allegorical *Four Saints* works as a composition in both the literary and the horticultural sense, revealing a formal garden conceived as a plan of knowledge. This work remains Stein's great achievement of the play as landscape.

When one considers *Four Saints*, or indeed any one of Stein's plays, alongside the more conventional successes of the period, the originality of her dramaturgy is breathtaking. Stein had no antecedents in the English language, and even within the context of the European avant-garde between the wars her dramatic style remained unique. The 1933–34 New York theater season featured productions by the Theatre Union, Theatre Guild, and Group Theatre, in addition to the standard Broadway fare, such as O'Neill's *Ah, Wilderness!*, Maxwell Anderson's *Mary of Scotland*, Sidney Howard's *Dodsworth*, and Sidney Kingsley's *Men in White*, which won the Pulitzer prize. There were also several Gilbert and Sullivan operettas, the Kern-Harback musical *Roberta*, and plays by Ibsen and O'Casey. The following season two important dramas opened: *Waiting for Lefty*, by Clifford Odets, and *The Children's Hour*, Lillian Hellman's debut in the theater. The serious dramatists on this list constituted (and still do) what was considered the "modern theater" of the day. Stein has never fit comfortably into American theater history, and even today her presence in the university theater curriculum, much less on the country's stages, is more the exception than the rule.

As early as her first play, *What Happened*, Stein had decided that a play didn't have to tell a story. What happened was the theater experience itself. In other words, the creation of an experience was more important than the representation of an event. Stein had already eliminated nouns in *Tender Buttons*, deciding that she could make a portrait of an object without naming it. Around the same time in the visual arts, Marcel Duchamp gave up conventional painting to create art that was more conceptual. Both artistic giants of this century were to challenge the habits of the eye and mind and to frustrate memory—in Duchamp's understanding, "to reach the impossibility of transferring from one like object to another the memory imprint." If for Duchamp it was the viewer who completed the work, Stein shifted attention from the text to the reader (or spectator). In every sense, the perceiving intelligence took precedence over the art object, whose status as an autonomous, self-contained totality was diminished. The observer and the art object were not separate but interdependent, making art and life indistinguishable. In this way, both artists welcomed the "ready-made," the everyday, into their works, becoming part of the century-long avant-garde search for the real. Ironically, the rose figures in both artists' statements of identity: for Stein, her rose that is a rose, and for Duchamp, his Rose Selavy. Stein's virtual theater was an attempt to eliminate anecdote in order to conceive a drama that placed supreme value on the experience of the mind, and therefore presence, or, in her sense, the continuous present. She was always more interested in existence than in events. From the start, then, Stein and Duchamp recognized the significance of audience in the modern art experience, and now at the end of the century it is even more apparent how strongly modernity and spectatorship are linked in our era.

In the same period, Stein began to define her notion of the play as a landscape in a radically original book of nature trope. This spatial conception of dramaturgy elaborates the new, modern sense of a dramatic field as performance space, with its multiple and simultaneous centers of focus and activity, replacing the conventional nineteenth-century time-bound, fixed setting of the drama. The effect is a kind of conceptual mapping in which the activity of thought itself creates an experience. A more expressive understanding of this idea is the Roman sense of the mind as a field, that is, site of cultivation. Now part of the common vocabulary of contemporary practice, the concept of performance space, which opposes the character demands and causality of setting, really begins with her theater. Another way to clarify this difference is to distinguish between macro-space and micro-space. Thornton Wilder, Stein's friend and admirer who wrote more than one preface to her works, also understood, albeit less expansively, what experimenting with performance space could mean to theatrical vision, as his own plays demonstrate. Maeterlinck had been moving drama in this direction, breaking down conflict-based action in favor of a more static, repetitive structure founded on sense perception. Chekhov, who brought a new quality of light into drama, made early, tentative steps toward a pictorial, more open theatrical space, especially with *The Seagull*, which he described as "four acts and a landscape." It is tempting to speculate that the special interest Stein, Maeterlinck, and Chekhov took in the natural world influenced their new understanding of space in the theater, leading to contemporary conceptions of landscape and performance space. Any attempt to articulate a modern ecology of theater, which necessarily begins with the study of space, must surely explore their work as a starting point.

In her 1934 essay "Plays," which she wrote before seeing *Four Saints* staged, Stein attempted to explain what she meant by considering a play a landscape. "In *Four Saints* I made the Saints the landscape. All the saints that I made and I made a number of them because after all a great many pieces of things are in a landscape all these saints together made my landscape. . . . A landscape does not move nothing really moves in a landscape but things are there, and I put into my landscape the things that were there." A landscape is made up of things and people to be viewed in relation to each other. It doesn't have to come to you; you must discover for yourself what is there. This pictorial composition replaces dramatic action, emphasizing frontality and the frame, flatness and absence of perspective. The play is just there. It has no center. Whatever you find in it depends on your own way of looking. Similarly, if you observe a view outdoors, the landscape seems stationary, yet life or inanimate objects are moving inside the part of it your eyes frame. Little by little you see and hear more, until everything reveals an expressive quality. This scene, like Stein's landscape, makes itself known to you according to your individual powers of perception: you complete the view.

Stein was not concerned with creating a drama, but an image. In her world, seeing has nothing to do with remembering, which is why she wanted to negate memory and intensify the present, continuous sense of becoming in space. This affirmation of space and ontological process underlies the phenomenological thinking Stein brought into the theater, with its emphasis on observation and description, and the perception of an activity rather than its definition. She instinctively knew that modernity had to do with looking. Likewise, Stein was impressed by the cinema's ability to generate rapidly changing images that made it difficult to remember previous ones, and she liked to play with the idea of photographs as frames and suggestive sights that also confounded the past and present lives of images.

"Plays," one of the most remarkable essays written by an American playwright, though little-known, takes as its subject audience perception of theatrical experience. Here Stein considers the relation of sight and sound to emotion and time, rather than story and action. She refuses the classical ideals of catharsis and *communitas*, posing instead a non-Aristotelian drama that proceeds as a philosophical inquiry into mind, perception, and being-in-the-theater. How does one see and hear, do they affect each other, and what is the role of memory in representation? What has time to do with knowing? She situated the problem of reception at the center of her investigation: how does textual knowledge differ from performance knowledge. Like her mentor, William James, who was her teacher at Radcliffe College in the 1890s, Stein understood consciousness as a rhythm, the constant process of change. She had a similar probing, empirical style when it came to questions of human thought, as if to corroborate James's contention that "the mind is at every stage a theatre of simultaneous possibilities."

Stein never stopped asking questions of dramatic form, and virtually every one of her plays poses them in a different way. Even the text on the printed page announces itself as a unique spatial composition, each play evolving another arrangement of words and sentences and sounds. She loved series of words and the fragment, preferring parts to the whole (it made the modern sensibility) and, perhaps mindful of her reputation, explained that repetition was actually insistence. Her advice in *Tender Buttons*, to "act so that there is no use in a centre," applies equally to her plays. Between the start of her interest in the theater and the premiere of *Four Saints*, she wrote plays that consist of lists, objects, letters, sentences, and aphorisms. Their characters include cities, circles, religions, mountains. Acts or scenes could speak, and often there are many of them in the plays, just as in her stories Stein made fun of the more traditional literary propensity for long tomes of many chapters and volumes. Sometimes an interlude, a narrative, a nursery rhyme would drift into a play, perhaps lily of the valley, or a bird. Then there are the Stein friends who appear as characters, at times alongside historical, political, and literary figures or saints. In one sense, a grand theme of her work and life is making acquaintance. Not knowing who the people in the plays are only makes them more charming and their tales no less beguiling than the stories of strangers. An extraordinary sense of good humor and playfulness comes through the work, showing just how much Stein loved to experiment with dramatic form. It isn't the meaning that counts, but what happens and how.

Anyone or anything can make a play. *Photograph* is simply the construction of an image. *A Play Called Not and Now*, made up entirely of stage directions, has characters who all look like famous personalities. *Short Sentences* is precisely that. In *Dr. Faustus Lights the Lights* narrative passages alternate with dialogue, a ballet of lights, and a singing dog. A complicated play such as *Listen to Me* unfolds like a detective story, one of Stein's favorite genres. Characters seem to get lost in the play and wonder how many acts, or characters, it actually has. "I feel I know now what a play is there are many kinds of them," she teases in *Byron A Play*, which is a play about writing plays. Stein always rearranged the elements of dramatic structure and laughed at the idea of acts, scenes, chapters, pages, and volumes, which she spread throughout her plays, frequently disregarding numerical sequence and breaking any linear flow by moving from the exaggerated buildup of some scenes to the brevity of others or to the constant interruption of the curtain. She loved to frame events and used photographs, doorways, windows, curtains, words, portraits, and interludes as framing devices. Who would have guessed that silence is windowful. Stein was obsessed with trying to contain an image or an activity within a frame or stage picture. What you see is what you know, sight is insight. The lessons she learned from painting grounded all her literary studies, organizing her work in the forms of portrait, still life, and landscape. Like her contemporary Brecht, Stein created a dramaturgy that would bracket consciousness, but if his aims were pedagogical and political, hers were experiential and formal.

Within her frame Stein played constantly with the idea of the authorial voice, the author's intention, and authority. Her plays demolish arguments about the correct way to do a play, because the relations among author, text, reader, and spectator are confounded by the structures of the works. More often than not it is unclear who is saying what, what is a stage direction, what a speech, and who or what a character. Perhaps the water faucet in the early *Turkey and Bones and Eating* is a character and not part of a stage direction. Who can know? Usually there is only a voice or voices in a work. But whose? Are they male or female, animate or inanimate, and does it matter? Early in the century, Stein rethought the dynamics of voice/text, of reading/staging. Two very different kinds of modernists, both English-language writers who came to live in Paris, Stein and Beckett have been the dramatists most concerned with voice in this century, in part due to their philosophical meditation on the question of ontology.

One of Stein's great dramaturgical innovations was to incorporate aspects of daily life around her into the actual writing process, in this way bringing together documentary time and dramatic time and introducing a new narrative approach to autobiography and the personal in the theater. Remarkably, she managed to make domestic space the scene of avant-garde writing, and bourgeois comfort seem bohemian. Stein's texts were always open to the world in which everything was experienced as continuous delight. Any activity, if it occurred at home in the city of Paris or at Bilignin in the Rhône country, whether a birthday party, a walk in the garden, looking in shop windows, watching a cow in a meadow, or eating dinner with friends, anything could find itself a part of a play. Pansies, roses, dogs, butterscotch ice-box cookies were there too, and bird song mingled with conversation, lamplight with the moon. In *The Autobiography of Alice B. Toklas* Stein confides: "She was much influenced by the sound of the streets and the movement of the automobiles. She also liked then to set a sentence for herself as a sort of tuning fork and metronome and then write to that time and tune." It was essential to create the perfect spatial configuration of a sentence, the rhythm of anyone's personality.

Stein viewed all aspects of writing as natural phenomena, things existing in themselves, the time in and the time of a composition. She absorbed everything around her and turned it into writing. After her trip to America she observed, in *Narration*, that "anybody is as their land and air is. Anybody is as the sky is low or high, the air heavy or clear, anybody is as there is wind or no wind there." That sense of living in writing and writing living is what gives her work its organic quality. Earlier in the century John Dewey described this coming together of art and experience as the natural history of form, though for Stein it could just as well be the natural history of writing. The world of Stein's words is biocentric, encompassing with equanimity the lives of all species in a continuous present of boundless space and time. She always tried to find the exact word for the air and sky and light and people and to describe precisely their climate of existence. Her plays are site-specific, she herself a site-seer.

In her nonhierarchical approach Stein rescued the commonplace as subject matter. Sherwood Anderson, who wrote the introduction to her *Geography and Plays*, instinctively understood her accomplishment, which he praised in this marvelous passage in the book: "For me the work of Gertrude Stein consists in a rebuilding, an entire new recasting of life, in the city of words. Here is one artist who has been able to accept ridicule, who has even forgone the privilege of writing the great American novel, uplifting our English speaking stage, and wearing the bays of the great poets, to go live among the little housekeeping words, the swaggering bullying street-corner words the honest working, money saving words, and all the other forgotten and neglected citizens of the sacred and half forgotten city."

Stein gave herself an extraordinary amount of freedom to experiment in dramatic form, even if one considers the number and quality of theatrical works produced around her. On the European continent, especially in the period between the two world wars, when Stein wrote the vast majority of her plays, in addition to the volumes of poetry, portraits, fiction, memoirs, and essays, her playwright contemporaries included Maeterlinck, Pirandello, Brecht, Lorca, Witkiewicz, Giraudoux, and Kaiser; and in Great Britain, Shaw, O'Casey, and Yeats. The more aggressively avant-garde poet-playwrights of Europe and the Soviet Union, namely, Marinetti, Mayakovsky, Tzara, Khlebnikov, Apollinaire, Schwitters, Breton, and Aragon, were revolutionizing the word and the image. Isadora Duncan, Nijinsky, and Mary Wigman were imagining modern dance, and Cocteau, Picasso, and Satie, a new artistic theater. If elsewhere in France Artaud declared, "No More Masterpieces," Stein, who sometimes referred to them as "mater-pieces," was asking, what are they and why are there so few of them. By 1920 she had witnessed three of the most famous artistic events of the early twentieth century: Henri Rousseau's notorious banquet, the premiere of Stravinsky's *Rite of Spring*, and the staging of *Parade*.

In Paris the air was filled with the talk and art of cubism, futurism, dadaism, surrealism, and the last vestiges of symbolism. It would be a disservice to Stein not to read her in the context of these literary and visual styles, though cubism is the only one she acknowledged as an influence on her work. Ultimately, her own writing had a longer list of words-in-freedom than the futurists' accomplishments, and just as their leader Marinetti's work had symbolist roots, Stein too wondered what made a word a word. Was it made by the meaning of the word or the word itself. If you looked at something, did you see sound, and how did image and sound relate? Though she always preferred facts to symbols, Stein pursued in radical directions the symbolist interest in the relationship of words and sounds and space, along with the disinterest in naming, which led to abstract art. She extended much further the significance of the poetic voice and the polyvocality of the symbolist aesthetic, creating more languages of the stage, more voices, than the symbolists ever dreamed. The drama of perception, the drama of the individual mind, and the self-dramatizing characters of symbolism, as they begin to create the avant-garde and the idea of conceptual performance, are elaborated in Stein as the beginnings of performance art in this century. And here too is the discovery of the compositional field that would later define performance space. Generous in recognizing Stein's central place among the makers of modern literature and its important movements, more than sixty years ago the critic Edmund Wilson celebrated her accomplishment in "registering the vibration of a psychological country like some human seismograph whose charts we haven't the training to read."

If some aspects of symbolist and futurist literary pursuits can be traced in Stein's work, she was never a member of any movement. They were simply a part of the intellectual milieu of her time, particularly the infatuation with the senses and individual response. Her writings were not printed in the infamous avant-garde journals and magazines of the day. And even though she counted friends among the dada and surrealist poets and painters, she was not one of them. She worshipped rational thought and the mind and went out of her way to distance herself from any connection to automatic writing. Consciousness was her theme, not the unconscious. Their leftist politics, defiant gestures, and attraction to deformation and dream states, especially their pornographic interests, did not attract her. Nor did she frequent their cafes. She preferred the tranquility and routine of bourgeois life.

The most open minds of the age came to Paris, from numerous European countries, America, Great Britain, South America, and Russia, to discover, perhaps like Stein, that it wasn't what Paris gave you but what it didn't take away. They had all gone there to create the twentieth century or see what it looked like from the Eiffel Tower. Many of them visited 27 rue de Fleurus, where she lived, surrounded by good food and sturdy furniture and the paintings of Cézanne and Picasso, whose broken lines and shifting planes she would follow into her own writing. Years later, after she had been to America and first flown in an airplane, in a moment of deep reflection Stein observed:

> When I was in America I for the first time travelled pretty much all the time in an airplane and when I looked at the earth I saw all the lines of cubism made at a time when not any painter had ever gone up in an airplane. I saw there on the earth the mingling lines of Picasso, coming and going, developing and destroying themselves. I saw the simple solutions of Braque, I saw the wandering lines of Masson, yes I saw and once more I knew that a creator is contemporary, he understands what is contemporary when the contemporaries do not yet know it, but he is contemporary and as the twentieth century is a century which sees the earth as no one has ever seen it, the earth has a splendor that it never has had.

Thinking of her own sense of contemporaneity, she decided, "It made it right that I had always been with cubism and everything that followed after."

Still, Stein was always a different kind of modernist. She did not turn against the mind or set in conflict mind and body. Her writing is so sexual, her relationship with Toklas so often quoted and sexually coded, if ever there was a writer for whom textuality is sexuality, it is Stein. But her writing is sexual, not sensual, for it revels in declaration, not desire. In more ways than one her life is an example of the continual search for pleasure: of the text, of the word, of the body, of the world. Stein's body of work, and truly it is that, is a virtual catalogue of pleasures, enjoying a playful, celebratory lesbian erotics that is a marvel of formal invention.

Stein did not oppose nature and culture or reject the idea of civilization to exalt the primitive. She was not given to despair or pessimism or nihilism, nor did she search for mystery or transcendence. She manifested no real anxiety of the age or psychological malaise. Unlike many of her contemporaries, she was interested in the world more as paradise than as wasteland, in the miraculous, not the tragic. Unusually for her time and milieu, she was absorbed in the study of emotion and beauty and intuition in artistic experience. Stein represented, in her way, a heroic modernism that was still bound to Enlightenment values and even more so to an American optimism. That she loved the things of the world gave her work a special bliss and abundant sweep. In a Whitmanesque way she explored the tension of the self as a world and the self in the world. Stein had Whitman's expansive breath, which accounts for the primacy of the voice in her work, carrying his legacy of the human voice, the feeling of speech as song, into the theater.

There was much of the nineteenth century in Stein, something of the monumental. "I was always in my way a Civil War veteran," she once characterized herself. It seems fitting that for a woman who always wanted to be "historical" one of the works she is best remembered for, *The Mother of Us All*, unfolds with all the pomp and oratorical flourish of a historical pageant, with Susan B. Anthony at its head. The opera's famous refrain, "when this you see remember me," has been echoing for nearly fifty years, along with the equally insistent "listen to me," the two phrases articulating here and elsewhere the tension between seeing and hearing in the theater that so preoccupied her. Finally, at the end of her life, Stein brought together the writer's struggle and the feminist struggle. Before she moved to Europe her theatergoing had consisted mainly of old melodramas, operas, and touring companies of the classics and nineteenth-century repertoire. She always retained her love for melodrama, which she managed to update through the detective story to make some of her plays interrogate their own structure. For her the writing process was like the movement of a detective story: who did it, what was done, how it was done.

But Stein's nineteenth-century quality was demonstrated most rigorously in her passion for classification, the grammar of things existing: how to know everything there is to know about parts of speech, a punctuation mark, narration. She disliked the question mark. If you don't know a question is a question, what's the use. To her, commas seemed rather servile. "A comma by helping you along holding your coat for you and putting on your shoes keeps you from living your life as actively as you should lead it." She loved long, complicated sentences that forced themselves on you and made you know yourself knowing them. Stein tried to write the history of everyone in *The Making of Americans*, to know how any one is that one. Her work in its own way continues Mallarmé's desire to contain all of human existence within a book. She also shared the symbolist ideal of an art of grace and godliness, mindful that writing is a kind of sacredness. Mallarmé's words on the page with space and sound around them, as Stein's would later, floated in a meditative space, all mind. This is the source of their spiritual energy. Her own book of the world would be energized by a series of difficult sentences that start off, back up, and move in several directions, stopping from time to time, like an afternoon walk in the city. "The pleasure of concentration on the final simplicity of excessive complication" was what Stein wanted from the sentence. She would write the hymn of repetition.

Gertrude Stein, a dictionary. The young girl who sat reading in the window seat at the Marine Institute Library in San Francisco never lost her voracious reading habit. But Stein, it seems, was not widely read in French and wrote next to nothing in that language. "One of the things I have liked all these years is to be surrounded by people who know no english. It has left me more intensely alone with my eyes and english." The life work she set for herself was to render experience in precise English and to live inside this language as if it were her home.

Mainly, Stein tried to live her life in looking. The intensity of existence was what occupied her. She always preferred looking to remembering, hoping to bypass memory, which is to say, the consciousness of having previously experienced or thought about a fact or event, a person or object. Knowledge should proceed from the activity of being totally absorbed in the present moment of looking at someone, something. That is why Stein valued what she thought of as the flatness of the human mind, its continual presentness, over the contours of human nature, which she considered to be representative of the past, of memory. Experience was privileged over history. Her long meditation *The Geographical History of America*, which grew out of her experience of flying over the United States, takes up the theme of difference between the human mind and human nature. A great part of this complex book, in its own search for definition, concerns itself with identity and the nature of writing and the desire to make a play of just the human mind, that is, the drama of thinking, intercutting philosophical passages with short plays and occasionally addressing, or referring in the text, to Thornton Wilder, who wrote the book's introduction. Indeed, shortly after the work was published the dramatic sections were presented in Detroit as a puppet play, *Identity A Poem*. The idea of geography, as state of mind or place and personal mapping, is a major theme of Stein's writing. Her earliest plays are gathered in a volume she called *Geography and Plays*, and after her American tour she again used *geography* in one of her book titles. If landscape refers more to her notion of a play, geography describes her nondramatic works. The play inside the frame (landscape) and the land mass outside it (geography) are different spaces of consciousness, but each is a site/sight of knowledge.

Stein was always concerned with identity. Her success with *The Autobiography of Alice B. Toklas* and the triumphal visit to America caused her to be anxious about the demands of celebrity. "Was I I when I had no written word inside me." Yet here was a woman who wrote largely in isolation and suffered years of neglect. (It is interesting that in the same period, in one of the last plays he wrote, *When Someone Is Somebody*, Pirandello also took up the increasingly modern subject of the author/celebrity and the public.) A few years after her months of traveling, lecturing, and partying coast to coast as the famous Gertrude Stein, and after completion of *The Geographical History of America*, she wrote the opera *Dr. Faustus Lights the Lights*. In this seemingly whimsical but exquisitely personal tale, Marguerite Ida and Helena Annabel, one or two women, is bitten by a viper in the woods, then gains the knowledge to turn night into day. Now that a woman can do it, Faust isn't the only one. Against the setting of her growing reputation and the commitment at last of a distinguished American publishing house, the prolix Stein reflects on empowerment and vision, the soul and sin, recasting the Faust legend as a drama of contrasting light (daylight, electric light, candlelight, sunlight, starlight, twilight, moonlight, lamplight). Like many artists in the early decades of this century, she used light as theme, theology, technology. In one of Stein's fabulous frames, Marguerite Ida and Helena Annabel is revealed behind a curtain, an artificial viper (now a symbol of cosmic, female energy) beside her and a halo above her, lit by candlelight—as if she were a saint. A grand ballet of lights appears, and with a charming touch of self-irony a voice announces:

> They come from everywhere
> By land by sea by air
> They come from everywhere
> To look at her there.
> See how she sits
> See how she eats
> See how she lights
> The candle lights.

Was Stein thinking about her life at rue de Fleurus?

Ultimately, Faust's electric light cannot compare to Marguerite Ida and Helena Annabel's candlelight. He has sold his soul for this kind of light (art), but no one is interested in it anymore. There are other ways of seeing (knowing). Darkness envelops him as the opera draws to a close, but Marguerite Ida and Helena Annabel finds her own way clearly lit: "I can be anything and everything and it is always always alright."

In Stein's hierarchy of feeling, foremost was the desire to know all there was to know about the life of writing, about life as writing: the conduct of life made a composition. For her the writer's life is the good life. In this way she brought together the ontological and the epistemological. What Marguerite Yourcenar once observed pertains just as well to Stein: "To some extent every writer has to balance the desire to be read against the desire not to be read." No understanding of Stein is complete without an awareness of her real subject matter: the writing life as a spiritual struggle with the materiality of words. A study of her work is the study of process, not object. In the final analysis, it is this emphasis on process, and the unwavering commitment to experimentation, that has been so decisive a factor in the longevity of interest in Stein by vanguard artists in America.

Now, as the half-century anniversary of her death approaches, it is indisputable that Gertrude Stein is the great American modernist mind. No author has been a more inspirational figure for more generations of nonmainstream artists in the worlds of theater, music, dance, poetry, painting, and fiction. This is not to say that Stein has generations of imitators or that a Stein school is easily traceable. Instead her influence has been that of a visionary presence hovering over the artistic landscape, radiating a grandiose personal freedom, delight in invention, and intellectual courage. For decades this patron saint of the avant-garde has provided an example for those who came after her of the space an artist can make for herself in the world and of the manner in which an artist can create a new world in a work. Even a cursory outline of the history of contemporary performance in this country establishes her as one of the strong links between modernism and the evolution of an American aesthetic in the postwar period. The performance art and new opera/music theater lines begin with the influence of her work for the stage. Just as Stein's writing to a great extent developed from her reflections on painting, so the most innovative performance work was influenced more by art-world values than by American theater traditions.

The beginnings of the American avant-garde, in any formal, educational sense, were at Black Mountain College, where European avant-garde drama and American poetic drama had been introduced to the artistic community. Charles Olson, one of the Black Mountain poets, defined the composition by field of his "Projective Verse" in a geography of spirit that resembled Stein's. John Cage, who was there after the war, had written music to Stein texts by the 1930s, as had Virgil Thomson a decade earlier. Coincidentally, when Cage began to compose music he was in Mallorca, the same place Stein began to write plays. By the end of the forties *The Mother of Us All*, with Thomson's music, had its premiere at Columbia University and Stein's work was appearing in volumes published by Random House and in Selden Rodman's widely read 100 *Modern Poems*, which excerpted her *Four Saints in Three Acts*. At this time too, as The Living Theatre was just organizing, among the first works the group presented were Stein's *Ladies' Voices* and *Dr. Faustus Lights the Lights,* which Judith Malina directed. Cambridge's Brattle Theatre Company, whose members in the early fifties included the poets John Ashbery and Frank O'Hara, early admirers of Stein's writing who would later become prominent New York poets, was also producing her work. The first audiences for Stein were the poets, visual artists, and performers who would define the American avant-garde of the fifties and sixties, particularly what was to become the New York School, and who knew her writings from available books and alternative literary magazines. Stein's work, while it was ignored by commercial and establishment theaters, was performed almost exclusively in off-Broadway spaces and university theaters.

She became a more visible presence in the downtown arts scene in New York in the sixties. In 1963 the Judson Poets' Theatre staged *What Happened,* which featured Judson Dance Theatre members Lucinda Childs, Yvonne Rainer, Aileen Passloff, and Arlene Rothlein, with Lawrence Kornfeld directing and the Reverend Al Carmines composing the music. As an unmistakable homage to Stein, her play was published a decade later in the comprehensive *Off Off Broadway Book,* an anthology of plays that featured the most influential writers of the sixties. In newspaper accounts of the Judson Dance Theatre some of the dancers' own work was compared to the circularity and repetition of Stein's writing. In the sixties and seventies the Judson Poets' Theatre was to stage several of the author's plays (*What Happened, In Circles, Listen to Me, A Manoir,* and *Dr. Faustus Lights the Lights,* among them), setting a standard for Stein productions. Around the same time, the dancer and Judson mentor James Waring choreographed a piece based on her long work *Stanzas in Meditation.* Curiously, Stein's theatrical reputation rests largely on her work as opera or music theater, though she didn't like music and expressed an interest in seeing her work done without it.

In the context of the explosion of avant-garde performance in the decades after World War II, with the blurring of boundaries between the arts, the close-knit community of artists and audiences who supported experimental work, and the influence of European modernism, Stein's legacy found its way into many new directions taken by writers and performers. Some discovered her poetics of performance, others her poetry, still others the erotics of her texts. The aesthetics of the sixties had natural affinities with her own work, especially the emphasis on process and repetition, the attachment to the idea of the ordinary, the fascination with objects, an insistence on presence, and experiments with new formal vocabularies in all the arts. These issues were appealing to the generation who created happenings, Fluxus, the Judson Dance Theatre, and the Judson Poets' Theatre. One of the members of Fluxus, Dick Higgins, who founded Something Else Press at this time, began to publish a number of Stein's out-of-print books, making them available to a new generation. Until the recent reprinting of several Stein titles, as a result of renewed interest in her work, his decades-old editions of some of the books have been the only ones around.

It has long been acknowledged that in this period of the new American arts the major source of performance ideas was John Cage, whose writing, composing, and collaboration with Merce Cunningham infused all the arts with a new energy, vocabulary, and provocation still evident today. But if John Cage has been the father of the American avant-garde, surely Gertrude Stein has been its mother. Together the two of them are the progenitors of the last half-century of American avant-garde work. Stein did for the theater what Cage did for music: completely rethink the art, its manner of composition, and audience reception. Both are marginal figures in the fields they represent in the sense that they are outside the canons of official culture. But if one looks back over the entire twentieth century, they remain the wellspring for American avant-garde artists, even if their original works are at times not as well known as the circulation of ideas around them.

Their affirmation of life, untouched by modern and at times fashionable alienation, is a joyous modernism that influenced the definition of an American performance aesthetic in profound, enduring ways, setting it apart from European practice in its formal and personal rather than political preoccupations. What Cage declared early on as his credo applies equally well to Stein: the world is excellent if we would only wake up to the life we are living. Both tried to live in looking and listening, erasing for themselves the borders between art and life, object and experience. They went about their work as if creation were a kind of song. When art means more as experience than production, everything exists as a world of possibilities, in continuous variation and multiplicity. Everything is usable. If Stein determined to let words be themselves, Cage let sounds be themselves: what counts is that each one is given the freedom to be itself. Stein's melody of existence is Cage's harmony of nature: her landscape as play, his field of sound and imaginary landscape. Together these marvelous, exuberant naturalists have left us a twentieth-century field guide to the sights and sounds of our world.

From the perspective of ecology, Stein and Cage formulated strikingly like-minded biocentric worldviews in their treatment of all material for composition as natural phenomena. The sounds of birds interrupt the human voice, plant life shares the environment with human life. Their reaching out to the natural world, to nature as process, creates the feeling of the open air in their work, the importance given to space as a luxurious field of activity and wonder, a landscape of unlimited centers of focus. This spatial unfolding of composition distances itself from linearity as time flows into space: duration, not sequence, is what matters. Both Stein and Cage conceived ideas about art by observing nature, making art more like life rather than the other way around. For them life itself made a composition. In their generosity of spirit they were interested in everything that came their way, a quality of worldly engagement that led to a deep regard for inclusiveness and differentiation and a fondness for the "found" phrase, object, event. They gloried in the ordinary, Stein in the lives of words, Cage in the lives of sounds, and more lovingly, in their writings the everyday activities and comings and goings of friends—in short, the pleasures of company—are casually recorded as text. In particular, their longtime companions, Alice B. Toklas and Merce Cunningham, are embedded in words. Conversation is the key to their compositions.

If Stein eliminated story and made the play the thing, the essence of what happens, Cage refused to structure music, but let the sounds themselves happen. The play, the sound: it is just there. Stein understood that what is seen in a composition depends upon "the enjoyer," and Cage let "people" decide what to listen to and how. Along with Duchamp, they shared an absolute devotion to the idea that a work exists beyond its status as an object, that it is experienced in subjective space. Stein's continuous present is Cage's process, their obsession with time the center of their provocative essays, her "Composition as Explanation," his "Composition as Process."

What grounds their work, infusing it with the feeling of spiritual wholeness, is a reverence for the presence of mind in everyday life: experience honored as a constant rhythm of enlightenment. Remarkably, both artists were drawn to the concept of emptiness, Stein through the writing process and Cage through his study of Buddhism. There is much complexity in the simplicity of their thought but no mysticism, not in these down-to-earth artists: they were in search of the real. What "emptiness" allowed was a freeing of the mind from memory in order to let the immediacy of experience take over. Freedom from memory and habit and history were fundamental principles of the grand projects Stein and Cage realized in their ecstatic lives.

Stein's influence moved into a new phase in the theater with the emergence of Richard Foreman and Robert Wilson as important artists in the 1970s. Richard Foreman's early work was written very much under the example of Stein as he began to incorporate in his plays autobiographical notes and personal experiences recorded at the time he was writing the plays and, like her, subverted memory and associative thinking in art. Perhaps the strongest linkage between Stein and Foreman, as America's foremost philosophical theater minds, is the significance they give to perception as the subject of art and to audience emotion in the theatrical experience and their subsequent attempt to break down into the smallest elements aspects of art and experience. Their philosophical tendencies have led both authors to the ultimate belief in writing as an expression of faith, in a deeply spiritual, secular sense. Foreman staged Stein's *Dr. Faustus Lights the Lights* in Paris and Berlin more than a decade ago.

The presence of Stein has always been apparent in the construction of Robert Wilson's texts, even in their typographical design, which allows words with space around them. His own interest in textuality seems closest to the poetry in her plays, especially the emphasis on sound rather than meaning, the disorientation of syntax, and the attraction to repetition, quotation, and fragment. He also puts historical figures in his pieces with the same freedom from chronological time Stein assumed for herself. But the more significant Stein legacy in Wilson's theater, and here the two share a visual arts sensibility, is his extension of her conception of a play as landscape. His sense of composition parallels Stein's: space as a field of revelation and surprise.

Like the Living Theatre, the Judson Poets' Theatre, and Richard Foreman, in Berlin a few years ago Robert Wilson also staged his own *Dr. Faustus Lights the Lights*, which seems to hold continuing interest for avant-garde generations in its eccentric confrontation with the themes of identity, enlightenment, and illusion. Over the years Wilson has reimagined opera and music theater, his *Dr. Faustus* offering a new model for staging Stein, vastly different from the Judson revue style and closer to an American opera experimental tradition based on imagery and movement. His production of *Four Saints in Three Acts* will premiere in Houston in 1996.

Other generations of artists after Foreman and Wilson continue to turn to Stein, particularly at the start of their careers. *Photograph* was an early James Lapine project, as an adaptation of Stein's *The Making of Americans* was for Anne Bogart. Perhaps the most enchanting homage to Stein is the biennial marathon reading (alternating with James Joyce's *Finnegans Wake*) of her great work *The Making of Americans* at the Paula Cooper Gallery in New York's Soho district on the occasion of the New Year. The twentieth annual reading was celebrated in 1994 with the Stein text, which takes approximately fifty hours to complete. The ambience of the gallery offers a warm, meditative space into which curious passersby wander and where aficionados of the event make their holiday appearance, everyone lounging on floor cushions along the bare walls or lying about the polished floor, listening, dreaming, while dozens of readers take their turn all day and all night, measuring out the long narrative in Stein's rolling, recalcitrant sentences.

Her friend the poet Mina Loy understood the way Stein could get inside a word. She had a very special appreciation of such astonishing literary gifts:

> Curie
> of the laboratory
> of vocabulary
>   she crushed
> the tonnage
> of consciousness
> congealed to phrases
>   to exact
> a radium of the word

Stein herself knew what she was doing, because she set her own achievement on the level of scientific discovery. "Einstein was the creative philosophic mind of the century and I have been the creative literary mind" is the way she defined the times. Her orientation reflected the new world of physics in its development of composition as a field of innumerable centers, and like her avant-garde contemporaries, she was aware of the new thinking in non-Euclidean geometry and the fourth dimension. If artists create worlds before science can find proof of them, then surely, looking back over the century, it is now obvious that Stein's technique has affinities with what has come to be known as chaos theory. Many of its defining features describe her writing: the pattern of self-similarity, words acting as strange attractors, the importance of scale, deep structures of order within unpredictable systems. Stein is a master of what can be thought of as the "fractal text," which makes her theater an exacting guide to a dramaturgy of chaotics. From the start her world has been ruled by its own natural processes.

There is no sense of ever coming to an end in Stein. Reading her is like wandering the Grand Canyon, trying to search a way out only to become drawn back into it, continually absorbed by the pleasure of tracing the endless diverging lines impressed upon constantly transforming surfaces, and at every turn discovering winding, wider pathways leading to ever more mysterious corridors of experience. Her work has the grandeur of the inexhaustible, the self-sufficiency of nature, a resistance to being known given only to special things.

Much of what Stein wrote and thought was set down in notebooks during the long nights at the rue de Fleurus. Down the block from her home is the western gate of the Luxembourg Gardens, and through the entrance to the left a statue of Paul Verlaine, to the right a smaller version of the Statue of Liberty. France and America at either elbow. Pigeons are still on the grass. She followed this pathway for three decades, often with her little dog, Basket, wondering what made any one that one, why any word was that word. As Gertrude Stein walked the lush allées that diagram the splendid park into long pleached sentences, now and then in the verdure of solitude perhaps her own words came to mind, *I had really written thinking.*

(1995)

Originally written as the introduction to a new edition of *Last Operas and Plays*, by Gertrude Stein.

The Mus/ecology of John Cage

||||||||| "If when I am in the woods, the woods are not in me, what right have I to be in the woods?" Thoreau's words inspired John Cage as a field guide to the life he would live in the world, which is to say, the life he would live in sound. If Thoreau elevated walking to an art form, Cage took the next step by declaring himself a walking concert. Both men were enamored of things as they are in their natural habitat, always becoming, changing, surprising, sounding. To live under the sign of wonder required inner silence, alertness, independence of mind, and a feeling for simple pleasures. Thoreau found the riddle of life in a bean field, and Cage sought his answers by a toss of the dice aross an imaginary landscape. In the natural world a life was worth living.

Sentient or nonsentient beings, rocks or trees or plants or people, Cage considered them all equally "world-honored," as one of his Buddhist expressions explained. A man of the most contemporary diction, he chose a wonderfully chivalrous, gracious vocabulary when he spoke of the things he valued. Equality for him was a matter of nobility, and with tranquility, devotion, and dignity it described worlds of meaning in both art and life. Cage embraced a view of the world as free and purposeless, oblivious to any separation of the elements, the air and sea, the sky and earth, a person or flower. His biocentrism encouraged Cage to remark on the dignity of sounds, the feeling of compassion for them, just as one might speak of the integrity of forms in sculpture. He didn't differentiate between nature and culture, or sound and space. He loved nature in art, nature as art. Most of all, he reveled in the swirling freedom of a field of sound where musical time turns into space and sound becomes a substitute for time, so that one lives in sound as if it were time.

A composer as naturalist, Cage didn't merely write musical notation, he documented the sounds of the world, bringing human, animal, vegetable, mineral, industrial, meteorological, natural, and artificial sounds together just as they exist in the environment. In its erasure of borders between the natural and social sciences his music metamorphosed into the socioecological, a different kind of anthropology, reporting on the life that was lived in the second half of the twentieth century, the vibrations of plants and peoples' voices, the objects around them, the tools people used and the art they created, the climate they lived in, their machines and modes of transport, what they listened to on the radio. He was in love with the ordinary. In his radical way of redefining science and art, Cage expanded the meaning of natural history by transforming music composition into an ecology.

Sound was conceived as an environment, another kind of landscape, sounds themselves as points in space, each one creating its own space and the spaces constantly multiplying, yet everything a part of everything else. The sounds of traffic could wander into a composition, or wind, rain, thunder, the touch of paper pressed against cactus, water floating in a conch shell, bird calls, clocks, striking matches, wire coils. One composition was patterned on astrological maps, another plotted as a "garden" of sounds, yet another created from a rubbing. Who more than Cage demonstrated that sound travels? He made music attentive to geography, or rather, he brought the sense of place into music.

What made a piece of music or a painting modern was the ability to live with a disruption of its surface by ambient sound or light. In other words, it had to be free to acknowledge the social along with the formal rather than close itself off to experience. It had to forgo privacy and accept the theatrical. Every event could be an occasion for interaction, as if nothing in the world existed so well as in the company of others. Oh, things could be appreciated for their own sake, but it wasn't the same without the heightened pleasure of conviviality. Cage dreamed of listening to a mushroom grow and a table sound like a table. He planned a project for children that would attach microphones to all the plants in a park and envisioned music performed by animals or butterflies. The list of objects that he amplified alone comprises a catalogue of artifacts from contemporary material culture. He let things perform themselves. Everything had a spirit, a sound. His great insight into silence is that it doesn't exist.

Cage was intrigued by the voice of anything, anyone. In the broadest, metaphoric sense his work celebrates in music and in writing the primacy of voice and, therefore, ear. He praised the random, open movement of conversation, based as it is on the quality of the individual sound/voice, over the resolve of communication, which encouraged him in his large body of writings to disregard the conventional style of the literary essay in favor of forms that appeal directly to the ear, such as letters, diaries, lectures, stories, jokes, poems. He brought all of these species of writing into the essay, along with the many friends and his parents, to whom he referred affectionately in humorous anecdotes, some of them the subject of visual poems he called mesostics, spaced across the page in the radical typography he described as a waterfall. Whether linguistic, musical, or social, Cage's poetics was always in revolt against syntax. His *Mushroom Book* appears as part of *M*, another collection of writings, overflowing with notes, recipes, the names and characteristics of numerous mushrooms, and the detail of personal relationships enjoyed. Since making music meant being sociable, writing was simply a form of conversation. There are voices everywhere.

Cage's belief in the unique sound of each thing bears some analogy to the medieval doctrine of signatures and symbolism's equally religious *correspondances*, the latter influencing many artists and movements in the early decades of this century, including Kandinsky, who believed that "the world sounds," even titling an early work for the stage *The Yellow Sound*. Among them was the filmmaker Oskar Fischinger, with whom Cage once worked and who, he acknowledged, introduced him to the idea that each thing in the world has a spirit released through sound. Whether as noise, spirit, or soul, acoustic or mediated performance, Kandinsky's inner necessity or Cage's chance, sound holds an increasingly recognized complex place in the development of modern artistic thought. In this respect, the significance for Cage of the work of Satie, Russolo, Cowell, and Varèse has been often acknowledged. But Cage took sound/noise to a level that had not been attainable for the composers who earlier identified its potential, since it was possible for him to experiment radically with magnetic tape, synthesizers, and computers.

Even more exceptionally for the history of the arts, Cage brought to the realm of technology what previously had been understood as the realm of the spiritual. The correspondences of the previous century were now transformed into feedback and digital sampling in a total environment of disorganized sound that needed electronic technicians more than a harmonic choir. Here was an opportunity for the "instantaneous ecstasy" Cage sought in his glorious life.

Cage always had more of the nineteenth-century clergyman than the alienated modernist in his heart. Though the Buddhist influence on him of D. T. Suzuki and *The Huang Po Doctrine of Universal Mind* is well known and he himself has commented on the initial relevance of Sri Ramakrishna, Coomaraswamy, and Indian philosophy before his turn from Hinduism to Zen Buddhism (it was less expressive), the substantial Christian imagery and beliefs in Cage's work have not received as much attention, although they are considerable. He might have been a Methodist minister like his grandfather, and if he devoted himself to the betterment of humankind through art instead of religion, nevertheless Cage conceived of his project very much as an aspect of the Christian way of life. His several installments of "How to Improve the World" and many of the lectures he gave are close to being sermons. Sprinkled in his writings are references to biblical teachings and a particular fondness for considering the lilies as a metaphor of silence.

A constant source of inspiration was the Catholic mystic Meister Eckhart, whose thinking reflects certain similarities to Buddhism in its praise of detachment and the now-moment, in the importance given to action without self-consciousness. If Eckhart represents a starting point for idealism, Cage exemplifies its significance in contemporary art practice. His renowned work 4' 33", originally titled *Silent Prayer*, surely was written in grace notes. Looking back over his career, it is remarkable how Cage so thoroughly interwove Protestant, Catholic, Hindu, and Buddhist thought and imagery within an avant-garde vocabulary free of a symbolist/mystical language and any feeling for harmony. He found a way to keep his dissonance and experience a spiritual transformation anyway.

Historically, the avant-garde has always shown this universalist, intercultural, and ecumenical range, in which intellectual tradition is absorbed and repositioned in a contemporary setting. Cage's own life is best understood within the century-long attempt of artists to redefine spirituality, especially in the turn to the East, for he was an exemplary figure in whom spiritual discipline was inseparable from creativity. His union of art and spiritual feeling in a profound cosmic awareness represents a high point in the secularization of the spiritual in the twentieth century. In more ways than one, Cage has led music from harmony to paradox.

Cage looked on the world as "Creation," his Lord's Prayer: Give us this day our daily noise. He regarded the natural world as a theater of sound in much the same way as the early naturalists saw it as a theater of plants. When decades ago Cage asked the rhetorical question, "Where do we go from here?" he answered himself, "Towards theatre. That art more than music resembles nature." Here, together, sounds are sounds and people are people: life itself is theater. He exalted the theatrical because it welcomed the social aspect present in the spectator/listener experience, envisioning a future of music that would offer a new example of social interaction. World as theater was all process, potentiality, splendor of chance meeting in the presence of music. No American artist more than Cage embodies the idea of the *theatrum mundi* in his philosophy and work.

It was only a matter of time before Cage's conception of theater was to make an immense contribution to the history of performance ideas. Together with Merce Cunningham, his companion of nearly half a century, Cage created a new performance paradigm in which music, movement, text, and design could exist in space as autonomous elements, each with its own vocabulary, even created separately and in isolation from each other. There were occasions when they were only together in the same space for the first time at the premiere of an event. The bringing together in a new situation of things that already are always fascinated Cage. Here was a vision of theater counter to and as powerful as the Wagnerian *Gesamtkunstwerk* that had influenced so many generations of artists, establishment and avant-garde: a new ecology of the arts linked to the Cagean belief in the "right to space" of dance or music. Astonishingly, in this aesthetic, formal way he made performance address rights issues. Since his death in 1992 at the age of seventy-nine,

the legacy of Cage can now be seen beyond the musical works and writings he left to the world in a vision that at its most sublime articulates
an ethics of performance.

The ecological perspective also characterizes the intertextual aspect
of Cage's method. He constantly recycled his own words and sounds in
the writings and music and spent many years "writing through" Joyce
and Thoreau. Cage used as a sourcebook for his compositions what he
called the "library" of recorded sounds drawn from the natural world.
In a poetic sense, what he really discovered was a contemporary, technological metaphor for the book of nature, his field of sound activated
as a space of revelation. Cage had as little concern for authorship (he
valued use over property) as he did for self-expression, emphasizing from
the start the disappearance of the composer (and the conductor), along
with the author. What mattered was not the origin of a text or composition but how it might suggest new possibilities to open the mind.

For Cage each sound was alive, a living organism. All species were
welcome in his landscape but were left uncultivated. It is as if they were
"escapes" from the garden into the wild. *Let sounds be themselves.* Seen
in this light, groups of sounds can be comprehended as ecosystems,
which in turn are linked to sociocultural systems. Whether animate or
inanimate, they are all equal voices in the environment. Cage's bio-
eccentrism led him to treat sound virtually as a matter of free speech. As
a holistic development, this philosophy of composition embraced the
movement from sound system to ecosystem to social system. He preferred to think of the audience more as *ecological* than *sociological* fact.

Even among the most ecologically minded, it would be unlikely to
find anyone who, like Cage, has embraced the "rights of sounds." Yet,
in contrast to many of today's "deep ecology" believers (as one wing
of the most radical environmentalists are identified), who have written of the rights of trees, grass, nature, and so on, he has none of their
anti-technology, anti-modernist, authoritarian, or misanthropic tendencies. As a radical avant-garde thinker with no interest in apocalyptic
pronouncements, Cage looked forward to the universal distribution of
available technology as a matter of world improvement. Global interconnectedness would create the landscape he imagined as World Mind,
this Oneness different from the "deep ecology" dream of Wholeness.
It was not a question of distinguishing between the natural and the

artificial realms of experience but of recognizing the infinitely various interactions between human beings and the landscape, each transforming the other in time and space. He simply didn't see human beings in conflict with nature or glorify nature as separate from society, nor was he a romantic in search of the lost wilderness, but a futurist at heart.

He believed in progress through technology, and as much as he enjoyed country life, he was a man of the city. Ultimately, Cage wouldn't judge bird song more valuable than the sound of a passing car, because he refused to make value judgments about sounds. Who else but Cage could learn to fall asleep to the sound of a burglar alarm by translating it into Brancusi-like images? He had no sense of the Fall, but considered the world as paradise, a garden of mushrooms and innumerable other delights. Accordingly, the world was so excellent and would reveal more of itself if only one would become fully awake to it. If the art of listening could be applied to all domains of social life, he would show how all the world could be made into music, and he dedicated his life to bringing this about by adding the character of space to music, so that if you could hear more you could see more: a sound field is also a visual field. The eventual goal was freedom of human creativity, everyone an artist.

What distinguished Cage's way of being in the world was his constant striving for *a climate very rich with joy*, coupled with an abiding optimism in world improvement. There's no stopping once you get interested in it, he eventually admitted, setting a wide range of issues in a global context, starting first with local concerns. In some ways Cage is a contemporary link to nineteenth-century self-improvement populists, for the flip side of world improvement is self-improvement, though Cage conceived of it as self-alteration. He was always thinking of ways people's lives could be made more efficient and mind-expanding, whether promoting new types of housing dreamed up by his friend Buckminster Fuller, or new conceptions of communities identified by his friend Marshall McLuhan, or new visions of a free society dreamed of by his friend Norman O. Brown. Cage wrote frequently of the utilities (let the humanities take care of themselves, he thought), of usage rather than ownership, envisioning a future when food, energy, and shelter would be distributed at the global level. Because Cage was a visionary who acted like a pragmatist, his declarations have an air of unreality about them, just as his technological openness brought the babble of talk radio along with the democratization of the airwaves. Who can say what kind of political future the globalization of communications systems will ultimately lead to?

As early as twenty-five years before his death Cage thought that for the twentieth century art's work was already done and it was now time to turn to the environment. His way of making music would be a way of changing the environment and thus of changing people. It was important to make music that was useful to society, to move from musical needs to social needs, from the self to the world, from the private to the public, a mission that led Cage to devise an open method of composition—the noncoercive play of interpenetrating, undifferentiated sounds, erasing borders between the sounds and experiences, and encouraging process rather than structure—that would act as an alternative model of society. Likewise, the principle of distribution of sounds would carry over to his social philosophy based on the global distribution of resources. Embedded in his democratic, pluralistic sound environment is a dream of enlightened civic space and of citizenship as good listening. Here was another incarnation of modernity's "New Man."

Cage is perhaps the last major artist of the twentieth century, after Joseph Beuys, to have had such unwavering philosophical roots in the avant-garde, utopian faith in the popularization of modernist aesthetics as a force of social change, the transformation to occur through the creation of a total aesthetic environment. Though their work went in very different and often contradictory directions, both Cage and Beuys shared a belief in the organic interrelationship of the social, natural, and spiritual worlds. If one perceived society as sound, the other thought of it as sculpture. Cage wanted to turn everything in the environment into art: *The whole world must be made into music.* In this profoundly idealist perspective, the evolution of society is inseparable from the evolution of art. That view of progress would demand of its human embodiment vast reserves of blessedness. Cage was such a man, so truly at home on earth was he. Coincidentally, the other joyful American avant-gardist, Gertrude Stein, with whom Cage shared so many aesthetic values and who had been an inspiration to him, demonstrated the same world-feeling. What gives their work and thought its sense of inexhaustibility and charm is a quality of attentiveness to the natural world, so that life and art are constantly replenished by the fullness of human experience.

If life was always more important to Cage than art, he wanted it to have art's best tendencies: freedom of thought, creative energy, invention. What could be more wonderful than "the bringing of new things into being." Now, at the far end of the long modern era, as the century draws to a close, the need for the kind of visionary ethos the avant-garde at its most protean represents grows ever more urgent. The heroic modernists are dying. Cage left as his legacy the unceasing rhythm of human passion searching for new sounds of life. In the beginning was a walk in the woods.

(1995)

Robert Wilson and
the Idea of the Archive
Dramaturgy as an Ecology

|||||||| In the twenty-five years since he first began a life in art, Robert Wilson has created an extraordinary number of works in theater, opera, video, furniture design, sculpture, painting, and drawing. Yet most of his theater productions of the last decade or more have rarely been seen in the United States, outside of New York, Boston, and more recently Houston. He spends the greater part of each year in Europe, producing works in the different media for its major theaters, opera houses, and museums. No contemporary theater artist's work travels from country to continent with such frequency or assurance.

The dislocation of contemporary artists and artifacts is duplicated in the lives of texts, increasingly at home on these transcontinental routes, dispersed from their own cultures. By that I mean the dispersed texts from lost civilizations, those of unknown or forgotten authors, the texts of books languishing on library shelves, exiled or censored texts, world classics. They are always at risk of becoming endangered species of writing. Time erodes their historical meaning; or, they can literally crumble and fall into pieces, like ruins. But there are those that find a home in today's world, preoccupied by preservation and travel. If the idea of the "dispersed" describes the lives of texts, Wilson's own manner of living and working in so many cultures and languages only stylizes the contemporary condition of relocation in literature. Today the natural state of writing is translation.

34

I

In elegant figures of speech Wilson has formalized a *dramaturgy of the dispersed text*, "dispersed" because the word suggests not only the feeling of "pieces" that travel and socialize but the migrations of human populations. This cosmopolitan dramaturgy is especially evident in the making of a recent work, *The Forest* (1988), for the 750th anniversary of the city of Berlin. Structured in seven acts, with music by David Byrne, it draws on themes from the first part of *Gilgamesh* and intermixes texts by authors extending from the pre-Columbian period up to the nineteenth and twentieth centuries, including the writings of Charles Darwin, Jean-Henri Fabre, Edgar Allan Poe, George Lichtenberg, Fernando Pessoa, and Hans Henny Jahnn. Both in Berlin and, later, at the Brooklyn Academy of Music, where I saw the production, it was performed in German and in English, with translations from the several languages of the literary sources.

The texts of Wilson's productions have not been explored as persistently as his staging, though he brought modernist theatrical interests in language, sound, and the voice into them more than two decades ago. Already in 1970 fragments from his first large production *The King of Spain* were published in *New American Plays*; in 1974 he made his first DIA LOG pieces and the text-rich *A Letter for Queen Victoria*, which was initially published in France before appearing in my anthology *The Theatre of Images* (1977). The text of *I Was Sitting On My Patio This Guy Appeared I Thought I Was Hallucinating* accompanied the London production in 1978 and was printed a year later in *PAJ* 10/11. When Wilson made *The Golden Windows* (1982) for the Munich Kammerspiele, the text was published in the theater program, as it was in Berlin for the Schaubühne's *Death Destruction & Detroit* (I, 1979; II, 1987) and for *The Forest* premiere (1988) there at the Freie Volksbühne.

It is not necessary to trace Wilson's entire publishing history to underscore that, even before the elaborate programs of texts, interviews, drawings, and dramaturgical materials prepared for the European productions, from the start of his career he published his texts. Moreover, it is worthwhile to note that if Wilson entitles many of his works "opera," a significant number are designated "play." One result of the lack of attention to Wilson's texts is the fact that though *the* CIVIL wars: *a tree is best measured when it is down* was the unanimous choice for the Pulitzer prize for drama in 1986, the Pulitzer board would not grant him the award, in large part because no conventional text existed for the work.

Yet, the spoken word has been a characteristic feature of his productions over the years, and increasingly since he went to Europe, the interest in classics. But Wilson does not merely stage a text; he transforms it into an architecture of sound, which is also apparent in the studied typographical organization of the printed texts and their titles and in the geometry that shapes the distribution of individual speeches. Furthermore, not only do the contemporary texts substantiate this authorial gesture but classic texts too are "adapted" by Wilson, and their speeches rewritten and revisioned on the page. The issue of authorship is central to Wilson's dramaturgy.

The Forest goes so far as to pose a distinction between the "Text" and the "Book." Credit for the text is given to Heiner Müller, a portion of whose play *Cement* is excerpted in it, and to the American writer Darryl Pinckney, who contributed a number of sections. In addition, Müller and Pinckney collected several texts of other writers. There is also a visual book composed of drawings for lights, costumes, and gestures, research for which is drawn from photography, film, painting, and architecture sources, originating in Wilson's initial sketches and theatrical concept. Text and image are brought together in the formation of the book as the visual and literary structure in which the texts are arranged and fitted and on which the staging is made. The Book, then—in actuality an anthology—is the basis of the production, and Wilson, as designer and director, its author. In this sense, direction can be considered a kind of redaction.

The emblematic concept of the Book is developed in a unique way by Wilson. At the start of a project he makes drawings showing what each scene will look like. His creations for the theater are truly *works on paper*. During the workshop stage that follows, all of the blocking is set without a text, according to the story boards. This "dumb play" is videotaped, and the text and music added separately by other artists to fit into the silent formal structure already devised by Wilson. So it seems that there are several books (visual, audio, literary) inside of the Book/Work, each offering independent stage languages (image, sound, word), themselves different and autonomous readings of its fundamental structure. This process is made more complex by the ironic fact that one has really to read the Book in order to make a comprehensive reading of the production.

The bibliography of text fragments that make up *The Forest*, its recuperation of dispersed, often arcane, texts, reflects not only the attraction of allegory in conceiving theatrical narrative in the present but an attitude toward the past as an archive. The theatrical realm unfolds—and why not consider the proscenium as an upright book?—to present an anthology of texts and images, as it were, framing classics for contemporaries. It also recontextualizes Wilson's personal vocabulary of imagery: grid, chair, forest, cave, angle of light, window, table. The subject of this theater is not history but memory. It lingers in myth and dream, the liminal zone between literature and history. Wilson's modernism is of the quality exalted by Baudelaire: modernity that can eventually claim its worth as antiquity. This way of making theater opens up an entirely new approach to the idea of the canon.

The narrative style of reprocessing scattered species of writing to envisage glorious new performance worlds is a prelude to Wilson's very special ecology of theater, inscribed in the treatment of space and time and the figure. Landscape is not merely a setting or scenery but a real geomorphology of spirit and value, site-specific, whether it is the beach in *The Life and Times of Joseph Stalin*, the river in *Alcestis*, the open field and outer space of *Einstein on the Beach*, the vast hillsides of KA MOUNTAIN AND GUARDeniaTERRACE, *Orlando*'s snow, HAMLETMACHINE's leafless branches, the tree that serves as trope for his monumental *the* CIVIL wars; the deserts, the cities, the moon. Wilson is a geographer, but in the special way Gertrude Stein conceived of nature and turned it into a concept of space: as a bountiful field of revelation where bird calls mingle with the human voice. Just as her view of nature was influenced by painting, so Wilson draws from the archives of art, his imagery continually revising the teleology of the relationship between nature and culture. In one sense, Wilson's theater leans toward landscape architecture.

Here in *The Forest*—woods are the ideal mythic space—animal and human metamorphose. Bird song fills the air. People, birds, fish, and rocks cohabit—in desert, city, forest, shore—in ancient and modern times. Adaptation is the cornerstone of natural selection. The large population of *The Forest* includes as its *theatrum mundi*, besides Gilgamesh (the ancient king and builder of great cities and temples, now updated as a nineteenth-century German industrialist) and the wild Enkidu (his cherished friend), a lobster, a dragon, a Japanese farmer, a Renaissance Man, an ancient Mother, four lizards, a ballerina, a porcupine, a Figure with Moon. Relationships are heterosexual, homoerotic; there's talk of a Pope in love with a whale and the Queen of England panting over ship propellers. When Gilgamesh is indoors with his Whore, a lion quietly waits beside him; an aquarium is positioned nearby. The Wilson bestiary and the plenitude of plant and mineral life, here and elsewhere, challenge criticism to act as taxonomy. More than a half-century ago, in one of the most moving passages in modern drama, Pirandello unwittingly philosophized on the origin of species: "One is born to life in many forms, in many shapes, as tree, or as stone, as water, as butterfly, or as woman. So one may be born a character in a play." In one of his late plays a writer turns to stone.

Linked as it was by the ancients to human behavior, the climate of scenes is as influential as it is changeable: here there are arid and icy landscapes; heat and fire; wind, water, mountains. After a brief prologue, in which a crescent moon turns full, *The Forest* opens onto a desert where an Old Man sitting on a rock begins to tell a story of long ago. Birds caw, women in long dresses slowly glide by with ravens perched on their wrists, a mysterious Hooded Figure threatens violence with the slow, stylized movements of a sword, and a little boy called Berlin is building a city with blocks. Here and there on the ground are stones, a geode. An odd beached marine creature keeps watch at the edge of the scene. The nature imagery of *The Forest*, alternately literary and pictorial, is most pronounced as rock, moon, river, tree, desert, lily. In the distance a tree (inevitably there is one in a Wilson production) floats sideways in the air. In the natural world of the third act it looms larger, upside down; in the fifth act the forest comes indoors.

The biodiversity of Wilson's theater lyricizes both space and time. All species—flora, fauna, human—enliven narrative in this advanced stage of theatrical evolution. He frames their adaptability and process of hybridization in scenes that visualize the insistent nature/culture theme as a structural feature of the work. If Wilson loves the city, he needs woods. What is a theatrical landscape but a species of desire?

In the new theatrical (and scientific) Enlightenment Wilson proposes, natural history shares the scene with human history. His landscapes stage the passage of time. To some extent, this is an aspect of his symbolist heritage. It was Maeterlinck who a century ago joined his affinity with the natural world to the human drama, dematerializing space into time. The manner in which the symbolist impulse in theater enfolds abstraction, the prominence of the human voice, and liquid thought into an intense spiritual longing and sense of cosmology is a legacy very much a part of Wilson's visionary aesthetics. This contemplative mergence of cosmic time and theatrical time (the macrocosm and microcosm theme are elaborated in his special attention to scale) outlines the utopian dimension of late-twentieth-century performance, which Wilson so consummately elucidates.

One of the subtle turns in the continuation of symbolism in the theater is that it took the advanced technology of our own age truly to realize the simple emotional aura of "illumination" in the natural world that symbolism discloses. Effortlessly, the world of Wilson welcomes organic form and high tech. Now, at the approach of another century turning, the symbolist impulse foretells once more the new frontier of consciousness and creativity, this time the union of spirit, art, and science. Symbolism was the first modern movement to take an interest in myth and the origin of cultures as it began to piece together the collective mind from its archive of cultural memory and artifact. If symbolism dwelt in the past life of an image, it also assured that image's future in the unconscious. Now, in the world theater of images, in which the local has become the global, Auerbach's words have a prophet's urgency: "Our philological home is the earth; it can no longer be the nation." Likewise, the itinerant Wilson's transcontinental vocabulary of American, Japanese, and European stage languages globalizes theatrical form, heralding the cosmopolitan nature of his style.

II

In the wide sweep of his search for stories in the dreams and archetypes of cultures, Wilson adds a new chronotope to theater: the *archival*. (Ironically, his unrealized magnum opus *the CIVIL wars*, which was prepared on three continents, exists now only in archival form—video-

tapes, texts, notes, drawings—in Wilson's own Byrd Hoffman Foundation offices.) Painting has always acknowledged the history of objects
and images, but the theater did not until Wilson brought an art sensibility to it. He is the one laying the foundation for, in Gombrich's
timely phrase, an "ecology of the image." For *The Forest* he and his col-
laborators have compiled a new encyclopedia of texts and images that
tells the story of the earth and its peoples, and those beyond the earth,
an encyclopedia made up of stories written in the past and rewritten in
the present, images inscribed in the monuments of world cultures in
other times and places that also tell of our time and our place. Even
the sculptured hands of the performers challenge the proficiency of a
chiromancer. Circles, triangles, lines, rhomboids shape yet another language. Texts are everywhere.

Intuition is the way to this book of knowledge, and one must have
the watchfulness of Benjamin's angel in the library. Its compositional
style is much more than that of pastiche or collage, and the concept of
intertextuality alone too limited to encompass it. There is a vast difference between technique and worldview, drama and dramaturgy. The
divagations in *The Forest* reveal a remarkably baroque hidden order: an
entire narrative world resonates in the organization of literary and visual
material, as even a small amount of research reveals. If this creation sat-
isfies Nietzsche's notion of redemption in illusion, then there may be
earthly reward in his belief that "only as an aesthetic product can the
world be justified to all eternity."

Gilgamesh, the great epic of Assyrian-Babylonian culture dating back
to about 2600 B.C., and rewritten by many authors over a period of two
thousand years, was discovered buried in the ruins of Ashurbanipal's
library in the Mesopotamian city of Nineveh in the middle of the nineteenth century, then deposited in the British Museum. The last formidable king of the Assyrian empire, Ashurbanipal was an antiquarian
whose scribes searched the archives of scattered intellectual centers of
the region, translating for him the older Sumerian historical, scientific,
economic, literary, and religious texts. In Ashurbanipal's library there
was a collection of proverbs. One of them offered this observation:
"Writing is the mother of eloquence and the father of artists."

Gilgamesh began to be written down only centuries after the invention of writing in Sumer, on twelve clay tablets. Parts of one of the

world's great lost texts, which has never been completely recovered, were found in the Near Eastern cities of Ur, Sippar, Uruk, Megiddo, Sultantepe, and Ashur, composed in Sumerian, Akkadian, and Hittite. The tablets that survived were pieced together to decipher the epic, which by then had been literally written into the earth. *The Forest* does not use the textual material of the actual epic, but responds poetically to its themes. Similarly, the historical Gilgamesh is not likely to be the man in the text of the epic, because over the millennia it was written down, and rewritten myth and history were indistinguishable in the human mind. At every turn *Gilgamesh* itself deflects any attempt at accurate historical reproduction and interpretation.

Another literary work collected for *The Forest* is the *Florentine Codex (General History of the Things of New Spain)*, a pre-Columbian document of the Aztec civilization written originally in Nahuatl, then completed in Spanish in 1569 by the missionary Fray Bernardino de Sahagún. Its twelve books, ordered by both literary and visual texts, were scattered during the Inquisition and later found in the 1880s in the Laurentian Library of Florence, where they have remained since the 1790s.

Darryl Pinckney based the knee plays (unspoken in the New York production) on ancient Assyrian texts and wrote several comic speeches on animals, trees, and a Lisbon earthquake. Their visual source was the book *New and Curious School of Theatrical Dancing* by the Venetian ballet master Gregorio Lambranzi. This recovered text, a manual with fifty engraved plates of dancers in remarkably modern-looking movement, was first published in Nuremberg in 1716 and then discovered in the British Museum in the first quarter of the twentieth century. The effect of the knee plays was to recall Bauhaus performance style. One text by Heiner Müller appears in *The Forest*, the section entitled *Herakles 2 or The Hydra* from his own 1972 play *Cement*, which is based on the 1928 Russian novel of the same name by Gladkov. Herakles, who some have thought to be based on the figure of Gilgamesh, had twelve labors, the second in the forest. In Müller's nightmarish fragment a man is running through a war-torn landscape, its trees distorting into the shapes of snakes, the ground sucking him into the forest as he follows the tracks of his own blood.

Moving further into the texts inside of texts inside of cultures a structure emerges. Two stories echo through *The Forest*, enunciating its powerful organizing frame. "Silence—A Fable," an 1839 work originally called "Siope," opens the production. It is a tale from the Magi whose stylized Oriental setting evokes the ancient world of myth, cursed nature, and unearthly forces. Here narrative time is geologic time, and writing a kind of sedimentation. Through a sickly crimson mist its author reads the word DESOLATION on a huge gray rock. In "Shadow—A Parable," from 1835, a fragment of which closes *The Forest*, a writer recounts his story from the realm of the dead, and it too is cut into stone. The story tells of seven men who grieve at the ghostly deathbed of their friend during a time of pestilence: outdoors Jupiter and Saturn conjoin, disturbing the sky. Poe's story was written during an American cholera epidemic that coincided with the appearance of a comet, which frightened people even more. In another bizarre coincidence, 1988, the year of *The Forest* premiere, was a year of natural disasters around the world, and a deep red Mars was visible in the night sky.

The elegiac words of "The Shadow," appearing in the Poe tale when a mysterious phantom enters the death chamber, are now spoken in the last moments of *The Forest*, after the death of Enkidu: "The tones in the voice of the shadow were not the tones of any one being but of a multitude of beings and varying in their cadences from syllable to syllable fell duskly upon our ears in the well-remembered and familiar accents of many thousand departed friends." The allegorical level of the literary material crescendoes to an intense emotional drama set beside the legend of Gilgamesh and Enkidu, the first story in the world that is known, the story of a great love between two men, for the specter of AIDS lingers in the last, haunting moments of human speech sounded both live (by Gilgamesh) and on tape (by Wilson himself). The contrapuntal narrative lines are cross-grained in the terrible winds of loss. A slow-moving chorus of black hooded figures takes on the appearance of funerary sculpture in the white-cold space of death, grief echoing through centuries. The last image of *The Forest* is the silent scream of Gilgamesh, who, like Orpheus, has turned for a final look at his friend. In the epic the hero mourned seven days and nights, for the Sumero-Semitic world recognized the seven lunar divisions and days of the week.

It should be clear by now that the numbers seven and twelve figure prominently in both *The Forest* and *Gilgamesh*. One way to understand

Wilson's spiritual style is through its numerical order, which also manifests his deep feeling for structure. He is the most Pythagorean of theater artists. So significant in the numerology of world cultures, the number seven is that of the universe, perfection, synthesis; it connotes the cosmic stages, planetary spheres, and Pleiades, the directions of space. It is a totality, containing the temporal and the spiritual. There are seven branches of the Tree of Life. The legendary Gilgamesh and Enkidu had cut down the seven cedars of Lebanon to build a city. The number twelve signifies cosmic order, the hours of the day, the fruits of the Cosmic Tree. Many of the great books of civilization are divided into twelve, and notions of time and space derive from this number. Twelve also alludes to salvation.

Adding to this subtle numerical resonance, the composition of *The Forest* elaborates a highly refined poetic narrative—an architext—built around voices. Wilson's own voice on tape is distinctive among them, dispersed in fact throughout the entire production. In the first four acts of the work he narrates parts of "Silence," and in the last three, sections of "The Shadow." At times the narrative voice (the Old Man, or Wilson as the Voice in the text) appears only briefly for a few lines, at other times, such as in Act IV, Wilson gives a longer powerful story fragment by Jahnn on male bonding; in portions of Act II and Act III his voice takes on the gnarled poetic texture of isolated sounds, rather than commentary.

Turning from the single narrator to the manner of group speech, in Act V, where the forest (now evergreen) fills the great hall of the mansion, Fabre's treatise on the need of plants and animals for air is distributed among the characters, who separately speak a word, part of one, or a phrase. Act VI, in which Müller's *Herakles* text enters, shows Wilson using a technique that is not infrequent in his work: a cacophony of nature sounds and human screeches, cries, whines, fills the space, the disorder of human society embodied in the breakdown of speech.

The Forest, with sound design by Wilson's frequent collaborator Hans-Peter Kuhn, is full of sound effects, overlapping voices, noise, wordplay, talking, squawking, word fragments; narration, taped and live voice, chorus, solo; accented English and Wilson's crisp recitation. Sound environments crackling with a multitude of voices and pitches scramble syntax and deny the semantic value of language, reconstituting words as sound poems, in a continuous process of texturing/layering. The voice acts as a form of punctuation. This technique of stratification calls to mind Robert Smithson's analogy of word and rock, each containing "a language that follows a syntax of splits and ruptures," the word itself fragmenting into a "series of faults." Byrne's music slinks through this dense groundwork of sound, quoting vocabularies of modern music from Romantic to pop. Each scene expresses a distinct style of diction, with Wilson's own peripatetic voice placed as the unifying authorial voice, the activity of storytelling by nature lending a certain intimacy to the work. When it occurs, his very counterpoint with the Old Man, each telling and retelling different parts of a Poe tale, in two different timbres, occasionally alternating German and English, heightens the sense of time, which is the motif of the production.

Since the beginning of his work in the theater Wilson has been acclaimed for the sublime grace of his images, while the prominence of voice, the speech styles, and the sound poetry in the same pieces have gone largely unremarked. Yet, words and letters have covered his curtains and backdrops and as discrete units of speech filled his spaces, often as anguished words or screams. It is commonly known that Wilson had a serious stuttering problem well into his teenage years, eventually corrected through body-awareness training by a dance teacher in his native Texas; he would later name his Byrd Hoffman Foundation after her. Speech acts, though never the dialogue of conventional drama, have a substantial impact in Wilson's conception of theater: speech and gesture together, but as autonomous compositions. On one level his work plays out the tension between the spoken and the seen, the aural and the pictorial, in the theater experience, rightly addressed by Stein earlier in the century as an issue of emotion. To overlook the rhythm of speech in Wilson's work is to deny the rhetorical interplay of text and image, hearing and seeing, in the process of "articulation." Indeed, these emotional relations converge in the several kinds of "books" that constitute the production: literary, audio, visual.

The promiscuous forest of sounds, with its polyphony of human and animal voices, and "tongues in trees," rejoices in the plenitude of species, speech styles, and text material. For Wilson text equals texture. One of the essential dynamics at work in *The Forest* is the distinction between voice and text, which is elaborated in the opposing rhetorical styles of myth (based on orality) and history (based on the written word). At the level of diction the work analyzes its own dialectic.

III

Like John Cage, the great naturalist of contemporary American performance, Wilson seems to love the potential of sound in the open air: sound with space around it. In his method of composition he incorporates speech as text as naturally as Cage welcomed sound as music. (In his frequent use of bird song Wilson is on his way to becoming the Olivier Messiaen of the theater.) The Cage text, lost or found, made a landscape. Wilson's own forest is a library. In fact, this analogy is related to the deeper meaning of the book itself. According to the *Oxford English Dictionary*, the Latin root of *library—liber—*means bark (of a tree), which the ancient Romans used as writing material. This poetic linkage of imagery, with its cosmic overtones, is not without precedent in Wilson's work and thoughts on the idea of the Book: The transformation of a tree into a book is the resonating metaphor of the entr'actes in *the* CIVIL *wars*, conceived a decade ago. In Wilson's library, the voices of its authors fall to the ground like leaves, cultivating our world and its memory with organic matter, the very decomposition revealing the double life of the book as nature and culture. It was the woodsman Thoreau who observed that "decayed literature makes the best soil."

Trees are everywhere in Wilson's theater world axis. Indoors, outdoors, floating, standing upside down, right side up, withered, full of leaves, simply a branch or trunk; deciduous, evergreen. The tree is his *arbor philosophica*, rooting him to the great depths of human consciousness, where myth, religion, science, art, history, and geography are one, and drawing from it creative inspiration. In his production of *The Forest* the image of the tree is powerful in its mythical, historical, and ecological implications, extending from the ancient world to the present, because Wilson created it in Germany, in whose cultural imagination the forest plays so prominent a role, even as its forests are dying of progress. Tree symbolism, the teller of time, is a constant of humankind—Tree of Life, Tree of Light, Celestial Tree—signifying the epic of life and death on earth, and afterlife. The inverted Cosmic Tree of the *Upanishads* and Kabbalistic writings, a magic tree, appears frequently as an image in Wilson's work, not just in *The Forest*. This symbol of inversion illustrates the reflection of celestial and terrestrial worlds in each other, but also the path of knowledge traveling back to its roots. Beyond its symbology of the life process and feminine principle, Wilson's own tree of illumination is a line of energy that parallels his signature bars of light, and classical pillars.

If in the Western tradition Greek cosmology viewed the earth as a living organism, suffused with intelligence, the coming of Christianity, and with it the power of the Book (Bible), brought together the influences of the early Hermetic writers and church fathers, which led in the Middle Ages and the Renaissance to making the "book of nature" one of the great tropes of Humanism. Wilson gives to the theater its own book of nature, removed from its religious connotations, now in secular form, as if it were inscribed with the wisdom of Paracelsus, who exhorted humankind to study the geomancy of the earth, whose every element bears the sign of its essence; the earth, that book "in which the pages are turned with our feet." The discovery of new worlds is always accompanied by a new understanding of natural science.

In Wilson's eloquent dramaturgy the poetics of analogy transforms drama from its contemporary status as a local phenomenon to an international event, subverting the notion of making or viewing art from one's own cultural center. He gathers up the texts of world cultures and repositions (reprocesses) them in other climates and epochs, in new cultures and continents, transforming the national (and potentially nationalistic) into the universal (as opposed to the mass) and cosmopolitan. Already for Novalis books were a "modern species of historical entities" that replaced tradition. Texts live their own lives in the world, yet as part of the collective heritage, expanding the magisterial archive that is the world text/book of knowledge. This great book of the human voice makes and remakes peoples and civilizations, in a continuous cycle of life (body of knowledge) that defies the natural aging of thought over time. Texts from other worlds coexist with those of the contemporary world as if they were interactive organisms in the same environment. In fact, in the breath of the performing voice, in the new (theatrical) culture each production develops, they are. If a text is considered as an organism, the collective of texts/images that make up *The Forest* can then be understood as an ecosystem. And this ecosystem is part of a cultural system.

Wilson's dramaturgy demonstrates how the ecology of intertextuality delineates a global and historical perspective. In this antidote to contemporary literary/art politics, attention shifts from the idea of consumption to conservation, and from the obsession with appropriation/quotation to a feeling for the text as a gift—an earthwork (the text as graft). This dramaturgy of memory (which extends further than popular culture) is rooted in the life of the mind, all the while acknowledging the fragile identities of those who have written its stories and analyzed its dreams. Wilson has always shown more interest in civilization than in society.

As long ago as 2000 B.C. an Egyptian scribe expressed the anxiety of influence: "Would I had phrases that are not known, utterances that are strange, in new language that has not been used, free from repetition, not an utterance which has grown stale, which men of old have spoken." Now, nearly four thousand years later, origins are less consequential than destinations.

IV

The "dramaturgy of the dispersed text" celebrates the worldliness and acclimatization of texts, conflating the intercultural and the intertextual in a new sense of the *liber mundi*. In a world of chaos the fractal text knows no borders; it is a global concept. The book is now a (tectonic) plate whose natural state is continental drift. In the performance worlds Wilson invents, his dramaturgy can be more expansively construed as an *ecology*. He chooses all manner of species of texts and images from the world archive, then stages their fertility and adaptability in new environments. Relationships in these worlds are largely a matter of visual association. These texts and images have no reason to be together, mating in the same landscape, miscegenating (theatrical production is always reproduction); some of them are escapes from nature into culture. More profoundly, Wilson's dramaturgy imagines a world in which it is possible to comprehend that a cultural system cannot be separated from an ecosystem, and that cultural change is impressed upon the landscape. His theater acknowledges the place of nature in human consciousness.

Suggestively, the concept of anthology (the lives of texts) that Wilson's dramaturgical style evolves is linked etymologically to the lives of plants. In its original Greek sense, *anthology* meant a "gathering of flowers" (of verse). The Roman world would later define *horticulture* from *culture*. So to cultivate the mind and to cultivate the land came to be understood as related activities in the development of a civilization.

Wilson's biocentrism shapes his understanding of natural history as part of the history of the world, a philosophical view that joins theater to natural science, biology to geology, and dramaturgy to ecology. It is not so difficult to move from a theater to a landscape. Each envisions a world in a place that reveres presence, and the fabulous confusion of nature and artifice, which is to say, reality and illusion. *The Forest* reveals why it is no longer enough to think merely of the play, but rather of the *archive*, as the revitalizing force of a new dramaturgy for the twenty-first century.

The Forest is part fable, part fiction, now epic, now science, as if genres were temperaments that shout across mountains and millennia in long-forgotten qualities of the voice. One by one the dispersed texts of human history are reflected in the Wilson moonlight, which turns old books into illuminated manuscripts for new audiences, numerous worlds.

(1993)

Revised, expanded version of "The Forest as Archive: Robert Wilson and Interculturalism," published in "The Interculturalism Issue," *Performing Arts Journal* 33/34, 1989.

St. Gertrude

For Robert Wilson

I

"Through a window with a grate covered by a veil, I spoke with those who came to visit me," St. Therese of Avila described convent life in her *Book of Foundations*. The sense of a framed life would appeal to Gertrude Stein, who brought together the painterly and the literary, changing nouns to verbs. In her *Four Saints in Three Acts*, in which St. Therese has more than three dozen companions, St. Ignatius is always worrying about who is "to be windowed." Nuns should observe enclosure, he had decreed in sixteenth-century Spain. "How many windows and doors and floors are there in it," asks St. Therese herself in the middle of the opera. She wants to know what kind of space will frame her.

Stein took great pleasure in the transcendent moments of human existence, which St. Therese, her literary sister, had called "spiritual delights." Inspired by her favorite saints—Therese, Ignatius, and Francis—Stein, a Jew, participated in the secularization of the spiritual, the long-lasting project of modernism, by aligning spiritual energy and creative power as acts of faith. Catholicism was an aspect of the intellectual landscape of France, her home from 1903.

Numerous books printed in France (and in England) from the turn of the century into the twenties offered studies of sainthood, mysticism, and the religious life, St. Therese or St. Ignatius the subject of most of them. It was then that Stein's mentor at Radcliffe, William James, published his great work *Varieties of Religious Experience*, though in it he criticized St. Therese as a bit of a flirt in her solicitation of God. Before

World War I, in painting and drama, the spiritual dimensions of human thought and feeling had inspired the vision of abstraction, which moves toward the same goal as religious feeling: the contemplation of absolute perfection in an instant of pure presence. In French letters Mallarmé had already conceived of The Book as a "spiritual instrument," and the Belgian Maeterlinck imagined a new conception of dramaturgy in the religiosity of symbolist aesthetics. Moreover, numerous French composers created works on religious themes or in liturgical forms, including Debussy, Poulenc, Satie, Massenet, and Messiaen, from the turn of the century to the period between the wars.

Saints, in particular, have long preoccupied artists, particularly St. Francis, St. Joan, St. Anthony, St. Paul, and St. Sebastian. There are many examples of works in the modern period that treat their lives: in painting, poetry, opera, drama, film. Even the avant-garde manifestoes of the era, mainly from the Catholic countries France and Italy, have a sense of the church litany in them, for repetition is as much a formal quality of avant-garde rhetoric as it is of church doctrine. The exemplary writings of Artaud, to be fully understood, should be read alongside saints' writings. Closer to our own time, Genet made of dramaturgy a liturgy, then Sartre turned him into a saint, and Barthes wrote a long essay on the language of St. Ignatius.

Stein's great friend and astute admirer Thornton Wilder, who himself had written plays with a fair share of angels and saints, understood that on one level her work could be read as a series of "spiritual exercises." Her Latinate writings were full of exhortations, codes of self-discipline, study of mental states, acts of contemplation, the cataloguing of the senses. Stein offers a manual for the writing life as rigorous as Ignatius's guide to the spiritual life. Like the lives of saints, her inner world leaned toward the ascetic, and like saints' writings, her own are full of repetition, for going forward always meant going backward, beginning again. If her guide wasn't quite the sort Ignatius had planned for his classic work, Stein's spiritual journey was nevertheless toward the perfect state of mind, her stanzas in meditation more joyful and wondrous in celebrating nature and being and creating. Ecstasy was always her subject.

For Stein, sainthood, like its secular counterpart, genius, celebrates the fullness of presence: aura. "Saints shouldn't do anything. The fact that a saint is there is enough for anybody," she said. A saint's life is quite like a writer's life, based as it is on the Word, revelation. A saint, like a classic, is just there. Perhaps that is why both saints and books enjoy canonization. A writer-saint's life, St. Therese's, is naturally a performance, because it is given to self-dramatization, this self-dramatizing quality of writing resulting in the primacy of the voice in the text. For St. Therese the voice was her link to God: to listen for the Word is at the center of Catholic faith. For Stein her voice was the link to the audience: "listen to me" is a constant refrain in her writings. She called *Four Saints* "an opera to be sung," emphasizing its vocal quality. The forms that characterize it vocally are those of the Church: antiphon, litany, polyphony, choral. Its structure of three acts alludes, significantly, to the Trinity.

Stein extended the condition of sainthood, the state of grace, into her conception of the play as a landscape. In the 1934 essay "Plays," she explains: "In *Four Saints* I made the Saints the landscape. All the saints that I made and I made a number of them because after all a great many pieces of things are in a landscape all these saints together made my landscape. . . . A landscape does not move nothing really moves in a landscape but things are there, and I put into the play the things that were there." For Stein, the life of a convent is the life of a landscape, nuns busily moving about but the scene remaining placid as a landscape, simply there. Still life. The walled-in cloister is a natural frame. It follows that the play/landscape evolves essentially as static composition, tableau, in which frontality is the defining visual attitude. Elements in the landscape—people, objects, or nature—only become meaningful to one when they are looked at. In deriving from nature, Stein's conception of a play as landscape joins the natural and the artificial in a topographical view of dramaturgy.

Though much less radically, and with altogether different intentions, Maeterlinck carried a personal, spiritual vision of the natural world into drama, breaking down the conventional action/conflict-based scenic structure into smaller units of nonaction, at times with repetitive, fragmentary sentences. Narration often substitutes for dramatic action, intuition for speech, the sign for the thing. The notion of the figure in a landscape is central to his static, abstract plays, as it would be for Stein. In Maeterlinck's quiet drama the most cherished element was sense perception. Chekhov, ever attentive to the world around him, had hinted at the idea of a new performance space with *The Seagull*, in which he made landscape an aspect of the dramatic conception. He made dramatic time seem like real time. Stein's remark that "conversation is only interesting if nobody hears" might well apply to Chekhov's plays. All three writers took great interest in the natural world, which influenced the philosophical underpinning of the works, Maeterlinck and Chekhov as horticulturalists, and Stein—she left the gardening to Toklas—in her special view of geography and the human mind. She elaborated the concept of a dramatic field as drama. For her, space became a scene of revelation.

At the same time that painting was moving toward abstraction and flatness, there was a parallel movement in theater. The fussy detail of setting was giving way to space, the text to the voice, closure to process. This theatrical shift was perceived by dramatists, who were evolving new attitudes toward space, object, and perception, in effect a philosophic shift in the relation of figure to ground. It is not coincidental that Kandinsky, whose paintings are among the earliest abstract compositions, in his work for the stage elaborated the scenic units as "pictures." The idea of the stage picture described a theater of tableaux and tableau objects, emphasizing frontality and the frame, the painterly and the contemplative. Kandinsky harmonized the abstract and the spiritual in a new spatial consciousness. Under the influence of cubism, which opened up other possibilities for abstract art in its decentering of subject and fragmentation of surface, Stein brought the techniques of abstraction and collage to drama, shifting it from the anecdotal to the pictorial, from psychology to mind.

II

Stein was more interested in soulfulness than in the soul, in natural processes than in nature. She invited the natural world into her work to express itself in a formal way, opening her pages to bird song and climate and plant life as compositional elements of the plays. They create the language of the plays, not merely functioning as description of setting or atmosphere. Bird song alternated with conversation, the moon with a lamp. John Cage, who early in his career set Stein's words to music, would decades later create music from the same impulse to have it imitate, not nature itself, but the processes of nature. Stein and Cage shared a passion for the sights and sounds of the world, and from this passion flows their spiritual energy: everything is experienced as mind, enlightenment. That Stein liked to sit in the front seat of her car "Godiva" and write to the rhythm of street sounds and traffic is the kind of joyful creativity Cage celebrated in his mus/ecology. Stein treated her own life and the lives of friends as "ready-mades." In the countryside she would at times write in the open air to the rhythm of life around her—a circling cow, a stream, the wind, a conversation. The sky was a sheet of paper. Her writing was repetitious and cyclical in shape because she wrote in nature, not of it. Repetition instilled in the words a sense of awe. As early as *The Making of Americans* she understood that repetition was a kind of wisdom. "Loving repeating is in a way earth feeling." For Stein, writing was always organic process.

In the glorious St. Remy period, beginning in 1922, five years before she wrote *Four Saints* back in Paris, when Stein composed such plays as *Saints and Singing, A Saint in Seven,* and *Lend a Hand or Four Religions,* in addition to other works that alluded to Catholic literary form—"Talks to Saints or Stories of Saint Remy," "Practice of Oratory," "A Hymn," and "Precepts"—she infused her saintly preoccupations with the worship of the natural world. When she first began to write plays, in 1913, she was in Mallorca. There she first called a play a landscape, and the early plays she gathered with other works in a volume called *Geography and Plays.* Already the compositional sense of writing as mapping was in her work. Geography and perception, and for a time Spain and play and landscape, would be inseparable.

By 1922 Stein was infusing more of the landscape in the emotion of her writing. "I concentrated the internal melody of existence that I had learned in relation to things seen into the feelings I then had . . . of light and air and air moving and being still." Her writing was rooted to daily existence in the Rhône Valley, where she had a country house. In the Mallorcan plays she was a tourist in the landscape, but in the southeast of France, at St. Remy and later at Bilignin, she inhabited it, and that made all the difference. Here the lives of Stein and her friends were indistinguishable from the lives of saints, and talk from prayer. She prayed to saints for rain in St. Remy. She went to Lucy Church amiably. She saw mountains of saints singing and religious faces on black currants.

She read flowers. There was beatitude in gratitude. The land was like an illuminated manuscript. What joined together the writer's life and the saintly life was that in her childlike wonder Stein was able to experience the world as miraculous. For a time she became St. Gertrude in ecstasy. "How a little nature makes religion, and how a little religion makes creation." Stein was never so musical as in the saint plays, her miracle plays. These were her years of the sublime.

III

Stein was preoccupied by creation, not representation. Things in themselves, the qualities, not the names of things. *Four Saints* works as a composition in both the literary and the horticultural sense, demonstrating as complex an idea of dramatic writing as one can find in twentieth-century theater. If Henry James had his figure in the carpet, Stein would have hers in the garden. Both writers wrote around a subject, not about it.

Hidden in *Four Saints* is the outline of a *hortus conclusus*. St. Therese is both the protected virgin and Stein's literary heroine in a garden. As much a plan of research as it is a play, *Four Saints* reveals a formal garden conceived as a plan of knowledge. With the constant interruption of her own voice in the narrative, Stein incorporates her ideas for the play, the choices for weather, objects, birds, flowers. Stage directions and remarks on design are also made a part of the text. "St. Therese could be photographed." More scenes, more saints. "A great many saints can sit around with one standing." Documentary sections of daily life and thoughts flow into the writing process, making real time interchangeable with dramatic time. "What happened to-day, a narrative." A bit of sexual innuendo. Two of them, longitudinally. More and more saints are added, even a St. Plan. Halfway through, St. Therese asks, "How many saints are there in it." Stein needs more time for research on Ignatius. "Continue reading." More wordplay, children's tunes, rhyming. My country tis of thee. Scenes run out of sequence, repeat in different order, go backwards. One scene is an adverb—"usefully." Sentences sing across the page. "Could Four Acts be three." A procession. "One at a time in rhyme." An exasperated chorus of saints wonders at last, How much of it is finished.

Curiously, St. Therese's own writings are full of digressions, repetition, movements from singular to plural, first person to third, missing punctuation. "But what disorder in the way I write," she interjects in *The Way of Perfection*. More self-recrimination. "So many days have gone by since I wrote the above." Stein is just as anxious in *Four Saints*. "A narrative to plan an opera." Then, "Come panic come."

Stein's grand design is a fabulous subversion of plot. The English word *plot*, which in the medieval period first defined a patch of land set off from its surroundings, by the sixteenth century describes a plan for writing. Like Stein's window, it can be both noun and verb. The topographical conceit of the opera elaborates her idea of dramaturgy: the play as landscape or dramatic field.

What Stein does in *Four Saints* is transform the idea of theological space into a spatial conception of drama. Read as an allegory, the "four saints" of the title act as the four pathways of the garden, echoing the biblical four rivers of Eden. (In her autobiography St. Therese describes the four kinds of prayer as four ways to water a garden.) The garden is Stein's perfect universe, a paradise, a frame. The Persian word *pairidaeza* (paradise) means enclosure, and from this form the cloister garden plan of Catholic monasteries took shape as a place of learning and meditation and cosmological principle. In *Four Saints* the garden space is now a performance space, the plot of a garden the plot of a play.

If in the earlier *Lend a Hand or Four Religions* the four religions serve as four roads in the play (sign/posts), now the imagery outlines a garden that is walled in, enclosed. The garden is filled with flowers: hyacinths, pansies, violets, fragrant roses. Herbs too. And hedges. It has fruit trees—pear, cherry, apple. An arbor. To piece together the images of the play one has to discover the words dispersed throughout it, because they don't appear together as a description of an event, but in an all-over effect, as field. Reading Stein, being an observant Stein reader, is looking for her words on a page the way one seeks out wildflowers in a meadow. She likes words in the open air, words with space around them. It's as if the words have been windblown through the text. A robin here, a magpie there, snow, rain, soil, a bench, a plateau. "Exercise in mastering pieces of it," she advises in the rapturous *Saints and Singing*.

In *Four Saints* there is a "garden inside and outside of the wall." The frame inside of a frame inside of a frame—the walled-in garden in the walled-in cloister inside of the walled-in city of Avila. Here is the perfect principle of containment for Stein to pursue inner and outer reality. Even her stage directions follow the pattern of the wall. "Who mentioned that one followed another laterally." Two geographies: Avila for Therese, Barcelona for Ignatius. Walls, water. Pigeons on his grass, alas. It's only the Holy Ghost. Stein called *Four Saints* "a perfectly simple description of the Spanish landscape."

A play is a landscape. In Stein's plan the preferred landscape does not imitate the natural, flowing line of the English school, but the more formal, stylized continental design. The same can be said of her writing. With the elegance of Poe, Stein's own philosophy of composition equals her structural plan for the work itself. Her "landscape" collapses the time/space frame of sixteenth-century Spain and Paris of the twenties, the baroque and the modern—cultures of sight.

Here in her garden as text Stein reconciles nature and society, her private and public lives. Play and work. The blank sheet of paper on which she plots her play opens up as a land of wonder. To write is to worship.

(1994)

Natural Histories
of the Drama

A Cosmography of Herself

The Autobiology of Rachel Rosenthal

⁘⁘⁘⁘ Nowhere more evocatively does performance art express the ecological condition of contemporary life at the end of the twentieth century than in the works of Rachel Rosenthal, elaborating as they do the polemics of harmony and chaos, which so many seek to moderate in their lives and in the world around them. This antinomy is at the heart of her dramaturgy, and since performance art is primarily a solo form made on the body of the performer, it is, more significantly, a function of her physiology as a woman in her mid-sixties. What comes through in the performances of Rosenthal is her worldliness in the acceptance of natural history as a part of the history of the world and part of her history. Because performance art is not a tragic form, nor Rosenthal's nature tragic, comic irony is the mood of the all too human *commedia* that is the natural history of her own life.

All of these themes come together like fibers of a nervous system in the kind of performances Rosenthal constructs around body, biology, and gender. She transvalues the routinely autobiographical form into what I call the *autobiological*, making performance a life science. Her feminism evolves a profoundly philosophical system that impels feminine principles toward an ethics of performance. Then human ethics is made symmetrical with environmental ethics, opening up a historical perspective that moves beyond the merely personal to the more broadly global. The very precise spiritual focus of her work collapses human time into cosmic time, aligning art and science, poetry and performance.

59

In effect, Rosenthal fuses the controversial Gaia hypothesis, the view of nature described in chaos theory, and the perspective on geology described in the study of plate tectonics to trace the autobiology of her life. Drawing upon issues raised by these scientific ideas, her performances are oriented increasingly around ecological themes and animal rights. But more than that, the face of the earth has become a metaphor for her own physiognomy.

In an early piece, *Grand Canyon* (1978), Rosenthal transforms into a vampire who flies over the canyon on a snowy winter day. She reads it like a topology of her life. The canyon's faults, erosion pattern, plateaus, and rocks act as signs of her life in this personal journey of metamorphosis: a geological fault is for her a matter of guilt. As narrative strategy, the journey is both real and symbolic in her work. Rosenthal's family fled Hitler's Europe, first to Brazil, then to New York during World War II, and so she became a refugee, a traveler, homeless, an immigrant. Rosenthal, who lives in Los Angeles and speaks English with the New York City accent of someone who once spoke another language, has always made geography—which is to say, walking across the earth— her subject. She brings the feeling of travel into performance.

Another one of her works named after a specific topography is *Death Valley* (1988). More metaphoric in name, this *J'accuse* solo is accompanied by dissonant violin and vocal work consisting of animal sounds, Jewish religious rhythms, speech-song, and chants. The operatic reach of the piece links it to the avant-garde arias Cathy Berberian was known for in Europe a few decades ago. In any case, music has always been an essential element in Rosenthal's performance style, based as it is so freely in the timbre of the voice. Her declamations often assume the character of song. In this piece she develops the theme of collaborator: "By being alive I have tacitly agreed to . . ." Dressed in a long blue, white, and black robe and long black gloves, wearing black lipstick and eye shadow, the elegant, bald-headed Rosenthal recites a litany of horrors that includes "obscenity of the food chain," "carnage of the earth," "stealing habitats," and "chemical warfare." At times Rosenthal takes on the cry of a coyote. She feels constant pain in her knees. The world is disjointed. Indeed, the year 1988 brought worldwide ecological turmoil.

A large-scale piece with live animals, *The Others* (1984), takes up the issue of animal liberation, a prominent motif in later performances.

Here Rosenthal attacks the Cartesian view of animals as "thought-less brutes" without consciousness. She speaks for their victimhood, or otherness, focusing their exploitation by science as a rights issue.

Some may find problematic Rosenthal's biocentrism because of its inherent antihumanist view. But it is at the core of her performances, the philosophical foundation of their "deep ecology" perspective. Within the ecologies of theater that I have been outlining in recent years, Rosenthal has affinities with the biocentric worldview reflected also in the works of Meredith Monk and Robert Wilson. These artists elucidate the utopian line of thinking in late-twentieth-century theater, creating nonhierarchical performance worlds populated by human and nonhuman species. Even more than that, they share an interest in cosmology.

Biocentrism helps to illuminate Rosenthal's interest in Gaia, the ancient earth goddess of the Greeks and the poetic essence of her personally revealing work L.O.W. in Gaia (1986) Here, in the true spirit of performance art, centered in the body as text, Rosenthal takes on the persona of Gaia herself. James Lovelock, whose two books on the Gaia theme draw on contemporary thinking in geology, geochemistry, evolutionary biology, and climatology, offers a view of the earth and the life it bears as a "physiological system." He regards it as a self-regulating organism rather than inert rock upon which plants and animals live. In this scheme of things the health of the planet matters more than that of individual species or organisms. If the word *theater*, like *theory*, derives from the idea of spectatorship, then the Gaia hypothesis is at the heart of Rosenthal's definition of the theatrical. I think of her as the Great Mother of Performance.

Lynn Margulis, Lovelock's colleague in first putting forth the challenging idea of Gaia, views symbiosis rather than the random accumulation of mutations as a source of evolutionary change and diversity. The reciprocal action between organism and environment—in sociological terms, a partnership society—is favored over that of competition among individuals. Margulis's contention that the earth is *autopoietic*—self-maintaining—sits comfortably with the contemporary psychology of self-actualization that Rosenthal affirms. This perspective on Gaia—its rebuke to the belief that environment dominates life, or humans the environment—is emphasized in Rosenthal's noncoercive dramaturgy, based not on the Aristotelian notion of interactive conflict but on a more process-oriented, open, nonhierarchical model. It is documentary rather than dramatic in nature, chaotic rather than unified. Scientifically based Necessity overrules Fate.

If in the earlier *Gaia, Mon Amour* (1983) she assumes the persona of the earth goddess in a series of interlocking monologues that catalogue human violence toward nature, the more expansive and dramatic *L.O.W. in Gaia* is a chronicle of a three-week vacation Rosenthal took in the Mojave Desert. In this work she shows color slides of herself there in a rented van and recounts her adventures hiking and preparing meals, even brief encounters with humans. She praises the beauty of the stars in the dry, silent night and the enchanting sound of a coyote concert. But Rosenthal is no sentimentalist. Little by little the haunting scenes of the desert landscape shown in the montage of slides give way to images of the desert floor littered with the detritus of the civilized world. Accompanying voice-overs and visual texts—by Gary Snyder, William Catton, Aldo Leopold, and others—provide commentary on nuclear radiation, pollution, technological profligacy, human irresponsibility. Here in the desert are the unmistakable allusions to ancient religion and myth and, in our own time, to nuclear testing and missile sites. The voice of the sagebrush whistles in the desert wind: nuclear crisis is one of metaphysical dimension.

One of the profound themes in Rosenthal's work is the understanding that the ecosystem is inseparable from the cultural system of a people. This insight returns to the ancient view of the world in which history, myth, religion, ecology, philosophy, and aesthetics were considered together in any reflection on human affairs. Rosenthal is simply forcing performance to accept its place in the history of ideas. The feeling for landscape is at the very marrow of the American psyche. Rosenthal's diaristic performance problematizes the town-versus-country theme—she is drawn to the desert but lives in Los Angeles—so familiar to nature writing and the myth of the sublime western landscape with its boundless resources. She brings into high relief the very real possibility of ecological catastrophe.

L.O.W. in Gaia, then, is no mere eclogue singing the praises of desert solitaire, but a cry of rage to Gaia, in Rosenthal's adopted voice of a Crone. A ritualistic mood transforms this performance conceived in part as a meditation, in the small altar of bones she constructs around her, close to which she places a candle, and sanctified by her incantatory language. Rosenthal's totemism also gives a feeling of the sacred to her performance, which is more of a rite. Her head, on which she will trace in lipstick the number sixty (for her sixty years when the work was created) as a kind of magical act, only serves to enhance her mystique as a woman of special qualities. Indeed, she is a Crone.

In prepatriarchal mythology, linked as it was to ecology, the Crone —the force of life and death—formed part of the three-in-one unity that comprised Virgin, Mother, and Crone. Rosenthal weaves around the concept of time the condition of her own aging body, and that of the earth, her linkage emphasizing personally the importance given to the contemporary consideration of ecology as an aspect of biology. So human time is apprehended in the sweep of cosmic time, and myth joined to history. Furthermore, Rosenthal develops the theme as a cosmography of herself, drawing upon this suppressed women's history to articulate an autoecology.

However appealing the Gaia hypothesis is as a way of explaining life on the planet, I am somewhat skeptical of Lovelock's recent book on the subject, *The Ages of Gaia,* in which he invokes comparison between Gaia and the Virgin Mary. Though she certainly regards the earth with a sense of the sacred, Rosenthal's own ethos is nondenominational, fully secular, even pagan.

In the ancient stone of Marble Mountain she sees an anthropomorphic likeness of the Death Crone. She reflects on death and dying. A sequence of slides is projected on the back wall of the performance space, unfolding in a series of portraits of Rosenthal in her own "Ages of Woman." While the autobiographical images unfold behind her she takes an electric razor over her bald head as if to fully erase history, and with it the seductiveness of youth, of woman, of victim. Then she speaks in one of her characteristic Euripidean women's voices:

> I am the Crone
> The third aspect of the Triple Goddess. The one you fear.
> You can accept the Virgin,
> barely stomach the Mother,
> but me, you have attempted to destroy.

I am your death.
Not the glamorous death of battles, of heroism, of blood
    spilled for a cause.
No, I am gout, ulcers, rheumatism, Alzheimer's, and cancer.

I am Nemesis of the Greeks.
Morgan Le Fay of the Celts
In India I am Kali the Black
In Scandinavia, Hel—Queen of the Shades
I am the Night Mare, the black mare-headed
    Demeter, Demeter Chthonic, the Subterranean.
Your culture turned me into a devil.
You reject me. You despise and fear older women.

If one of the most profound philosophical implications of theater is
the moment-to-moment dying of the performer's body before the eyes
of the audience, Rosenthal carries this thought to an extreme by making
it the subject of her performance. Moreover, she then links this theme
to the aging of the earth, of Gaia, and the desecration of the earth's
body through the forces of commodification and relentless human de-
structiveness. In its compelling model of ecofeminist performance she
brings together the exploitation of women's bodies and the body of the
earth, that is, women's rights and biotic rights.

The origin of the universe at the Big Bang now seems certain, but
Rosenthal sees its destiny as the Big Crash. Her nightmarish vision of
the future is physicalized in the fortieth-century Monster she imper-
sonates at the beginning and end of the performance: an androgynous
creature who is bent over, jaw fused open, lipless, hands bereft of their
tensile ability. The Monster will find in the ground bits and pieces of
disks marked with a warning symbol announcing waste disposal nearby.
The waste remains, but not the human race.

In Rosenthal's work, not only *L.O.W. in Gaia* but those pieces that
address her grand themes of nuclear holocaust, pollution, consumer-
ism, the forces of nature, the myth of progress, such as *Death Valley,
Was Black,* and *Pangaean Dreams,* she condemns developments in history that have led to humankind's separation from the natural world.
She evokes the opposition between nature and culture even as she
humorously explores her own contradictions in the face of it. But Rosen-

thal is not anti-technological (her performances demand a sophisticated use of technology), she is not anti-Western (all cultures' wanton destruction of their land is acknowledged), and she is not anti-modernist (her work sits comfortably in the century-long tradition of avant-garde performance). All of these positions have found a place in the environmentalist critique, but not with Rosenthal. In fact, she is more materialist than mystic, despite her conviction that the crisis of culture is a spiritual one.

Rosenthal offers a model of the performance artist who can imagine life-sustaining images amidst the imagery of extinction. She transforms the Death Crone into the creative force of the death-defying artist who can generate essential new myths for today. In a perversely classical sense, L.O.W. in Gaia is a public enactment of the myths of the community, a feminist satyr play to be considered alongside the classics.

Rosenthal dares to expose herself to the certain beauty in facing terror, the evil that is human, dreamed of by Artaud in his own radical autobiology. Singularly, she carries his disturbing chaotic spirit into American performance art, where she is author, director, spectacle, signaling through the hot air of global warming, if not its flames. Her bald head becomes a blank surface on which to reflect the history of the world, a mirror of its horror. The Crone is the ancient presence of the Other in her body: her double. The foreground of the performance is her own agonized body, now a theater where Artaud's "spiritual therapeutics" is acted out for the social body. Her body politics reaches out toward healing. Where else can one go with the final image of *Was Black*, a response to the Chernobyl disaster (and a literal translation of the Russian word), when the performers wrap around her torso and face a long cord whose tiny bulbs light up suddenly, reflecting in gruesome metaphor the radiated body.

Rosenthal projects from her body a special kind of performance knowledge, a womanly knowledge, the physiological understanding of images that is the powerful inner light of visionary performance. It is the spectacular autobiology of a performer one wants to know and to learn from, the very embodiment of the kind of illumination a body of knowledge bestows.

Yet all the while Rosenthal walks in the realm of myth she is demythologizing herself. A highly self-conscious performer, more theatrical and literary than most performance artists, she is forever finding "another self-made myth to explode." Among her favorite devices is the double or split self in dialogue, and the sudden about-face from a serious political diatribe on a social issue to a personal revelation of her own complicity in the problem. How to pursue further the possibility that the Great Mother mystique may unlock the possibility of a mother-daughter story?

The ironic play between masking and unmasking is nowhere more poignant than in Rosenthal's exposure of the very subject of performance art—the body—to laughter, even pity, and, more frighteningly, fear. Here is a performer confronting aging, one of the great taboos of performance life. Her body, she allows, is not the perfect instrument it is supposed to be *as a performing body*. "Why is every performance so hard? Why do I suffer like this?" Rosenthal personalizes the condition of chaos theory's fractal self in *Pangaean Dreams* (1990), a piece about motion: What could be more difficult for Rosenthal, with her decades-old knee problem (Wilson has his knee plays, she has hers). Osteoporosis is acknowledged as structural principle in the body of pain. With her wheelchair entrance and talk of plastic knees, back trouble, and fractured vertebrae, Rosenthal only underscores the lithe, puppetlike quality of her performances, in all its tragicomic implications. Rosenthal has a marvelously trained body, a mime's light-footedness and legerdemain, and one watches in performance a body struggling to act—the way one looks at aging dancers or listens to aging singers—with a heightened awareness of nature's competitiveness with art.

Given that performance is a function of the body, and with an aging, still-active avant-garde, it is surprising that this subject is not more important to artists, especially women, who stand to gain so much in the lifting of taboos on the aging female body/performer/image. The biological is the dangerous staging ground for the struggle between theory and praxis, or desire and experience. Rosenthal positions herself in this dialectic, creating for it a frame of reference full of poetry and panache. The performances constitute her own natural history.

If in *L.O.W. in Gaia* Rosenthal draws a metaphoric parallel between her own aging body and the earth, in *Pangaean Dreams* she considers the breaking apart of her body in the context of continental drift and plate tectonics. Again, the personal is extenuated to the global. As a resi-

dent of California, she can't help but anticipate the Big Rift. In this recent work, subtitled "A Shamanic Journey," Rosenthal descends into the
underworld to search for answers to the mystery of existence. An accom-
panist beats the drum that induces her altered state of consciousness.
Rosenthal chants and rattles to the four corners of the earth. Roaming
around the bowels of the earth inside a video image she discovers the
workings of plate tectonics. It shapes for her an entirely revolutionary
worldview.

Scoffed at for decades, Alfred Wegener's idea that the surface of the
earth is divided into a small number of rigid drifting plates on which
continents, driven by hot, upwelling fluids, move and interact with each
other, has become in recent times a fully elaborated perspective on the
distribution of mountains, earthquakes, and volcanic activity. In fact,
the earthquake in the Mojave Desert in June 1992 gave scientists a look
at what they believe is a new tectonic system that is cutting California
away from North America and moving it toward Alaska. In a development not without its cultural irony, the Baja region of Mexico is pushing northward on its Pacific plate, unnerving the San Andreas Fault. So
Rosenthal's sense of continental drift has real repercussions in her life,
as well as scientific legitimacy. She, Rachel Rosenthal, living at the end
of the twentieth century, is part of a process that began about 250 million years ago, when the continents of the world formed a single mass,
called Pangaea, which broke up into several continents that have been
drifting ever since. As she reads the signs of her life in the earth itself,
the semiological swells into the seismological. Nothing is what it seems.
But now she has a radical understanding of time and space and personal upheaval. In another light, the discovery of the workings of plate
tectonics was largely circulated during the period of cubist painting,
which captured the fractured, shifting planes of reality on an unstable
surface. It is this cubist vision, which in fact destroyed perspective as it
had evolved since the Renaissance, that adds a metaphysical footnote
to the scientific findings.

The knowledge that Rosenthal received about the earth on her
underworld travels is presented in the form of the shamanic trance as
the Big Picture, a moving picture projected on the surface of a long
robe she wears, unfurled by sticks that stretch the robe wide as she
opens her arms, unmistakably recalling Loie Fuller's grand gestures a

century ago. It is a collage of dinosaurs, flocks of birds, ships, refugees, cowboys, Indians, cities, trains, factories, bridges: dislocation—a theme of the work—as life principle. Everyone is on the move.

If Rosenthal formerly longed for unity, *rapprochement*, now she accepts the way of the world as constant flux. Call her the Heraclitus of the performance world. Plate tectonics defines a state of mind, and Rosenthal considers all of its convulsive realignments "a learning experience." A simple event can turn into a groundbreaking perception. In a fantastic California-inspired image she sees the plate as a skateboard weaving around everyday activities. Even the structure of *Pangaean Dreams* seems to be affected by the idea of the plate: separate parts of the stage space act as plates (planes) in which different kinds of performance occur, the shamanic journey or Rosenthal as herself. The concept of the plate also evolves into the plane surface on which slides or video are projected throughout the piece. In this context, plate tectonics suggests a provocative interpretation of collage, which has always been the organizing principle of Rosenthal's work.

Added to this view are the lessons of chaos theory, which, in this context, allows for the comparison of human relationships to earth's tremors, magnetic fields, strange attractors. In other words, predictable turbulence is the law of nature. These scientific metaphors are joined to an all-embracing Gaia image to form a comprehensive ecosophy, which declares indivisible the ecosystem and the cultural, economic, political, and psychological systems of a people. The human body will share the same nervous system as Gaia, because nature and culture cannot be disjoined into separate environments. It is this split in "human nature" that Rosenthal's work addresses.

Themes of conflict and duality are explored in Rosenthal's dialogue with her male double, the personification of her pain, which she refers to as the Autonomous Being. He challenges her to account for her conflicting selves: Rosenthal is a worshipper of the Great Mother who disdains childbirth, a nature lover who cannot do without the amenities of conventional hygiene, a celebrator of womanhood who hates its biological imperatives. The most provocative exchange between Rosenthal and her Autonomous Being comes in a discussion about gender in which he questions her feminism. Rosenthal answers that she is "a gay man in a woman's body." Autobiologically speaking, her identity crisis is a provocation of enormous complexity. "Men don't want me, because they sense something funny. Gay men don't want me, because they see me as a woman. Women want me, but I don't want them, because I want men —but not as a woman. . . !" Formidable seismologies erupt from the rhetorical body in this chaotic discourse of signs and shifting surface texts.

In another section of the performance Rosenthal talks about men and women and love in the style of a thirties French film: taunting, seductive, pushing to extremes. Love is flaccid, feminine, and amorphous; hate is vigorous, masculine, linear. Rosenthal is a feminist who can make feminists uncomfortable with their sexual position because she gives voice to the unmentionable subjects, as Carolee Schneemann has done in her own pioneering autobiology. And, she is close in spirit to the mocking sophistication, even decadence, of Pina Bausch. These women eschew the frequently girlish, politically safe attitudes in performances by women for a more dangerous worldliness and womanliness where Eros and Irony share the stage.

What is especially engaging about Rosenthal is the great, good humor that characterizes her performances: quite simply, the comedy that is always attached to the biological in human drama. Rosenthal has a real earthiness and scatological sense that, when accompanied by the release from etiquette age can bring, leads to a decided freedom of expression. Who but she would worry about the methane content released into the environment by human beings? "From the Gaian perspective, we may be only as important as our farts," she confides to her audience.

Part of Rosenthal's "aura" is the multiple imagery of her own persona—the sense of glamour she exudes; the very sensual gestures of the long hands; her redoubtable femaleness, always flirting with androgyny; the drop earrings; the remnants of French sweetness in the voice. All of these qualities coexist with the bald head and deliberate dressing down, cross-dressing, at times in army fatigues; and the raunchy language and cutting through of taboos, the disturbing thoughts. Rosenthal is as much a personality as a performer, in the expansive modernist sense. Her performances stylize her desire for an out-of-body experience. Or is it Artaud's dream, still alive today, of the body without organs?

Dismemberment is part of shamanism, and in *Pangaean Dreams* this component of the journey is transmuted into Rosenthal's frequent digging up of bones and body parts throughout the performance. Bit by bit

they are fitted together on an armature, until at the end of the performance the (partly) reconstructed body is hoisted about the performance
space. Rosenthal has unearthed her own remains. The Autonomous
Being had told her she was "part angel, part dinosaur," but most remarkably, part of the great chain of life since prerecorded history. It's the
structure—the bones of a thought—that has always mattered to Rosenthal.

If, as Mircea Eliade has written, shamanism is a technique of ecstasy,
then so is making art, following as it does the same trajectory of dismemberment and resurrection. The unmistakable allusion is that artists, like
scientists, give themselves up to the quest for new worlds, and often they
are ridiculed when they attempt to describe them. *Pangaean Dreams* is
Rosenthal's *Tempest*.

For Rosenthal the new worldview is plate tectonics, which can, at
last, explain her own body/continent of restless desire. Not for her the
dance of death in the face of chaos. She prefers the tectonic boogie,
one of the new *lazzi* for the twenty-first century.

> When one plate moves, all move. That's the law of Chaos and I ac-
> cept. I nod *Yes*. I will live my allotted time torn apart by my duality,
> kicking and screaming all the way. With the violent love of Gaia.
> With fear and trembling and loving care. With the Pangaean dino-
> saur ensconced in my brain. In the Earth. Of the Earth. In the world.
> Of the world.

Rosenthal's ecological testament reflects her profound understanding
of the life force. In her search for enlightenment she discovers an ironic
lesson: wisdom is insecurity. *Learn the tectonic boogie / Or you've had
it, Baby.*

(1993)

Despoiled Shores

Heiner Müller's Natural History Lessons

|||||||| Like seaweed that shifts restlessly from shore to shore, green hope of the future, his words stretch out in the vast ocean of texts that is the world, sweeping its depths.

I

For the Europe of 1992 Heiner Müller has already prepared a drama of no borders. He has dramatically realigned the political order. He has rewritten the stories of East and West, the Old World and the New, and the Third one. In the common marketplace of ideas *posthistoire* is a hapless consumer item, for Müller has not yet finished writing the history of the world. Backwards.

In his *Lehrstücke*, which are unlearning plays, Müller outlines brutal new history lessons. His narrative is set at the end of Western civilization, his book a Baedeker for the nuclear age, unmoved by proud architecture, priceless collections of art, scenic excursions to romantic capitals. If he pauses at Berlin's Landwehrkanal, it is only to remark that Rosa Luxemburg's body was dumped there by her murderers. If he points to a street in Jamaica, it is only to show the slave exhibited in a cage. Müller describes places drama has rarely been, his words captions for snapshots that quote the history of violence. He is the last traveler in Europe, our Odysseus, his guidebook to be read upon ruins.

The monuments are already crumbling, whole cities cry out in putrefaction, people disappear into landscapes at the moment of catastrophe.

Heroic figures of myth and history walk alongside the living in cities around the world. But their stories are different from the golden tales of ancient epics, of Shakespeare's and Schiller's royal tragedies, nor do they resemble the revisionist histories of student textbooks. From a lake near Straussberg Jason and his Argonauts begin their walk through the city of East Berlin. Gandhi sits in a Nazi prison. Prospero turns into a desk in the brave new world of socialism. The time between history and literature melts in the unbearable heat of Müller's poetry, skewering fact to imagination in a new kind of horror story.

In bloody, cruel ink Müller retraces the classics in contemporary scenes, framing the violence and dislocation that is commonly celebrated as their poetry and passion. His texts are satyr plays attaching themselves like bindweed to great works of the Western tradition, trailing over the fourth wall of Berlin, prolific morning glory. A homeless man who lives at whim either East or West of the wailing wall, Müller, a man split in half, is the disembodied emblem of his divided country. At home here or there, he lives best in literature.

Müller uses the texts of the past like found objects from an archeological dig, dreaming in them, reshaping, recasting them: burnt offerings from the altar of war. Everything is material. His writing, a history of imagery. He scratches behind the pentimenti of historical portraits in the museum of Europe. Somewhere, in an homage to Stalin, Caesar and Napoleon are chewing on the dead corpses of soldiers. Lessing meets the last American president, a robot, in an automobile junkyard. Müller tells of the life of cities in mourning plays (*Trauerspiele*), his sorrow that of architecture. Already vines reach to the ceilings of ruins, whose inhabitants act out their agonies, great allegories of decay. Science fictions spin out of time machines, the audience extinct races. When the sun is at its zenith Alcestis comes back from the dead, in a long-forgotten dramatic structure that gathers in a single sentence a random drawing, *The Odyssey*, a Noh play, and an Alfred Hitchcock film. Intercultural—its form is its content—this explosion of memory lives its own life in the world. Between time and space and culture, the continental drift.

Now one can speak of an anthropology of drama, the dream life of nations. The world is not one because human beings have the same body parts and live and laugh and love and give birth astride a grave; rather, it is that in the world of global trade, of common markets, everyone consumes the same imagery. Multinationals have colonized Olympus and turned Fate into economic Necessity. If once great books and their heroes unified cultures, today it is Coca Cola the classic that generates myth, forging a new collective unconscious. Coke brown snow of conformity, bottled rage.

Müller writes of countries and continents, of myth that turned into history, troubled fragments of a once-shared past. In a world where Hamlet is a machine his critique of culture erases the difference between science and the humanities. He writes plays for an age of computers, unsettling artificial intelligences. The worldliness that is missing in the greater part of writing sprawls in Müller's conjugation of history: to be or to have been. His plays are the stammer in Beckett's silent rhythms, the shadows of history between the images. They are history writing itself, not the decorous commentary about it. Poetry, which in its awesome courage studies, then passes through the immense horror of human history, carrying the newly initiated to the more distant shore of reflection, where first there is the shattering joy of acquaintance, then finally the peace that accompanies art.

Müller expands the range of history in drama by adding geography to it. Until the life of societies fragmented into separate branches of knowledge, geography had always been part of the narrative of history. But the sense of place was gradually overshadowed by the domestication of dramatic form, trapped in its agoraphobic four walls. Müller writes of civilizations, not towns, of cultures and classes, not personalities. His subject is at once collective and historical, unconcerned with the fleeting interests of individual chronology. In this meltdown of time the notion of dramatic subject is on its way to being reinvented. Even when Müller writes of himself his subject is Germany.

His drama is a kind of travel writing: essayistic, narrative, intimate, ethnographic, surveying the *battlefield of tourism*. He walks through the world, his Doppelgänger in Greece, in Rome, in Jamaica, in Peru, measuring the distance from utopia that shapes the history of Western civilization. His world is that of curved space-time, his unities past, present, and future. Who has walked more in the streets of cities, his figures in foreign landscapes, addressing the loss of future as a dream. Nelson Mandela on his *Way of the Cross* is a guidepost. Polypheme's one eye a traffic light.

Müller has already begun his walk into the twenty-first century, a pilgrim who howls at progress. His plays are journeys, his companions voices. Unidentified speakers surround him. The voices are like winds, shifting direction and scattering language debris from continent to continent. It is the cold, terrible wind of a nuclear future that might include the swirl of bodies, a tree, a piece of Antarctica, and fragments from Euripides. Or A *shred of Shakespeare/in the paradise of the bacteria.* If as a disillusioned young socialist he once wrote, "No image contains the sky any longer," now that nuclear war is capitalism's answer to communism, he finds a new alphabet in the clouds. Dramatic syntax can make history when the sky is a blank page.

II

In Berlin he wrote me a poem.

> Shakespeare the
> > tourist
> From Stratford to
> > Stratford
> via London
> In his heartbeat the
> > greed of the epoch
> In his blood a tiredness
> > to come
> a grip for the sun
> a jump into shadow
> > > 22-5-84 Heiner Müller

In New York he wrote another.

> without hope
> without despair
> > for the next half century.
> > > to Bonnie
> > > April 28 (1986)
> > > year of terrorism
> > > Heiner Müller

Then I wrote one.

For H(i)M

I sing of arms and a man
Continents radiating texts
Heiner/Janus
Wallflower
thistle in Brecht's side
weed in Etruscan tombs

O Wanderer
You have come to the new world
Electra-pen in your suitcase
Shakespeare in your heart
Myth-maker, image-taker
under a Soho moon

> May 5, 1986
> (after Chernobyl)

III

Always Müller returns to the landscape. The attitude toward nature is finally one of politics. In the timepiece of evolution, what is human history to natural history and where does the concept of presence begin.

Müller's writing fiercely acknowledges natural history in the history of the world, until now one of the many histories whose narratives have been left out of History. That knowledge suggests an entirely new perspective on theatrical space, the behavior of character in relation to environment, as radical a change as naturalism once brought to the age of determinism. (It is not surprising that Müller and Robert Wilson should have come together to work at this point in theater history, because it is the idea of landscape that joins them: men for whom the natural world is part of the conception of the theatrical event.) Müller attacks scientific objectivity at its core by subverting the notion of historical truth. Chaos theory has replaced natural selection, Aristotle's poetics a whisper before the big bang. One day the ecology of theater will have to be written, with performance space a branch of the sciences.

Farces in their second life as history, Müller's plays act as dramatic counterpoint to the court dramas of an aristocratic age that once staged masques in outdoor theaters. But even as the once royal theatrical system has brought drama indoors to houses of couture, Müller's plays return the theater to its original scene, the landscape. (One could write a bestiary of the different animals he lets roam in his writing: birds, serpents, dogs, wolves, boars, tigers, roosters.) The proper home for his plays is the parterre of Charlottenburg Palace, or beneath the triumphal arch of Brandenburg, gateway to paradise.

The end of human history, the end of a species, will first occur as a destruction of the landscape. In the great sweep of DESPOILED SHORE MEDEAMATERIAL LANDSCAPE WITH ARGONAUTS the history of the world leaps from the beginning of colonization to nuclear war. Here in the theater of his death Jason watches his body merge with the landscape, just as the Pompeiians were sculpted in monuments, their bodies their gravestones, just as the flesh of the Jews turned the sky a sinewy red and the atomized victims of Hiroshima paved the streets where they lived. At such times it is impossible to separate the drama from natural history. The ecological theme subsumes all political issues. It is the final solution.

IV

Finally, it will be a war of the landscapes.

> DEBUISSON: Why aren't we born as trees, Sasportas, to them this is of no concern. . . . Why can't we simply exist and watch the war of the landscapes.
> SASPORTAS: The rebellion of the dead will be a war of the landscapes, our weapons the forests, the mountains, the oceans, the deserts of the world. I will be forest, mountain, ocean, desert. I—that is Africa. I—that is Asia. The two Americas—that is I.
>
> THE TASK

The Frenchman Debuisson gives up the revolutionary struggle for the liberation of Jamaica and returns to France. He trades revolution for the sensual life. Treason is a woman. (His dilemma, Danton/Müller's dilemma: the choice between the austerity of political commitment and the sensuous life of the imagination. It is always played out on the bodies of women. This is the image unable to fall out of the skies of Müller's texts.) The black man Sasportas continues to fight for Jamaica. For him no deterministic laws of nature: the landscape has its own version of history. Nature has a political life. In the latest view of the apocalypse, the final war will be between species. Even the stars will make war.

There is another war of landscapes in Müller's worlds, equally significant. These landscapes are the bodies of women, the other colonies of the world. Sexuality is its own kind of natural history. It is not so difficult to move from the idea of the world as a body to the actual human body, another landscape: from the public to the private. Medea writes a play on the body of Jason's new wife in poison ink. Ophelia's body is a blank text on which a new women's history will be recorded. Alcestis is a country. In Müller's work Woman is spirit, nature, womb, Plato's cave, the black hole in space, a prison, a snakepit, a one-way street. She is also the landscape of utopia, his grand theme. Woman, like nature made to embody the ideology of the eternal feminine, passive, fated. But nature is not a still life, nor is the earth a receptacle.

Müller himself, who masks his personal obsessions in the foreplay of literary allusion, envisions new lives for women. In a drama that takes place less than two hundred years after Debuisson's revolutionary disengagement, Hamlet finds himself unable to act out his prepared text in the streets of Budapest. Echoes in the landscape of literature: Hamlet, HAMLETMACHINE, Heiner Müller. A man sickened by the theatricality of his tragedy. The intellectual whom privilege has marginalized. He does not want to be poet of the revolution. *In his box, the prompter is rotting.* Death of the Author.

Into this landscape, the Europe of Women, walks Ophelia, who criticizes the role she has been given as a dramatic type. *Yesterday I stopped killing myself.* She has grown into Electra, wrapped in white gauze, now a trembling sheet of paper, wedded to violence. *I eject all the sperm I have received. I turn the milk of my breasts into lethal poison.* The tragic heroine of Greek drama has waited centuries to see herself in the streets of the twentieth century, even now acting out the archetypal dramas. Rewritten classics shout art's contribution to politics.

Müller brings to drama the strongest female characters since Greek tragedy. He moves women from the stifling homes of bourgeois drama's well-made beds to the city, from domestic space to urban space, the realm of history. For him Ulrike Meinhof, *late-born bride* of Kleist, was the female protagonist in the last drama of the bourgeois world. In a landscape beyond death that describes his overpainting of *Alcestis*, a woman comes out of the earth to enter a prefab house where a man who waits for her will snap her larynx like a birch branch. (The bird he holds in his hand is the last of its kind.) This battered woman joins Medea and Ophelia in the new Europe of Women, their sisters in cities and suburbs waiting to inscribe the lost images of their lives, lost texts in the Book of History.

In Müller's recovery of suppressed narratives the history of women, of sexual relations, is part of the history of the world. Women and nature struggling against the careless myth of the eternal, their bodies landscapes ravaged over and over again by the germ of warfare. Colonized by monuments erected to immortality, impossible dream. Gyn/ecology is the child delivered by Chekhov a century ago. Müller, adoptive father, explodes the memory that ecology and the liberation of women from conquest are part of the same ethos. Chekhov, first to differentiate between the acts of a play and a landscape, understood that the earth is a body. He walks with Müller into the forests of the future. Still, marvelous Chekhov, when he gazed up at the sky a cloud looked to him like a grand piano.

V

Gertrude Stein called a play a landscape, and in hers she could envision the lives of the saints. There are no hagiographies in Müller's landscapes, his Lord's Prayer *Give us this day our daily murder.* His version of paradise a newer testament: one serpent each for the first, second, and third worlds. All narratives start from the garden where Beckett waits before the withering tree of knowledge, its apples polished by pesticide.

What is theater but the history of figures in a landscape, the earth itself a history, older than humankind. Müller welcomes Gaia to the theater, transforming it into a life science. Gaia, no longer the passive Ophelia of the world, but the new protagonist in the drama of the future. The greenroom now a greenhouse. Ozone peels away her blue mask. Nineteen eighty-eight, the year Persephone didn't spend her seasons on earth, year of the acid tears of fir trees, snakes swimming in the homes of starving Bangladeshis, syringes of affluent despair swept up on lonely beaches, spoils of undeclared war. Bloodshot eye of Mars oversees the century turning.

No full moons light Müller's cities. Artaud's *sun of torture* watches the earth's sleepless tossing and turning in the theater of cruelty that radiates all over the globe. The earth is warmer now, though the gentle breeze of human feeling is constantly threatened by the humidity of fear.

Long ago one sang another song to the radiant sun:

> Greetings, lord
> Be kind,
> > give me a life that is going to satisfy my heart

Not for us Homeric hymns. We are closer to the sun but great distance from modest prayer.

(1988)

The State of Grace

Maria Irene Fornes at Sixty-two

Early in *Abingdon Square* a young woman says to an inquisitive friend, "You have to know how to enter another person's life." In many ways that rule of etiquette has shaped the theater of Maria Irene Fornes, whose profound theme has always been the conduct of life.

This is particularly true of *Abingdon Square*, in which she creates a universe more Catholic than any of the other worlds of her plays. The teenage Marion marries a loving older man, has an affair with another man, a child with a third, descends into a personal hell, and in the end nurses her husband after his stroke out of a sense of compassion and remembered love. At a time when so much writing about women (and men) celebrates the joys of sexual freedom, Fornes is writing about sin, penance, forgiveness, the power of love. She does not deny her characters the choice and excitement of self-discovery in transgression—in this case adultery—but concerns herself instead with the repercussions of such liberating acts. *Abingdon Square*, then, is a counterreformation for our ideological age, in which responsibility for one's actions is regarded as a hindrance to personal fulfillment. Fornes's abiding humanism is in stark contrast to contemporary drama's moral relativism and contingency ploys.

Fornes is an unabashed moralist, which is why her thinking is so suited to the epic style she has been developing as a writer and director in recent years, at least since *Fefu and Her Friends*. Epic dramaturgy is rooted in the medieval morality play, which produced a synthesis of theatrical and spiritual style. If Brecht used this form to proselytize for his secular religion of communism, and the expressionists for the re-birth of modern man, Fornes makes it her own to represent the spiritual lives of women—the kinds of choices they make and why.

In her recent production of *Abingdon Square* at the San Diego Repertory Theatre she has brought all of these strands together in a staging of more clarity and evocativeness than the original production of the play in 1987, at the American Place Theatre in New York. The play itself has been considerably revised since a workshop at the Seattle Repertory Theatre in 1984 and Fornes's own 1988 staging at the Studio Arena Theatre in Buffalo. In San Diego it was performed on alternate nights in English and in Spanish.

Stylistically, *Abingdon Square* is a journey play, but more impor-tantly, another kind of *Lehrstück*, or learning play. Enlightenment must be spiritual, not merely the absorption of received ideas. Knowledge is understood in the Platonic sense, as absolute beauty, virtue. Fornes's moral tale is strengthened by its distance from contemporary life and values and its elaboration over a ten-year period in the World War I era. It exudes a willful circumspection and sense of refinement.

In such a universe a person must know his or her worth. Marion looks to Dante for instruction. She keeps a diary to chronicle "things that are imagined." Learning—the book, the diary, the act of writing—holds a special place in the work of Fornes, for knowledge struggled over is a form of empowerment, a way of mastering one's life, a guide to value, the cultivation of worldliness. A manuscript must be of the illu-minated kind, revelatory. (Kroetz develops this same theme in *Through the Leaves*, also using the epic form.) One of Fornes's preoccupations in her work is the evolution of a higher, transcendent knowledge from sexual knowledge. The body is a body of knowledge.

Fornes takes a very ascetic approach to life. It is important to live in a state of grace, and to save your soul. For there is a sense of heroism in the admission of shame. Her asceticism accepts the dualism of body and soul. Nothing must be extraneous, merely decorative, self-destructive. The good life is measured in terms of accountability, purity of heart, virtue, transformation through work and study. Chekhov had that code of ethics; his thought moved along the same bourgeois lines of self-improvement. The humor of characters who fail to achieve this grace-fulness, therefore, is never one of mockery or the grotesque. It is that of manners—humors—as when the dour husband Juster reads a long, suggestive passage about pollination from an E. A. Bowles garden book in a brief scene after Marion and a cousin gossip with "sinful" delight about a *menage à trois* they've heard of. How do the three of them make love? Fornes's laughter sometimes comes in threes instead of the usual comic pairs. One of her early plays she called *The Successful Life of Three*.

More than any of her other works, *Abingdon Square* develops rhetorically through a prayerlike formality. Sentences are simple, short, unequivocating. Very few contractions are used. There is genuine communication, not diversionary chitchat. Characters tend to understand themselves and reflect on their behavior, traits reinforced by the liberal use of the pronoun *I* in strong, declarative sentences. At times the language is confessional, transcendent. Therefore, the quality of voice is given primacy in the writing: it is the link to God. There is a certain sacredness attributed to the word because it expresses self-knowledge, which in Fornes's hierarchy of values is esteemed as a gift. The upper-class Marion shares this intuition, as well as the innate qualities of goodness and charity, with her later embodiment, the dirt-poor Mae of *Mud*.

Fornes's lessons evolve in a precisely defined horizontal space that emphasizes stations of a life. The lack of depth in the stage privileges the portrait, the still life of tableau, as an object of contemplation, accenting the iconic nature of the scenes. There are thirty-one of them, usually brief, some only visual, others in monologue, separated from one another by a blackout. The sense of miniaturization also enhances the dimension of scale, making the events on stage at times more dramatic. Every element of the staging moves toward a meditative rhythm, space to breathe between scenes, darkness and stillness to welcome thought. The stage space and the auditorium forge a single architectural unit.

The (didactic) pictorial frame, reflecting Fornes's early life as a painter, is well suited to the epic construction of the play. Doorways, windows, walls, glass panes serve to emphasize the sense of the frame. In one important scene—a frame within a frame—part of the center back wall gives way to reveal an alcove wherein Marion is practicing the mortification of the flesh, as it were, shaking, arms stretched heavenward, in a trancelike recitation of "Purgatorio" from *The Divine Comedy*. A concerned old aunt finds her and in the final moment of the scene lays her body over the conscience-stricken Marion, evoking the pietà-like resonance of a religious painting. Fornes's space is theological.

If this drama is positioned between heaven and hell, light and dark are its poetic counterparts. Before her marriage to the much older Juster, Marion rejoices, "In this house light comes through the windows as if it delights in entering. I feel the same." Toward the end of the play, when both husband and wife are at the brink of madness, Juster will say, "Paper would burn if it were held up to her glance. When I reached the door I saw her back reflected in the glass. She was so still that there was no life in her." The issue of enlightenment, which is so central to the work, is played out in the chiaroscuro effects of the staging. One can palpably feel the sensuous interplay of light and emotion in the visual style that characterizes Fornes's directorial intelligence.

Besides emphasizing the pictorial, the San Diego production, for all its quietude, was more operatic than the original. The highly emotional, taut quality of the writing, its subject matter of love, and the stylization of movements shaped the musical line of the production. Scenes were played in many different musical moods, at times hymnlike, on occasion ragtime, then nocturne, or adagio. The Richard Strauss song cycle, a touch of Vivaldi, or an aria from Purcell's *Dido and Aeneas* used between some of the scenes heightened their operatic quality, transforming the work's epic nature by provoking at times a wonderful, humorous tension between melodrama and expressionism. The human, high drama was then subtly contrasted to the indifferent life of plants on the stage and of trees growing in the garden, glimpsed through the parlor doors leading outside, and through which Marion and her lover initially reveled in their illicit affair, now turned from farce to tragedy. If more and more directors here and abroad are becoming attracted to opera and music theater, this is a rare instance of the operatic informing dramaturgy in ways that point to new possibilities of rhythmic experimentation within the epic vocabulary. Melodrama is a natural inclination in the highly emotional space of passion and its repression that defines opera because it addresses, to a great degree, heroism. In fact, the triumph of passion over negotiation (the subject of contemporary life) is perhaps what is making people (artists and audiences) turn now in increasing numbers to opera. The beauty of the soul *in extremis* is desperately needed on our stages ridden with role models instead of heroes, opinion in place of knowledge.

So is the imperative to create a greater place for artists with mature vision. It is one of the scandals of the American theater, obsessed as it is with "development," whether of the playwright or funding sources or subscribers (and the parallels between the real estate industry and the theater are notoriously striking in their attitude toward preservation), that at the age of sixty-two, after three decades of a richly committed life in the theater, Fornes is still working on the margins. Most of the theaters she works in, like the San Diego Repertory Theatre, which offered a home to this remarkable production, survive on the edge of bankruptcy. When *Abingdon Square* was produced recently in London it went from the fringe to the National Theatre.

At her age, and with such a long record of distinguished achievement entirely within the medium of theater, a fully elaborated directorial style, and a grand reputation as a teacher, Fornes should be given all that the American theater has to offer in terms of resources—choice of actors, technicians, designers, access to larger audiences, longer runs. Imagine what other artists might learn from Fornes. Imagine how her own work might grow under new artistic conditions. Yet, her work has never appeared on the main stage of any of the major theaters that pride themselves on providing an alternative to the commercial exigencies of Broadway—the Vivian Beaumont, the Guthrie, the Mark Taper Forum, Arena Stage, the American Repertory Theatre, the Public Theatre, among countless others. At the center of theater's exclusionary practice and arrested development is the absence of the mature dramatic voice.

For too long the American theater system has ruthlessly infantilized artists and audiences by coddling "new" playwrights and directors, falsely setting up gender gaps where instead we should be able to see theater artists develop in relation to one another, generation to generation. The new triumvirate of young directors at the Public Theatre (albeit under the artistic directorship of the more seasoned JoAnne Akalaitis) already reflects the problematics of the one-dimensional approach. Perhaps it might have been wiser to secure a more broad-based leadership there so that artists and theater audiences could benefit from seeing the work of several generations of artists, representing several stages of life and vision. An art form must carry on an internal dialogue with its own history, and the successive histories of artists and audiences, to honor cultural memory in any meaningful way. The American theater obscures the profound relationship between art and society at every turn.

Of a generation of playwrights who came to prominence in the sixties, including Rochelle Owens, Kenneth Bernard, Adrienne Kennedy, Megan Terry, Rosalyn Drexler, Ronald Tavel, Paul Foster, Jeff Weiss, Tom Eyen, to name only a few who created the idea of off-off-Broadway, only Maria Irene Fornes is making a living in the (nonmainstream) theater. Furthermore, their body of work is far more daring in its exploration of sexuality, language, theatricality, and politics than the vast majority of contemporary drama. Even Sam Shepard, one of the most gifted of this group, though younger, received greater recognition only after he became a film star. With few exceptions, his work is still produced strictly within the confines of the nonprofit system. Since those theaters that support Shepard only produce "new" American plays, none of his earlier work is revived in major contemporary productions, a situation duplicated for other writers as well. Compounding the problem is the fact that the fashionable theaters are closed to earlier generations of playwrights whose work is not of the mainstream. Thus, there is no attempt to create a repertoire of American contemporary plays. No space is created for American writers as they mature.

The American theater has never found a way to integrate its avant-garde into the larger world of theater as Europe did, by giving them a place in their major institutions after they've proved their worth, nor even the way that the film, literary, and art establishments/industries have done here. In theater the avant-garde spirit is made perpetual outcast. This dilemma increases as artists age, because they cannot constantly, to recall Lillian Hellman's good phrase, cut their conscience to fit each year's fashion, slavishly following the new hype of funding sources, theater publicists and boards, trendy "isms." Are you now or have you ever been an (avant-garde art)ist? The real twist in the theater scene is not that it pandered to the masses but that it pandered to the funding sources and their shifting "priorities." Both conservatives and progressives, the right and the left/liberal, have corrupted the funding process by politicizing culture at the most base level. Art has become a branch of journalism or the social sciences, and critical discourse mere publicity. Only the true artists of the theater can resist the grant hustle, the hype. They risk marginalization, obscurity, censure, unemployment. But then, being an artist is not a rights issue.

Fornes was in San Diego with her one-hundred-year-old mother Carmen, her frequent companion during theatrical engagements in this country and abroad. I hope that Fornes herself lives to be one hundred, still moving from place to place, bringing her work to the world without any trace of bitterness, simply considering herself lucky to be working in our economy of planned obsolescence of people and things, and that she may be fortunate in old age to have her own fellow travelers, if, that is, the light of our most courageous theater artists has not been snuffed out by the shades of official culture already appearing on the horizon of the twenty-first century.

(1992)

Performance World, Performance Culture

Culture is in the Body:
From Pirandello to Performance Art

It is impossible to consider this century theatrically without taking into account the impact of Pirandello, Brecht, and Artaud. I'd like to address their importance from the perspective of the *body as text*. Let me try to outline what I mean by reflecting on such things as body, mask, sign, presence.

We begin to see the drift away from the idea of the actor merging with the character in the plays of Pirandello. His characters develop an attitude toward, even comment on, the act of playing a role. Here the private world of the character interacts with the public world. Brecht follows by creating a theory that justifies separating the character and the actor. But he doesn't allow any tension between the private self and the public self: the Brechtian character is entirely a *social body*. Artaud, rejecting the literary text and the development of character altogether, sees theater specifically as the experience of the body; even the audience should have what he called "the physical knowledge of images."

What one can trace in Pirandello, Brecht, and Artaud is the status of the sign, that ubiquitous code that began to fascinate modern artists in the period of symbolism, when the reality of the phenomenal world was challenged. This was also the period when art began to have a feeling for abstraction. Pirandello, in some measure attached to symbolist interests, didn't have any faith in the sign, the seat of identity, and so he disrupted its logic by making the issue of representation the subject of his work. Brecht, on the other hand, based his whole theory on the sign. That was his idea of *Gestus*—how to show the conventions that define social relationships in a particular time and place. He viewed the body as a social text. Now Artaud also addressed the issue of the sign—it was in the actor's body, but as a metaphysics-in-action: a language of spiritual states that precede speech.

If we turn from the body to the mask, we find that Brecht didn't believe in the mask—he thought that everything could be shown. Pirandello had of course based his entire approach on the literary concept of the mask, which is, after all, a kind of writing on the face. And Artaud was drawn to the mask of the Oriental actor for its stylizing effect as language.

In all these developments the movement has been toward the separation of the actor from the role, which has led to the recognition of the actor's body itself as a text. But more importantly, we can trace a narrative style of performance that runs counter to the realistic acting tradition. (Theoretically, realism denies "presence" in the merging of the actor and character, while performance, which I am opposing to acting, affirms presence by acknowledging the split between actor and character.)

So the narrative style of performance includes the commentary on the act itself. Pirandello effected this by having his characters split into separate selves who could objectify, treat as an abstraction, and comment on the self; that's why the mirror concept was so important to him. Brecht and Artaud, for very different and opposite reasons, found the essence of narrative in the Oriental theater, in which the story was narrated by musicians on one part of the stage while being acted out by actors on another part. These developments start to shift theatrical ideas into the realm of performance art, which is primarily a narrative form, more often autobiographical, even abstract, disembodied.

The final step in the century-long tension between performance and acting is the use of the *self as text*. Spalding Gray, appearing in his film *Swimming to Cambodia*, based on his solo performance of the same name, is a character who is his own author and who doesn't represent anyone but himself, commenting on the events of his life. He doesn't do theater, but life. Like Wallace Shawn and Andre Gregory, whose *My Dinner with Andre* was a personal film in the same style, Gray also comes out of the experimental theater of the sixties, bringing avant-garde acting technique to a populist medium, film.

Gray reflects the glorification of presence, the interplay between private and public selves, the irony of the mask, the tension between the fictional and the real, the narrative and the dramatic, played out in performance. All of these issues outline the essential movement of theatricality, and the journey of the actor, in the twentieth century. In another odd way this theatricalization of "natural man" represents the culmination, even perversion, of the transcendentalist spirit inherent in Thoreau's how-I-spent-my-day reflections—minus the philosophical underpinnings that relate political issues to nature and the social body.

The Idea of Performance Culture

"Performance culture" is a phrase I use to articulate the tendency in American life toward structuring all aspects of individual and social activity around the paradigm of theater. From psychological therapies, politics, self-help books, and the training of athletes, to television programming, advertising, and video games, to big business and police techniques, the emphasis is on framing an activity in the triad of performer, audience, and event. Individuals are encouraged to structure and to view personal experience in terms of what I call "performance acts," a form of self-conscious role-playing linked to the projection of certain imagery. It seems ironic that the actor, despised and ridiculed by society throughout history, should be the model of the contemporary personality. (Pirandello, incidentally, was the first modern writer to understand the nature of the performance act in relation to group behavior.)

Theatricality is a primary human activity, even need. But beyond this fact, what does role-playing mean as a model of human behavior? How can it make one more conscious and critical in a life experience? What are the kinds of "performance acts" one can engage in? Is performance an art or an activity? Does it aestheticize emotions or draw one closer to them?

Theatrical paradigms can of course be construed to good or detrimental ends. We need to consider their full impact on human experience, to understand more fully the interaction between public life (in the public eye) and privacy (the private I). We need also to comprehend in a deeply political and social way how a society promotes and rewards socially acceptable roles. Finally, the performance act can and should be regarded as an ontological act, not merely a social one. The feeling for form, the will to transform and to control human images in dynamic settings, to compose dialogue, to structure social relations, to manipulate emotions—to make oneself a work of art—are human desires that need to be examined in all their complexity. If performance, that is, role-playing, is an ontological act, what is performing in relation to being? The larger, more crucial question is whether the individual "performance act" is aligned to a new liberation of the self generated by democratic society or rather a rehearsal for a totalitarian future of fixed roles in an exclusively public, regulated world order of the mask and the image.

I've chosen a few examples from contemporary culture to emphasize how certain activities are related to performance:

1. At a disco near my Manhattan apartment, every Thursday is Brokers' Night, when young stockbrokers and Wall Street types come by cab to the club—that is, when they're not trading coke for securities secrets. What's unusual about them is that part of their ritual is to come wearing dog masks. Is the mask—the body as text—a social critique by night of their life by day? Here is a grotesque recasting of George Grosz's satirical portraits of a society on the eve of destruction come full circle in the dada and neoexpressionism of today. Certainly it is now clear that the modern *commedia* sensibility is linked to the performance act.

2. The personals columns of today's magazines. *Attractive, warm, nurturing, caring, intelligent,* and *vital* seem to be the recurring adjectives in these advertisements for the self. Of course there are variations, depending on the venue: Women in the *New York Review of Books* seek men who are Jewish and love art, theater, concert-going, novels by Trollope; they're professors, writers, and psychoanalysts. In *The Nation* someone was advertising for a woman for a "laid-off communist pipefitter" friend in Philadelphia. The *Village Voice* is a great place to find Chinese-American, "disease-free," "un-Yuppie" types, if you're looking. *New York* magazine ads unashamedly seek out "self-made millionaires," "models," and "marketing professionals" who enjoy strawberries, presumably at a country house on Long Island. In all these cases and places we are presented with rather rigidly defined roles and outlines of desired scenarios. But these are all characters in search of an author. Which is the person, which the persona?

3. *Baby M*, the subject of a very private drama played out in the public realm. A series of reversals play about in this melodrama, which is not very well made. The question is, Who can best enact the role of parent? Here again the issue is that of representation.

4. *The Map of the Stars.* The scene is a Sunday afternoon in Beverly Hills, where hawkers are selling maps that pinpoint over two hundred movie star addresses. Public eyes ride up and down the streets all day taking videos and snapshots of their homes. The movie stars are trapped in their celebrity roles, hiding behind massive, electrified gates that act as their contemporary masks. Sometimes, when the star has died, we're allowed inside the gates to walk through a home that is now a shrine. To admire the props, setting, and costumes without the body. You all know Graceland, I'm sure.

5. *Nuclear theater.* The Department of Defense's *Dictionary for Military Terms* defines *theater* as a "geographical area outside the continental United States." In its original Greek (*theatron*) the word *theater* means "a place for viewing." There is a European theater but not an American theater or a Russian theater, so the implication is that we in the United States and in the Soviet Union are the audience, the Europeans the actors.

The kind of imagery rehearsal taking place all around us elaborates a profoundly disturbing mode of thinking because it regards history only in terms of spectacle. The growth of the media and communications in the evolution of society has made theatricalism into *the* twentieth-century political/art form: it subsumes both ideology and individuality as our way of being in the contemporary world. The social sciences have shown their limitation in creating a profile of the performing self. It is time to recover performance theory from the social sciences and return it to the realm of art and philosophy. What we need is an ethics of performance.

Another Look at the Theater of Images

When I began working on *The Theatre of Images* in 1975 my intention was to develop for myself a new critical vocabulary to approach a theater that was itself developing a new theatrical language. In one way it was a kind of critique of my life as a graduate theater student, because at the time I was receiving a traditional theater education at City University during weekdays and on the weekends watching early productions of Robert Wilson, Richard Foreman, and Mabou Mines. This new theater challenged, and was a radical alternative to, what I was studying.

The "theatre of images," the phrase I used as a kind of umbrella to describe contemporary experimental theater, reconceived the role of director, actor, writer; space and audience. It was a theater that turned away from such things as psychology, realistic conventions, and audience identification and instead reorganized the sense of space in theater, recast the actor, created texts in which words were sometimes used for their plastic qualities, and made technology an expressive feature of the work. Here was a theater in which imagery carried the weight of the narrative, which was usually dominated by dialogue. The *present moment* was emphasized, rather than there being an attempt to represent a past event. One of the chief intentions of those who created this theater was to cultivate a new spectator, one who would experience time and space and narrative in a more immediate, sensual way. With this theater a new visual style came into American theater. The theater of images, incidentally, did not exclude writing, but generated a textuality in which many more parts of the stage were emphasized as a language. All the elements did not have to serve the text. The works were highly self-conscious; they were about theater, about the act of creation, and, like much art of the time, they were very space- and process-oriented.

Looking back from the perspective of a dozen years, we can see that this generation of artists transformed our idea of experimentation in theater. But certainly they did not appear from nowhere, but rather had deep roots in the work of Pirandello, Brecht, and Artaud in traditional theater history, while also following the lesser-known performance history that begins with symbolism and extends through futurism, dada, and surrealism and such American influences as minimal and conceptual art, Merce Cunningham and the Judson Dance Theatre, and of course, even before them, the mother of the American avant-garde, Gertrude Stein.

I have outlined the idea of the "theatre of images" and its background only as a prelude to the real issues I wish to raise: the backlash in this country against Robert Wilson, the criticism of experimental work of The Wooster Group and the Ontological-Hysteric Theatre, and of the theater of images itself, as "formalistic," "reactionary," "apolitical," and so on. Much of the discussion of current experimentation, or the lack of it, revolves around the following issues:

1. accessibility—how complex should work be?
2. imagery's ability, or lack of it, to carry political content;
3. the appeal to emotions and/or intellect; and
4. the importance of experimentation itself.

These are just some of the points raised by audiences and critics who have come to question or be alarmed by the experiments of the seventies. I won't attempt to treat all of these complex matters now, except to say that I believe there is a danger in throwing around words such as *reactionary* or *fascist art*. One senses also a kind of revisionist history even by those who at one time championed the theater of images as a new step in theatrical consciousness.

We seem to be in a period when the very idea of the avant-garde is called into question; now artists themselves turn away from an adversarial position in an effort to reach out to broader audiences. But it is also a time in which art and other activities are being overpoliticized. It seems clear that there is a need on the part of many for less complex, intellectual work than that of ten years ago. There is an attempt by many to disassociate art from European modernism and to try to define a "populist" postmodernism. But from another perspective I find the criticism of experimentation, coupled with certain new tendencies in performance, problematic. Is there room for sensuality and beauty in today's theater? Is raw, directly political work a real desire of artists and audiences? How much is the shift a change in taste, how much is it economics? Finally, what are the deeper implications for the ideological shift in criticism and in art?

The Play as Landscape

It was Gertrude Stein who first called a play a landscape. On the surface a simple, poetic statement, and yet, if considered in depth, it appears more profound as the years pass.

If it is impossible to consider the century theatrically without acknowledging the impact of Pirandello, Brecht, and Artaud in relation to the history of the theatrical body, we cannot consider the future of theater without acknowledging the work of Robert Wilson and Heiner Müller. Their work, alone and together, articulates issues around which our current thinking about theater, about art, circulates: namely, the place of pleasure, beauty, imagery; the status of the artist or intellectual in society; the rewriting of classics.

But to go back a step, Wilson and Müller represent the culmination of modernism in the twentieth century. And Müller, especially, marks the contemporary link to the classical world—he calls his Medea play a "landscape with Argonauts," and here Jason walks through the streets of East Berlin. Wilson's theater gathers together the strands of experimentation that run through Wagner, symbolism, the futurist heritage, Artaud, and Stein to a theater of myth and spirit. Müller's work follows the opposite trajectory, from Büchner to dada to Brecht to political terrorism. They meet in the world of Müller's HAMLETMACHINE, where the actor, in an elaborately ironic pun, refuses to play Hamlet to audiences for whom classics have no meaning. And blood oozes from a refrigerator in an urban landscape colonized by Coca Cola and television, the daily nausea, where Electra is sister to Ulrike Meinhof.

All these modernisms, all these classicisms. Müller and Wilson end up in the same place—the landscape, a synthetic fragment of images from the classics, technology, politics, tourism. Beckett is already there, his characters sitting around a withering tree. Sooner or later all stories come back to the garden. Here earthly activities are united in the myth of the garden of paradise, the first scene of play, its actors the first to confront the concept of future: what to do next. We know who the Father is, but sometimes we forget the Mother of us all.

Writing at the Edge of Criticism

Lately I've begun to think of writing—and here I also include reading—as a form of travel. They have many of the same frustrations and pleasures. The problem for me is that all writing I really love, I want to live in, as if it were a wonderful landscape. Of course, this is impossible. One of the illusions of theater, I think, is the attempt to make audiences feel they can live in other worlds. I don't believe this. I prefer to acknowledge my differentness as an outsider, a traveler. So the idea of creating a world on a stage is problematic for me. I would go so far as to say that the great texts, such as Greek drama, Shakespeare, and Beckett, may not need a stage, they are so complete as writing. That is the paradox of theater.

Certain ideas about representation carry over for me in an attitude toward criticism: that perhaps it can move from having to represent something to being a thing itself. It is important to investigate ways to go beyond what we know as criticism, especially theater criticism, which cannot wait for a new theater but should take responsibility for its own future.

Some of the ways I've set for myself are:

> — to make criticism a critique of criticism

> — to incorporate fictional technique and other forms of writing

> — to move in the realm of the lyrical and philosophical essay or aphorism

> — to situate the essay between speech and writing

> — to convey emotional presence

> — to emphasize the voice over the text

> — to turn criticism into writing

(1987)

Delivered as a guest lecture for the Harold Clurman Professorship, Clurman Seminar, Hunter College of the City of New York, May 1987.

All the Football Field's a Stage

"You know what I'm doing—I think I'm doing 8 ½—a big Fellini movie—fifty thousand people running in different directions. No staff. No casting agent. No chauffeur. No backers." Lee Breuer is slightly hysterical at the thought of Mabou Mines undertaking to produce the finished version of *The Saint and the Football Players* in the giant indoor stadium at Pratt Institute. Nonetheless, propelled by that crazy, wonderful logic of theater people that involves them in productions they don't have sufficient time to rehearse or ample money to produce, he attempts the impossible.

The spectacle in the making, which features well over a hundred performers—football players, drill teams, referees, marching band, and six cars—has been briefly shown in various guises since 1973, at the Loeb Student Center and Paula Cooper Gallery in New York, the Walker Art Center in Minneapolis, and Connecticut's American Dance Festival. Still, many people have managed to miss the piece, so there's always been a great demand for it. Now New York will see the completed version, which has become rather like a work composed of "found objects"—a collage of performers and ideas gathered from several Mabou Mines workshops across the country in the last three years. People from more than a half-dozen states will travel to Brooklyn to participate in this "abstract Superbowl," as Breuer calls it, whose half-time features dancing cars in a parody of parade floats, a contribution of students from last summer's workshop in Connecticut, and a card cheering section and snowstorm at game's end contributed by Pratt students.

A conceptual art piece that blurs distinctions between dance and theater, *The Saint and the Football Players* had its genesis in San Francisco poet Jack Thibeau's Xerox poem of the same name, in which images of football plays cut from magazines and books mingle with a holy card of Saint Theresa in a metaphoric suggestion of the religiosity of sports events. Out of these images Breuer developed a performance piece that in effect suggests a kind of "high" mass celebrated before a gathering of worshipper-enthusiasts. Yet it is also a statement about movement taking place in real time, and posing real dangers for the performers. For Breuer the event is his realization of a dream to create poetry in the theater: "The whole idea of Mabou Mines is that it was to devise a method of rendering poetry on the stage—not the Yeats bit but to translate a poem into an image series. To have it end up not as a play made out of a poem, but a poem staged."

The result is a poetry in motion: a delicate balance between sports and dance energized by the interplay of authentic football moves in an absurdist show of power (one team fights itself across the field) and the high seriousness of football ritual abstracted in choreographic patterns. John Howell, one of the original "team" members, explains the effect: "The football movements themselves are very real, but they're organized differently—for instance, the line shift is about spatial arrangement."

Thus, transposed to another medium, in this case theater, football becomes sports art, in which its fundamental aestheticism is fully exposed. Sports viewed on television has a similar effect. On the screen football takes on an artiness when it is filtered through the slow-motion or freeze-frame effects of the "instant replay," and a golf stroke looks arty when a camera close-up emphasizes its formal elements. Sportscasters in these instances serve as narrators of performance.

Perhaps the most infamous example of sports as aesthetics (albeit fascist ones) is Leni Riefenstahl's *Olympiad*, a documentary of the 1936 Olympic games in Germany in which Hitler's personal maker of images filmed athletes in all their pristine elegance. Visions of supermen were easily accommodated in, and even created, Nazi ideology. Away from the bustle and anxieties of rehearsal at Pratt, Breuer and I discussed the aesthetics of dynamism over lunch in a Village diner. The sounds of "hut two" and "sweep left" and the crackle of two hands catching a pass were already far away. But the significance of sports icons remained, and this was our real interest. "All fascist psychology inclines toward a self-aggrandizement based on the images of strength," Breuer remarks, and I think of the acuity of Susan Sontag's statement from her recent essay on fascist aesthetics: "Certainly Nazism is 'sexier' than communism." Breuer reaches further back into history to make his point: "In the Hellenic period in Greece, statues started to look like superheroes in comic books. This is the associative pattern to the football hero — enormous shoulders from the padding, the steely helmet. Football is the Hellenistic imagery of statues pushed over to an absurdist category." A sport for the "he-man" is really about power, and football, after all, is nothing but a series of power plays — like politics.

The politics of sport is a central metaphor of *The Saint and the Football Players*, a most emphatic and timely one in this period of history, when the Olympics have become political events in which East battles West in stadiums that symbolize miniature battlefields. The piece was originally conceived in the Nixon era — remember Richard Nixon, who used to telephone coaches to discuss plays before the big game? — as a statement on politics. Breuer notes: "At first there were interesting political overtones because of Nixon running the country like a football team, and so one of the ideas was to do it on the White House lawn or in front of the Washington monument. But you can even make the same statement about Gerry Ford."

Later on he likens Knute Rockne's "Fight, Fight, Fight" pep talk to a Shakespearean before-the-battle speech. Associations with this piece are endless. Though Nixon's out of the White House, Breuer feels that *The Saint and the Football Players* makes even more sense in a bicentennial year. "This is the year for this piece, where it belongs. It reflects the values that went into the American Revolution and which have now come down to the football field." Not by chance he thinks of it as a war dance. Football players dress and make up for their slow dance on the killing ground.

If *The Saint and the Football Players* comments on the politics of sport, it also very much alludes to sexual politics. It implies a critique of the machismo ethic in football players, whose battered knees and elbows and blackened eyes serve as emblems of manliness. Breuer calls it a "total put-on on macho" — this coming from an erstwhile football freak who traveled to Rose Bowl and homecoming games when he was at UCLA.

Much of what *The Saint and the Football Players* explores is concepts of hero-worship, role-playing, players getting off on their own images of strength and sexuality—and the similarity between performing in a theater and performing in a sports arena. Underlying all of this is the transcendental romanticism of the sports experience. Sports columnist Wells Twombly hit the phenomenon on the head when he proclaimed, "Football is the state religion." Sports heroes have replaced God, and the stadium has become a giant open-air cathedral in which the faithful are transformed by the powers of magic and ritual. When the Redskins stop on the playing field for a moment of prayer they become supplicants at the foot of the altar. God isn't dead, he's at the Rose Bowl.

For Breuer the analogy between football and religion results in the piece's being a pun about yardage. "Football teams try to make horizontal yardage," he explains, "Here they try to make vertical yardage—yardage with God. Look at the sweatshirts that were worn by the basketball team at Notre Dame last year—'God Made Us Number One.'" Breuer laughs at the absurdity of it, at the same time recognizing how deep-rooted the impulse is. "We're simply going along with these associations. They're very much at the core of the country's mock heroicism." Isn't there a team, I add, called the New Orleans Saints?

The Saint and the Football Players is a metatheater that grabs the collective unconscious of America at its roots. It was the Puritan ethic that led to American imperialism. Founded on the pastoral ideal, baseball eventually lost its popularity because it wasn't violent enough; football, on the other hand, is about conquering territory, the acquisition of property, so it is the perfect game for a nation raised on the myth of the Wild West and territorial expansion. Just think of the names of football teams—they signify speed, conquest, and the Wild West myth: Dallas Cowboys, New York Jets, Buffalo Bills, Oakland Raiders, Chicago Bears, Denver Broncos, Kansas City Chiefs, Minnesota Vikings. Now compare these with a few of the mildly named baseball teams: Chicago Cubs, Baltimore Orioles.

Lee Breuer transvalued the comic book in his series of "animations" by giving them metaphysical content, and by satirizing the football game he offers a sociology of sport. In the best tradition of the avant-garde he radically refunctions popular iconography to produce a more intelligent and socially relevant work than found in most "political" theater. While Breuer admits he is interested in the art statement of the piece—that it is about movement in space—he also believes it is less an intellectual than a popular work. "I really am interested in trying to do art with popular imagery so that art is not totally effete the way some conceptual statements are." He's proud as hell that cops and kids enjoy his piece as much as his friends in the theater and art worlds do. Mixing metaphors on sports, politics, sexuality, big business, religion, and theater, *The Saint and the Football Players* is yet the virtual staging of a myth.

(1976)

New England Still Life

Fornes's Evelyn Brown

Evelyn Brown is an unusual piece for playwright Maria Irene Fornes because it is the only work of hers she did not write. Instead, using the "found" material from the diary of a New Englander, the woman of the title, who died in the early part of this century, she has fashioned a theatrical work that is more performance than play. A handsome, simple pinewood interior of a house serves as the setting for two performers, Margaret Harrington (an actress) and Aileen Passloff (a dancer)—both of them called Evelyn—who move about the nooks and crannies and the deep reaches of the performance space. The spatial structure collaborates with the textual material to reveal all aspects of inner, private space, for this is a piece about Evelyn Brown and her home. The text consists of the stark diary entries, which are simply the unadorned repetitions of the woman's daily activities. Live and on tape she recounted her chores of cooking, cleaning, and organizing a household, never including an observation of her own, be it joy, anger, tiredness, irritation, or desire. Her universe was founded solely on what work she did at home.

One might be tempted to believe that Fornes's piece, which she also directed, centers on the oppression of women by housework, but this is not the case. The precise, simple movements of the two performers, setting table after table, cleaning, and folding linens, sometimes even dancing, as the text is repeated create a pattern of a woman taking pride in a job done with a great deal of care and precision. Yet there are moments of quiet desperation in the performance of the dancer—

101

seemingly Brown's alter ego, whom Fornes as a contemporary woman imagines as the other side of the silent woman. She could be found staring into a wall, or muffling a scream, in what are powerful dramatic moments to counterpoint the lack of commentary in the execution of the tasks.

It is, however, the beauty and simplicity and pride in quotidian tasks that Fornes emphasizes, not the oppression of Evelyn Brown, and only those looking for a feminist polemic would think otherwise. Housework is belittled now, so Fornes offers something of a statement about another way, another time, of living, when the work that women did in the home was appreciated for its certain grace. Fornes is by no means calling for a return to premechanized drudgery: I think she is just reminding us of an attitude toward the home that is lost today. If you look at the handwork in a crocheted lace doily, do you admire its delicacy or think about a woman trapped in her home making gender-identified objects, which consumed much of her time and energy?

What is most rewarding about *Evelyn Brown* is its integrity of form, which at every moment shows Fornes's directorial care. No visual or technological gimmickry, no imagery outside the text, no dogmatism. Perhaps the fact that Fornes is a writer unaccustomed to working in this more performance-oriented area of theater accounts for the emphasis on text, when more imagery might have substituted for words. Still, I applaud this clean, honest work as I do that of Tillie Olsen, whose women, though often more politicized, inhabit the same universe of steady, silent workers.

(1980)

Self-portrait in Gray

|||||||| Spalding Gray's three solo "talking pieces," as he calls them, form a kind of oral history that expands upon the metaphoric treatment of the autobiography he presented in his trilogy *Three Places in Rhode Island*. I don't think the pieces would be as interesting in themselves if they weren't a part of Gray's ongoing anatomy of melancholy. Frank, direct (Gray is seated, and there is no setting other than a desk and chair), unpretentious, therapeutic, the solos create a portrait of an unexceptional narrator—Gray—in various stages of his life, from adolescence to manhood. The more imagistic trilogy strikes me as lyric poetry, and the solos as prose treatments of the same thematic ground: two sides of Gray—the performer devising a narrative self (role), the other unmasking that self.

The subject matter of the solos is fairly obvious from the titles, but *India & After (America)*, unlike the other two, which simply unfold linearly as stories, is an experiment in narrative strategy. In this teasing theater game, which requires the assistance of another performer, Meghan Ellenberger, Gray is given a word randomly chosen from a dictionary and a time limit in which to associate the word with a part of his story, in whatever sequence it relates to him. Though this technique is not new to the novel or film, it does open up new possibilities as a dramatic device, especially since very little attention has been paid to experiments in time in performance, most experimentation focusing on the use of space. Whereas *India & After (America)* has reverberations outside the world of the story, the other talking pieces simply compile data about Gray's life, offering crazy-quilt situations in place of a point of view.

The radical gesture of the solos as performance pieces is Gray's refusal to play a role for his audience, which is ironic in that, unlike most experiments in art, which point to their uniqueness, his emphasizes the sameness of experience between himself and his audience. It is art refusing to be art. Yet, by virtue of its setting it is art, and from that perspective what I miss in the new work is a mediating consciousness that transforms raw experience into a new equation between the artist and the world (the Other). Gray gives us only a self-portrait that merges his private and public worlds. David Antin has been doing his similar "talking poetry" for years, but he situates his personal experiences in an epistemological frame, whereas Gray is simply concerned with developing a personal mythology.

In a larger context, Gray's work pinpoints where performance theory is at the end of the seventies. One has only to compare his monologues with the earlier work of The Performance Group, of which he has been a member for ten years, to trace performance history in the sixties and seventies: from ritual to process, fiction to data, cultural anthropology to personal diary, the chorus to the solo voice. Gray's talking pieces represent self-absorption in a relentlessly pure performance situation and the concomitant refusal to make judgments about the world at large. It is an attitude that expresses no commitment to a future, being irrevocably bound to its own sense of loss of the past. What Gray is constructing is a geography of the spirit outlined by the images and feelings he attaches to certain events in certain places, namely, the psychic territory of his New England boyhood.

Gray is dangerously close to the kind of self-absorption that leads to breakdown or madness, most certainly beyond narcissism. His work is provocative as a theoretical model and for its reckless exploration of the increasingly imperceptible line between performing and not performing. I think Gray's solos are about the way an actor prepares to create that Other between the self and the role and as such only a stepping-stone to what he will do in his continuing conceptualization of the performer as material.

(1979)

PAJ, A Personal History

Editorial Review

▏▏▏▏▏▏ Publication of our tenth-anniversary issue suggests a natural occasion to stop and reflect on the conditions that shape the narrative of *PAJ*, how and why it happened, and, now looking back from the perspective of a decade, what hasn't happened, what may yet happen. So I will begin at the beginning. These conditions are part of a cultural history that is the larger shape of the life of a society, while at the same time being an aspect of personal lives, the smaller history of a culture. To what extent does *PAJ* make history? How does history make it?

In 1975 in a Greenwich Village cafe Gautam Dasgupta and I, then doctoral students in the theater program at City University in New York and also theater critics for the renegade *Soho Weekly News*, began to talk about starting a theater journal. I can assure you that the immediate literary reference to Paris in the twenties was not far from our thoughts. Who wouldn't be seduced by the idea of being geniuses together? What led us to think of this venture, which everyone subsequently advised against, was the absence of any commitment to an ongoing serious discourse in already existing theater journals, magazines, or books. There was coverage of events and personalities, and documentation of performances, scattered essays, even a few books, that did more than treat the established canon. But for the most part there was very little new critical thinking and commentary to accompany the avant-garde in the theatrical generation after The Living Theatre, The Open Theatre, and The Performance Group, namely, the work of Robert Wilson, Richard Foreman's Ontological-Hysteric Theatre, and Mabou Mines, which was beginning then to spark the imagination of theatergoers. In fact, there was widespread belief among both critics and audiences that this theater defied criticism because it was so sensual and imagistic and seemingly textless, that criticism somehow contaminated the pure experience of such theatrical events.

Our primary interest in those days, and it remains so now, was to create a forum for critical writing that would evolve a rigorous discourse wherein theater could engage the most imaginative ideas of our time. It would be a place to air and debate issues, methodologies, proposals, visions. We wanted to rethink the possibilities of theater in ways that would incorporate the critical dimension as an aspect of contemporary sensibility, beyond the singular field of theater. We wanted to see discussion in theater move from its enslavement to Aristotelian poetics to a new poetics of performance and text and to conduct itself at the more sophisticated levels of investigation that were changing thinking in other fields.

How were we physically going to do this? How would we reach an audience? What would *PAJ* be? We had the desire and a great willingness to work, necessary attributes, to be sure, but only a wishful prelude to the real effort of publishing a journal. Toward the end of 1975 we began to organize articles and writers for our first issue from the two sources that essentially described the different worlds we ourselves straddled: artists making the new theater, whom by this time we knew personally; and scholars and critics, many drawn from universities, already writing on theater. These specific sources would combine to produce material on contemporary theater experiments and theater scholarship that would uncover or rediscover lost and forgotten texts for a new historical time frame. The two aspects of publishing, we felt, should go hand in hand in any theater periodical that hoped to develop a comprehensive view of its subject. We never wanted to limit *PAJ* to one era, to one country (America), to one school of criticism. And as longtime students, we valued the rewards of scholarship and intensive study in a chosen field, just as we valued and were transformed by what I have previously called the "theatre of images," which would bring a new aesthetic vision to theater and provocation to criticism. It was simply our good fortune to be young would-be critics when a new wave of theater was being born. Furthermore, throughout the century, journals have emerged as forums for new art forms and styles, and the writings of critics have been identified with, and have helped to define artworks on the cutting edge.

I include these specific personal remarks because in recent years I have come to believe that it is important for readers to know and understand the hidden aspects of what they are reading: how positions or strategies are arrived at and what they represent. All too often the work of actors, directors, and playwrights is overscrutinized, while readers simply ignore the intellectual factors, the dynamics of power, the psychological dimensions, the ideologies that go into, say, theater criticism or the makeup of theater organizations. If theater were more a part of cultural discourse, these facets of theatrical life would be better understood for what they reveal. There is, to be sure, a real interconnectedness between, for example, the press and the making and breaking of reputations, careers, schools of thought, and modes of perception and acceptance of an art form in any historical period. Critical ideas, like art, evolve over a period of time in ways that should be openly examined and understood in an ongoing dialogue through which art and its audience interrogate themselves and their response to aesthetic and social change from a historical point of view. This is the way a field of study grows in proportion to the ideas of its time. In *PAJ* we hoped to present new forms of critical inquiry that would suggest the complexity of criticism in relation to thinking about theater, forms that would be as radical and liberating as the theater experiments themselves. If through *PAJ* we wanted to develop critical writers, we wanted more to develop critical readers. Just as we as individuals comprehend our own identity in relation to the group, so too does art in relation to its audience. Who would be the *PAJ* audience?

So far I have outlined our editorial approach. There still remained the biggest problem confronting us: how actually to produce the journal. Luckily, through the chance acquaintance of a Norwegian tourist/librarian, who later became one of our first subscribers, we found an inexpensive printer in New York. The larger expense would be typesetting the material, but this problem too came to be resolved in quite a miraculous way. As I mentioned earlier, Gautam and I were writing at this time for the *Soho Weekly News*, itself a fledgling publication, with no pretense of paying writers. One day the paper's publisher, who had learned of our plans, approached us with a deal. Essentially what he said was, you've written already a year without being paid; if you write for me another year for free, I'll typeset the first three issues of your journal. We thought this was a terrific deal—indeed it was. We considered ourselves to have been handpicked for special rewards from among an unpaid, or at best underpaid, editorial staff. Though not in the same category as the unfathomable kindness of strangers, a good friend, theater critic Cynthia Jenner, gave us a five-hundred dollar loan, which we kept in reserve.

During this time, 1975, Gautam was performing in Richard Fore-man's *Rhoda in Potatoland* at his Broome Street loft theater. Every one of the (if memory serves me correctly) sixty-six places on the bleach-ers would have a *PAJ* subscription form, which Gautam left there each night of the four-month run of the production. This is the way we got our first subscribers. More were added as we gave out flyers whenever we went to the off-Broadway theaters we frequented, sometimes as often as four or five nights a week in those days. The "offices" for *PAJ* claimed the greater part of our small Upper West Side apartment, where all the edi-torial and production work was carried out. Sometimes we would have groups of friends help stuff subscribers' copies of *PAJ* into envelopes, which we then had to zip-code. It wasn't until 1980 that we had our first office, a floor-through basement in the same East Village apartment whose fourth floor we were now occupying, having moved "downtown" to the center of arts activity. In order to cut down on *PAJ*'s rent, we acted as superintendents of the building. Among the tenants who had to step over the *PAJ* boxes lining the halls were Lee Breuer and Ruth Male-czech, whose own Re-Cher-Chez studio would eventually open up next door. On occasion we rented out a small room curtained off from our office to guests from abroad. The most interesting of them was a well-known Japanese anthropologist, Masao Yamaguchi, who was asleep one afternoon and snoring like a great man when the old Viennese gentle-man Thomas Sessler, head of one of the most prestigious publishing firms in Austria, came to our office to discuss the rights to Odön von Horváth's plays. We had to camouflage snores and try to act highly re-fined and respectable at the same time, which already was not easy, given the situation of our offices on the seamy side of St. Marks Place. Needless to say, we did not get the permission for Horváth for some years, though happily, his volume of plays will be published in 1986.

In any case, the first issue of *Performing Arts Journal* appeared in May 1976, paid for with a little bit of money we had received for our wedding the previous summer. (Historically, marriage and journals seem to go together: perhaps it is the allure of perfect binding.) *PAJ* began to lead its own life in the world, to develop its own relationships. The first issue outlined our editorial plans and philosophy in a note "To Our Readers," whoever, wherever they were. It read:

> *Performing Arts Journal* is dedicated to the contemporary spirit in drama and theatre. Though we will specialize in current theatrical events throughout the world, we take "contemporary spirit" to include any modernist experiments of the twentieth century as they have influenced concepts of performance and dramaturgy.
>
> We plan to publish a play in each issue, manifestos, interviews, dialogues between artists, and artists writing on their own work, in addition to critical and theoretical essays on a variety of topics.
>
> *Performing Arts Journal* is conceived as an open forum for new ideas and reinterpretations of accepted standards for judging theatre. It is our hope that *PAJ* will stimulate open, lively discussion of topics of interest and value to the theatre community, in the process expanding the parameters of what is conventionally considered theatre. . . .
>
> Our main objective is to offer a platform for new ideas and to develop a critical body of essays, interdisciplinary whenever possible, on the performing arts. . . .

Our aims and tastes were clear, I think, and we have never strayed from them.

PAJ: Texts/Contexts

As I look back over all the issues of *PAJ*, up to the current 26/27, I see four distinct phases of work:

1. Earliest volumes reflect orientation to publishing, struggle to articulate ideas about experiments in theater, to frame issues. Supportive of avant-garde theater, which is itself struggling to find an audience. Attempt to define a new performance vocabulary. Essays more tied to art works than free-floating "think" pieces. Academic

historical essays mix with less formal writing. Immediate international focus.

2. *PAJ* 10/11, "The American Imagination," a double issue (1979), inaugurates a more confident, independent tone. Critical writing moves to discourse beyond specific works of art. More controversial, polemical, expansive views expressed, even critical of trends and ideas in recent work. *PAJ* 10/11 addresses the most important ideas in theater of the '70s, and a growing new sensibility, set against the reconsideration of modernist values. More visual design format.

Announcement that *PAJ* is starting a new magazine, *Performance Art* (later called LIVE), to investigate the growing field of performance.

PAJ declares its move into book publishing. A consolidation of *PAJ* interests and goals to become a more influential, stronger voice in the theater world. Name expands to Performing Arts Journal Publications, with publication of first two books in May 1979.

3. *PAJ* 14–20 set a trend for subsequent issues to give new focus and insight to significant changes in contemporary theater. Closer to *PAJ*'s goal "to evolve a continuing critique of art and its audience in its historical setting" (*PAJ* 16), without becoming ideological or following any one school of thought. "Backtalk" section of *PAJ* begins as a place to isolate single, polemical topics. "Styles in Production" (later "Performance Notes") section initiated as an anthology of short articles to expand commentary on important international and American productions soon after their opening.

Increase in new approaches to critical writing. Attention to theoretical issues stirring in critical circles: semiology, postmodernism, textuality. Titled editorials added to engage more pointed issues, particularly theater and the literary culture.

4. *PAJ* 26/27, "The American Theatre Condition," a double issue reassessment of contemporary theater life in America: definition of theater strategies, crucial issues facing artists and institutions, modes of discourse. Opportunity to acknowledge and evaluate a national crisis identifiable at individual and institutional levels. Broad analysis of transformations in audiences, marketing, funding, production trends, off-Broadway and regional structures, approaches to criticism, science and technology. Entire issue written from the point of view of critical inquiry, representing several generations of writers.

Announcement of plans to establish a theater institute in 1986 to open up new directions in critical writing and theater scholarship. Institute to be a meeting ground for writers committed to reimagining theater discourse in America.

Not surprisingly, our three special issues on American theater, *PAJ* 1 (1976), 10/11 (1979), and 26/27 (1985), give a very definite sense of the changing shape of American theater culture over the last decade. The general shift in tone is from the celebratory mood of discovering new theatrical forms, to more critical understanding of contemporary work in relation to history, to a veritable explosion of discontent and frustration, even bitterness, concerning theater's structural composition and crisis of vision. The present moment reads as a great desire for theater to make an imaginative leap and rethink itself in proportion to its promise. In terms of content, there has been a big shift away from essays about specific works of art and artists' statements to our current issue, which is entirely given over to critical writing, not writing about specific works but writing about theater culture. The very body of work in *PAJ* reflects the process of aging in the American theater, which is no easier than aging in American society.

I want to go beyond outlining a history of *PAJ* to a more specific analysis of what I think are the journal's contributions, as well as its unfulfilled projects, because from these points of reference the general condition of theater and the writing about it will emerge in fuller perspective. I believe my outline makes clear that our major concern has always been to generate a body of critical writing on theater. More than anything, *PAJ* has tried to emphasize theater as a form of intellectual engagement in the world. Since Gautam and I are writers, that sense of engagement and, more personally, love of writing came to express itself in a journal dominated by critical writing. Conversely, had we been actors or directors, *PAJ* probably would have been oriented more toward working methods and process.

A journal has to have new writers, just as a theater needs new plays and new directors and each generation must have new forms. We have, simply by being here, extended an invitation to writers, but all too few have accepted. One of the disappointments, even failures, of the generation under forty is that it has produced so few people committed to writing criticism or history, and even fewer in new areas of research and scholarship. Economic factors and the general scarcity of publishing venues beyond small journals are not entirely to blame for this situation. The economics of inspiration is such that it always generates new modes of commerce. The rejection of criticism is a legacy of the sixties counterculture challenge to hierarchical thinking and categorization, reinforced by the historical lack of theoretical thinking in American theater. But it has also to do with the increased preponderance of intellectual equivocation and sheer refusal to commit to one side of an issue or to assign values to experience. The blurring of the boundaries of art and their de-aestheticization, the demolishing of categories of high and low culture, the general loss of moral perspective, the preference for participation over contemplation, and the immersion of modernist ideology in bourgeois culture are only a few aspects of this impasse, which has decentered critics of the arts.

The Idea of a Theater Culture

Approaches to criticism are inseparably bound to their historical epochs. I have been dismayed to find writers all too aware that negative comments might damage an artist's funding capabilities (artists themselves will sometimes point this out), and critics have too often gone to artists for interviews and other information, beyond the purely factual, in order to write their pieces. This later trend, a post-sixties phenomenon reflecting critics' disorientation with the crossover of theatrical forms and an unease with the critic's role, further diminishes the function of criticism, referring all analysis of art to the subjective criteria, even intentionality, of the artist who creates it. In such circumstances critics abrogate their positions as independent thinkers. The result is that there is very little good theater criticism or significant theater scholarship by a young generation of writers. It is also true that the proportion of important recent theater books to the number of Ph.D.'s in this country, the natural source for new energy, is low. Who will produce the work?

University theater departments must take part of the blame for weakening in recent years the place of criticism, theory, and history—conceptual thinking in general—in favor of acting, directing, and playwriting. (The current upsurge of dramaturgy programs in universities around the country is, I think, an attempt to reclaim analytical territory.)

Does America really need fifteen thousand playwrights? A dozen very fine ones will keep our theater alive. And from what quarters will the visionary directors this country sorely needs burst forth? Theater departments have scarcely strayed from Aristotelian poetics, which must rank with the Bible and the Koran in its influence on believers. Does theater need an urtext? The same tired genre courses still dominate theater study, realism is taught as if it were the only view of experience, little attention is paid to contemporary ideas of textuality and performance theory. The American theater tradition itself, when it does find its way into schools, is divorced from any grounding in American culture.

Though theater departments in this country are comparatively young, they are long past needing a major overhaul in curriculum and conception: the larger question is, how will the natural competition between theory and practice influence theater training? *Thinking* about theater has to be seen as being as important as *doing* theater. The study of theater must recognize the evolving shapes of contemporary thought inside and outside of theater in order to bring some life back into it, to make it a more rigorous and demanding pursuit of knowledge. The role of the theater professional in the university needs to be reevaluated. Now that we have gone through the phases of guest artist, artist-in-residence, and the workshop syndrome, isn't it time to return the study of theater to analytical and speculative thought? Nothing will kill it faster than the stagnation that results from the loss of ongoing conceptual dialogue and the absence of new texts that propose future theatrical models. Theater, the most dangerous of all arts because of its ability to bring imagination to behavioral reality, today has become a timid reproducer of banality in its misrepresentation of populist thinking. Every level of theater activity in this country is touched by the pervasive mediocrity in which theater allows itself to exist. Perhaps it is time to recognize it as the elitist, marginal form it is in American society and to try to recover the lost, intelligent audiences who demand more than to be entertained unless it is to entertain ideas. Why must theater be relegated exclusively to the "arts and leisure" school of thought?

We hoped *PAJ* would challenge this mentality through its main objective: to generate ideas connected to a cultural and historical discourse. We have, therefore, always been interested in the avant-garde historically, not simply as current innovation. Art, like fashion, ages quickly, perhaps because at one level it is fashion. For us an important facet of theater publishing is the introduction of historical materials, so we have published many of the modernist texts of the twentieth century—mostly in translation from foreign languages—in order to bring a wider perspective to contemporary work. (Referring again to university theater departments, I propose that they seriously consider a moratorium on certain overexamined dissertation topics unless they partake of startling new research or methodology and instead encourage documentation of archival material and translation of the world repository of texts that deserve wider recognition. To our great loss, the study of theater, but not only this subject, rests so narrowly on just a few preferred languages, which dominate scholarship.)

Along with the all-important link to the present that publication of historical material provides, and the generation of criticism and theory shaped by new work, it is important to include commentary on the theatrical productions abroad. This is part of the education of a theater person. *PAJ* celebrates the idea of cosmopolitanism, which is too often absent in the American theater, where so much attention in the last dozen years has centered on American plays, their funding and production. There has been scant coverage of works of art abroad in the theater pages of any major paper or magazine, further exacerbating the theater's myopia. New York, still the center of theatrical activity in the country, reflects this provinciality: its lack of high-quality productions of classics and its inhospitability to world-class foreign troupes make it an impoverished theater capital. It is no longer even possible for a theatergoer to get a first-rate theater education in New York.

We have tried to keep a certain amount of reportage in *PAJ*, letting readers know what is happening and where. Our "Performance Notes" section was developed to fill in some of the information gaps, about theater abroad in particular. As for work here, earlier on we had planned to have artists write or speak of their work rather than have it exclusively presented within the frame of criticism. But we have now moved slightly away from this initial impulse because too few American artists write about anything other than their own work, and this most often lacking a broad cultural context; second, we experienced a general boredom with the overemphasis on process in contemporary theater.

PAJ was founded not simply to give coverage to events, which is more the function of a newspaper or monthly magazine, but rather to undertake an investigation of an event, to ask the event questions. Even the answers are not as important as the questions. As I look back over the years of publishing, I find *PAJ*'s investigations bound up with the questions it has asked of theater, more importantly, its search for the hidden orders of art. What is theatrical experience in relation to life experience? How can we understand the idea of performance? What is the meaning of writing—where is it? The articulation of issues, problems, and concepts has been one of our strong points in a period of theater history not characterized by controversy and politics. I believe our most significant accomplishment has been in the area of critical writing. In fact, I would go so far as to say that *PAJ*, through the journal and the publication of books of essays on theater, has been influential in the recent growing interest in criticism and theoretical work by making essays available from which modes of discourse could evolve.

For us it is a question of philosophical principle that we never repudiated the text in favor of performance but treated textuality and performance theory as equally important contributions to theater. It is easy to forget that a decade ago there was little interest in avant-garde writing, with the attention of artists and audiences focused more on staging. As the early years of *PAJ* demonstrate, when it was necessary to find a performance vocabulary for the young avant-garde, there was more attention to writing about staging techniques. Now, under the influence of poststructuralist literary theory, critics and audiences have become more attracted to the text (and the idea of performance as a language), a shift *PAJ* has reflected in its pages. Artists too, in the last half-dozen years at least, are more concerned with narrative strategies than, say, spatial experiments, which were a stronger interest a dozen years ago.

This shift does, I think, connect to broader cultural implications. The earlier experiments with performance space in nonproscenium settings paralleled the loss of perspective on moral and social levels. The return to the proscenium, and with it the growing interest in the text, suggests a more reflective, evaluative attitude on the part of artists. (It may also be related to a change in audience taste.) Group theater pieces, previously defined by their lack of a spatially organized center and a text composed of image clusters, sought in their performances to give audiences the experience of an event. Likewise, audience and critical response then was highly impressionistic: the idea was to give yourself up to the performance—it was wrong to try to analyze or think about it— just let it wash over you. Today we are seeing more frontality, not only in performance but in the New Realism plays, which is conducive to a critical approach precisely because of its perspectival centering. Finally, the turn to theoretical criticism in recent years accentuates theater's return to visual and social perspective.

Alas, we have reached a point in American theater history where we have a marvelous, expansive avant-garde performance grammar and yet not enough substantial writing for the stage. The loss of the writer in the contemporary experimental theater is one of the larger reasons for the general discontent with the avant-garde, however ambiguously articulated, for those who, like myself, have followed it in the sixties, seventies, and eighties. Performance theory has not made significant and long-lasting contributions to writing or the understanding of the text beyond quirky, individualistic examples generally only stageable by their auteurs. As we look to the future of theater, perhaps younger artists will see the limitations of having playwrights with too personal a vocabulary. There is no reason whatsoever why experiments in performance technique and writing cannot now coexist on an equal level. (When I speak of writing I do not mean the group-improvised text, but a single-author work.) The battles of the text have been fought and won. We have been through a period of "collective creation," often to find that many groups left behind a text composed of no more than a string of images lacking an organizing focus. We have seen the differences between actorly texts and writerly texts. We have seen that all groups have a leader/director from whom the definable aesthetic derived: here was the new seat of (author)ity. From one perspective, it seems as if all we are left with from a period of feverish experimentation is technique. That is not enough.

Since we began publishing *PAJ* a few new areas of critical interest have developed, namely, theater anthropology, semiology and semiotics, and deconstruction. These theories have affected what has been written about and how it has been written, in the journal. What publishing books in tandem with the journal allowed for *PAJ* was a forum wider than either the journal or the book division alone could provide. Quite simply, books have a longer life than a journal that appears three times annually. In sheer productivity, books can encompass the number of plays and essays we consider priorities on a much larger and more public scale. Publication of the books has given us the opportunity to help transform theatrical publishing in the United States, to instigate change in the university curriculum, and to influence the dramatic repertoire in theatrical production. Our publications have made possible extended study in contemporary theater.

I am extremely happy to announce that as of January 1, 1986, PAJ Publications will be distributed by one of America's most distinguished publishers, Farrar, Straus and Giroux. This great leap for us means that our books will be available in bookstores nationwide. It will allow us to reach many more readers on a casual basis. [Under this arrangement, we published more than two dozen books, continuing our drama list with works of Heiner Müller, Victor Turner, and Rainer Werner Fassbinder, as well as collections of new American plays, cabaret performance texts, and European plays in translation. *PAJ* also expanded to publish several novels, including those of Harry Kondoleon, James Strahs, Kenneth Bernard, Giorgio de Chirico, and Klaus Mann, and a number of gardening books. Our limited resources and the difficulties of functioning as a small, nonprofit press on a national scale in the commercial publishing system made the situation unworkable. Our agreement with Farrar, Straus and Giroux lasted two years, and was terminated in 1988.]

Since we have operated independently of a commercial corporation or university bureaucracy (all other theater journals in the United States are university-affiliated), we have had the luxury to publish very special, sometimes unknown authors in translation, nonmainstream American playwrights, and specialized essays, and the opportunity to experiment with alternative ways of printing texts, in both *PAJ* and the books. My own experimentation with critical forms is bound up with the sense of personal freedom I have in *PAJ*. We now publish more plays than any other publisher in the country, 170 to date, and many of the recent influential theater books have come from our house. To be honest, we are not so concerned whether the plays we publish will ever see production; that is for directors and theaters to decide. Against conventional practice, we publish unproduced plays too. Dramatic literature should take its place alongside novels and other forms of writing, simply to be there for readers. For too long the worth of a text has been tied to its production history. Texts live their own lives and should be free to do so. Who can say what is playable until it is played?

Twenty years ago many more commercial publishers were bringing out volumes of plays and books of essays on theater. All of this has changed in the last fifteen years. At one time many of the off-Broadway plays appeared in volumes published by commercial houses. Now it is rare if they publish anyone other than a Pulitzer prize or Tony winner, at the very least the writer of an extended hit. Few, if any, critical books are published by them, and almost no foreign plays in translation. University presses bring out a few theater books, but the majority are published by specialized theater publishers, which, happily, have increased in number over the last few years. This was the situation in publishing when we began our book division in 1979, commercial publishers having all but abdicated their interest in the field. From the perspective of today it is possible to measure the negative effects of this situation on the supply of books, old and new, out of print and in print, available for teaching and research purposes; clearly, it led to a deterioration in the discourse and dissemination of ideas. Since several of our recent editorials (*PAJ* 19, 22, 25) have already addressed the nonrecognition of theater books in U.S. newspapers and periodicals, I won't elaborate on that theme, except to reiterate that theater people can agitate for change in the situation by declaring the problem in a public way and by devoting more time to reviewing theater books. If we don't, who will?

Apropos of what we publish, Gautam and I try to separate our roles and impulses as critics and as publishers. We do not necessarily promote all of the ideas in *PAJ* or the books. Often we disagree with the schools of thought, even the ideas or methodologies, they represent. I have come to learn that we can be overidentified with the writing in our publications. Readers at times don't distinguish between our own views and those expressed in essays of other writers. There is a tendency to lump everything together with the statement, "*PAJ* says." We try to be eclectic publishers, to make available a broad spectrum of what people are writing and thinking about and doing, within the parameters of taste and integrity that define *PAJ*. In actuality, it would be easier to publish a theater journal that promoted a singular school of thought. Ideology provides its own unchanging rhetoric. For us it is much more difficult to be in constant search of critical languages.

As *PAJ* lives its own life in the world, it has its own shortcomings. I want to turn briefly to the topic of what hasn't appeared in *PAJ* and why. Sometimes what on the outside seems to be a matter of ideology isn't always the case. At other times the absences are a function of choice. As a matter of preference we have tended to stay away from essays on a single play or production, favoring instead larger treatments of an artist's or group's work. Long essays on a single focus can quickly become overextended academic exercises, and we have been determined to keep such writing out of *PAJ*. We wanted more high-quality, journalistic writing, opinionated conceptual pieces on significant issues, not the overly researched "objective" writing in academic journals. At the opposite end of the spectrum, we are not receptive to mere description or documentation of performances, since we prefer to print analytical pieces that have a point of view. We want the essays to think on their own, not just chronicle activities.

As a publisher, editor, and writer I have become all too aware of the power, real or imagined, a theater journal that circulates internationally can have. It affects funding, it affects bookings (particularly abroad), it affects the ways art is evaluated and experienced. Like it or not, criticism does reflect, even set, standards by which art is judged in a particular historical moment. To my disappointment I have learned that published work is for the most part regarded by artists as on the level of public relations. Critics and artists are totally isolated from any real lines of intellectual exchange and mutual regard. The newspapers have contributed to this condition by moving reportage closer and closer to public relations. Rarely is there any discussion of theater within a broad cultural system, attention being focused largely on celebrities. This cult of personality and the overemphasis on work process, plus the general low quality of journalistic writing on theater, especially in the *New York Times*, which is read by and influences countless people across the country and in some very perverse way sets the tone for its reception, has contributed to the loss of serious public discussion of theater. This affects avant-garde theater, off-Broadway and regional theaters, and Broadway. The deterioration of theater life is inseparably bound to the deterioration of theater reportage and scholarship and the increased mindlessness of audiences.

There are many areas of *PAJ* that I would like to see expand. One of these is the attention to playwriting. However unlikely it may seem, in ten years of publication we have received relatively few submissions or inquiries by anyone wishing to write about plays. As attention turned to experiments in performance, mainly centered in groups, one result was a gradual disinterest in textual analysis of individual authors. Furthermore, contemporary playwriting itself did not excite the imagination of most critics. To be sure, there are plenty of conventional studies of dramaturgy that comprise theater bibliographies, but it is now necessary to go beyond previous knowledge of the dramatic text to the more complex levels of discourse continental literary theories of the past several decades have opened up. This move can benefit critics and playwrights alike. I am not, of course, advocating that we become obsessed with semiotics, structuralism, deconstruction, or hermeneutics, but we cannot ignore the discoveries such theories have brought to our understanding of writing and reading. Likewise, the study of the text should be more receptive to new theories and methodologies of cultural discourse developed in recent decades.

Perhaps if we allow a deeper knowledge of the text as writing and as a form of cultural production, it will be possible to comprehend on a larger scale the language of the stage that each director creates. There should be reflective writings on the work of directors that address larger issues than stage business: social relations, division of space, the situation of the actor's body, attitude toward stage directions, the vocabulary of images, uses of technology, internal relationships. Semiotics and semiology have suggested many new directions of research in these areas that, again, need not be swallowed whole, but can be absorbed into other critical languages.

We have seen very little work, if any, by writers in specialized subjects such as gay, black, or, more surprisingly, feminist theater and theory. We'd like very much to have essays on issues relating to Broadway theater and television programs, but these too have been largely absent from our submissions or requests. More kinds of performance could easily find a few pages in *PAJ*, articles on singers and comedians, for example. Another area the theater community has yet to pursue is that of investigative reporting, specifically patterns of grant giving, expenditures of public monies, hirings and firings, how theaters and organizations are run and by whom. There is none of this scrutiny of activities involving monies that are publicly accountable for, essentially because no one is interested in doing it.

During the period we published LIVE magazine, 1979–82, finding competent writers was a continual problem. We started the magazine because there was a proliferation of performance that operated on a formal realm completely contrary to theater, more attached as it was to the visual arts. It was a phenomenon we were intrigued by and wanted to investigate in a magazine. Yet, despite all the "performance art" activity, there never developed a substantial number of critics or body of criticism.

What came to take the place of criticism was documentation of performance and artists' statements about their work, or their critic friends' explanations of the work as it had been explained to them by the performers. All of this generated more hype than anything else, and indeed it created the artificial economy of the performance art world. Though we tried for a few brief years, up to LIVE 6/7, to generate critical writing about the form, I'm afraid the magazine was never up to the standard of PAJ, just as the form itself pales beside theater. We were disillusioned by performance art, short-circuited as it was by its ahistorical stance, incompetent performers, and a lack of theatrical knowledge, which, as a performance mode, it cannot hide.

Acts of Criticism

What for me are PAJ's "unfulfilled projects" that I referred to earlier, call them failures if you will, or unrealized desires, are not so easily isolated. They are more complicated and historically rooted, certainly more than a question of aesthetics, though that is part of it. They partake of the social world just as theater in its fullest dimension does. The first of these is the frustration, the lack of breakthrough, in seeing drama, its literature, and its ideas, completely disregarded in American literary culture, where it should be linked comfortably as writing. The lack of attention to dramatic literature by the literary culture has not been significantly analyzed as an aspect of literary politics. I believe the divorce of drama, American or foreign, contemporary or classic, from literary culture has resulted in the substantial diminishing and overspecialization of textual knowledge and tradition. It is also stupefying that critics who write so assuredly of the "performing text" fail to acknowledge dramatic literature, with all its exemplars of performance and textuality, the twin pillars of new literary theory. The natural place to study "representation" is in the relationship of drama to theater.

Theater in general is abominably isolated from intellectual cultural life. While, as I have written elsewhere, American scholarship in the last dozen years has been revitalized by the very idea of theatricality, few theater scholars have actually influenced this thinking, which has been largely taken over by the field of sociology. Every age has to find its critical focal point. In our time that center is the idea of representation, or, to frame it less literarily and more culturally, performance, just as at other times it was "reason" or the "sublime." Theater scholars and artists should be contributing to, if not leading, critical debate over representation: it is the very definition of theatrical life, not only textually but existentially.

Vigorous new ideas in theater simply are not a part of general cultural discourse, except at the most banal level. When literary critics write about literature they don't examine the bestseller lists; yet virtually all discussion about theater revolves around Broadway, ignoring the long, great Western tradition of writing for the theater. Another result of this situation is that people will often read writers' novels but not their plays, and publishers will offer the novels and memoirs and essays of their authors but ignore their plays.

Part of the interchange of disciplines has to be brought about by critics and scholars themselves. I deeply regret that we have not found, or attracted, or inspired more writers, though I believe we have found nearly all who are writing, or they have found us. What theater culture lacks is the constant, healthy reexamination of ideas and theories, the revisioning of texts of previous generations. What tends to happen in the theater world is that a new theory or approach comes along, say, Grotowski's "paratheatrics," or "the theatre of images," or "postmodern theater," or "ritual," and so forth, and critics, scholars, and audiences alike begin to use the terminology and absorb the concepts unquestioningly. There is little or no critique of the philosophies, ethical issues, values, and social conditions that shape theater discourse. There is no analysis of the channels through which new ideas enter theater criticism, how these lines of discourse come to challenge and replace others, how discourse is controlled by various forms of power in the theatrical structure, be it university, press, funding agency, or theater. This knowledge should be a fundamental dimension of theatrical thinking. People simply fall into camps following one rhetoric or another. It would be enormously beneficial to include in *PAJ* more intensive dialogue and debate on concepts and theories as they enter the theatrical vocabulary.

The theater public needs to be more cognizant of the strategies writing devises, the systems of values they oppose or propose, and how these influence reception of theatrical form.

What I on another occasion called "acts of criticism" must be related to theatrical practice, not only to situate art more firmly in relation to its historical moment but to move closer to comprehending the nature of writing about it. I believe criticism is a profoundly subjective gesture that is not merely an activity but a way of life in which the writer enters into the text and the two begin to lead a third life. We must understand how a critic arrives at specific views, what those views represent in the critic's writing life, and to what extent the critic is the critical text. I am suggesting that the critic is to criticism what the dramatic text is to theater. The question of representation is, therefore, a category of critical thinking. It cannot be separated from the question of audience. Nor can criticism be excluded from what is called writing if it is to be grasped in its entirety.

There is so much more work to do before we will be satisfied that we have done what we set out to do. Oddly enough, having written these words, I feel that we are in the beginning stages of a cycle in which critical writing is regaining respectability and its intellectual edge. Ironically, the loss of art is giving life to criticism. The feeling of discontent is giving form to critical languages. Theater has somehow lost its importance in our lives because it has become less important to itself. We know now that it is not enough simply to see theater to do theater: the seeing must become an aspect of being. What will theater be for us as we creep up to the twenty-first century?

PAJ in the Future Tense

It is difficult to reconcile a vision of the theatrical conditions I have described with the resources of a country as prosperous and full of potentialities as America. How can we use these resources to create a fuller theatrical life? We will try to find a new way. In future issues of *PAJ* we will make every effort to reach out to horizons of intellectual discovery by moving beyond the world of theater more than we have in the past. These expansions will occur chiefly in three areas:

1. Examination of concepts in scientific thought and technology. The separation of the humanities and the sciences is an intellectual

attitude we do not support, and we therefore intend to enlarge the perspective of *PAJ* to discover how new research in science may contribute to theater research.

2. Linkage of literary culture and theater culture. Since PAJ Publications publishes so many plays by leading literary figures, we feel that we have a natural link to this world and the world of letters, in the larger sense of the word. Theater critics share many of the same concerns as literary critics, as do playwrights and novelists, and all could benefit from the crossovers of textual knowledge.

3. Participation by scholars in the social and human sciences, including psychology, sociology, anthropology, and urban science. Forms of research involving the human being and his or her environment can create a fuller context for theatrical thought and practice.

Beyond the newer dimensions we expect to emphasize in forthcoming issues of *PAJ*, we will add to our regular coverage of theater by publishing case studies of individual productions. These studies will take the form of in-depth analysis of the contributions of writer, director, designer, and actor to a specific production: how each conceived his or her role and how it was actually realized in production. On occasion we will ask a dramaturg to give a detailed analysis of the conceptual approach to a play and to trace its development in the actual staging. We also plan to publish more essays on plays, contemporary and modern, so that critics will be encouraged to implement new theories and methodologies in the study of drama. It is time to rewrite the history of dramatic literature in a post-Aristotelian poetics. The areas of focus I have outlined mark our current interest in moving beyond the world of theater to the larger intellectual world defined by the many new directions contemporary thought has taken. Though *PAJ* will of course continue to be a "theater journal," we intend to make it more and more an interdisciplinary forum for cultural criticism and exchange of ideas.

If I have saved our most dramatic announcement for the last section of my commentary, that is not to give it the least attention, rather more to give it the largest context. We are making plans now to set up a theater institute affiliated with PAJ Publications, as a natural extension of our activities over the last ten years. The institute, which Gautam and I have long thought of, will comprise members taken from among the contributing editors of *PAJ* and from outside the journal. It will be a small group of people who will meet periodically to initiate specific directions and projects in theater research and writing and, beyond that, to address significant issues, developments, and conditions in theater. The institute will be a kind of "think tank" for writers, most certainly not a docile body set in an ivory Tower of Babel, but a group of people actively engaged by the significant ideas of our time. It will also give writers the chance to get to know each other and exchange ideas, a simple enough goal but all too regrettably unrealized in this age of isolation and specialization.

The institute will be an experiment for us. No such theater institute exists or has existed on which we can model ours. Furthermore, existing scholarly institutes are most commonly affiliated with universities. Ours will instead be attached to a publishing house. This circumstance can work to our benefit since we already have a group of writers on which to draw and the means to make our research available to a wider international public through books and journals. [The PAJ Institute for Theatre Culture brought together fifteen writers who met several times to discuss their work, current arts issues, and joint book projects, and on occasion an invited guest attended the meetings. Our major project was the sponsorship with New York University/The Center for French Civilization and Culture, of an all-day conference (November 1986) on contemporary theater entitled "Performance Worlds." We had several preliminary meetings to discuss the event under the auspices of the New York Institute of the Humanities. Due to the overwhelming responsibilities of our expanding publishing program and to the lack of necessary additional funds to pursue our dream of an institute, we abandoned further activites in 1987.]

The idea of theater has changed radically all over the world in the last two decades, in approaches to the text, actor training, audience reception and perception, uses of technology, experiments with space, and collective work, to name only a few areas of change. Easy access to travel and exchange of information has been brought about by advanced communications on a global scale. But that information must be turned into knowledge if it is to have any lasting value. All forms of scholarship have advanced incredibly under the influence of counterculture pressures, current research, and the organic changes in the world as we live it at this historical moment.

But theater scholarship, as I noted earlier, has rarely kept pace with these advances. The expanded knowledge of historical and cultural discourse has made our theater history books out of date, their approaches old-fashioned: new ones must be written to reflect more sophisticated and less exclusive views of culture and art. There are no American histories of theatrical space, or histories of the audience, or sociologies of theater. The classical and contemporary repository of texts must be rethought in light of the textual knowledge brought about by new literary theory and the extraordinary opening up of cultural discourse and methodology. We can no longer be content to think of drama in the categories of plot, setting, genre, dramatic action, conflict: there are now new possibilities for defining character or the lack of it, and performance space itself. There should be new books on acting and actor training that incorporate research in brain studies and feminist theories of gender role-playing. Studies in vision and visual perception need to become a part of thinking about theatrical design and production. Recent experiments in performance theory have much to add to theatrical knowledge on formal and social levels.

Theater has a long, illustrious past and a future that can be full of promise and daring if we all work together to reclaim its lost dimension in our culture and in our lives. Our dream is for *PAJ*, the publishing house, and the institute to become a meeting place for a new gathering of theater writers who will, like theater itself, imagine new worlds in which to honor the human spirit, which is so gloriously receptive to transformation.

I want to close my remarks with the words of one writer that appeared in the first issue of *PAJ*. It was Gertrude Stein who set the tone for a proper work attitude: "I begin again so often that I can begin again."

(1985)

The Controversial 1985–1986
Theater Season
A Politics of Reception

|||||||| One of the regular dialogues on contemporary theater published in *Performing Arts Journal* follows, with contributing editor Gerald Rabkin and theater essayist Johannes Birringer participating here

MARRANCA: The recent theater season was characterized by a number of productions that, while exploiting taboos, raised issues to which contemporary audiences are responding more and more, in all forms of art. Among these issues I would include the question of representation, particularly in relation to race and gender; an exploration of liberalism as a political philosophy; and uses of technology in performance. It seems to me that we might begin with any one of these topics.

RABKIN: I assume by the failure of liberalism you are referring to Wally Shawn's *Aunt Dan and Lemon*. That is an interesting question, particularly if you read the appendix to the published version. Here Shawn makes explicit his working by negative example through the quasi—and not so quasi—fascist mentalities of his central characters and the positive need for liberal values: the recognition of the individual human being within a liberal framework is the only guard against the acceptance of the monstrous assumptions Aunt Dan and Lemon "logically" develop. But we see the failure of liberalism by the marginality of Lemon's mother, the one liberal voice.

MARRANCA: She clearly has no response in the play. That's obviously deliberate, and in some ways makes the play less interesting. There is no dialectic; it's completely one-sided from the point of view of reactionary politics. It seems to me a little bit dangerous about the play, and it's part of the ethos of the appendix as well—this danger of not distinguishing between things in our world. In *Aunt Dan and Lemon* there is no differentiation between the kinds of killings that are spoken about. There must be a difference between killing criminals, Indians, Jews, and cockroaches. Lemon's point of view is faulty in that all kinds of killing are equated—you simply can't link killing cockroaches and Nazi philosophy.

RABKIN: I agree that there are certain moral premises, historical premises, that are problematic in the play. The very choice of Kissinger as Dan's idol is deliberately provocative: he hardly tops the list of radical/liberal demons, even taking into account his involvement with the overthrow of the Allende government. But the moral issue is ultimately larger: unless one accepts a totally pacifist position, you come down to the old question of necessary violence. Shawn deliberately fudges the question here.

MARRANCA: Shawn's point of view doesn't necessarily attach itself to a fully developed philosophy, and the person representing the liberal point of view is completely inarticulate. Shawn makes the point that we have a certain freedom because other people in the world don't, that our freedom is dependent on their oppression. Aunt Dan's philosophy suggests to her that Kissinger takes responsibility for his action, while journalists and other detractors enjoying the freedom in American society simply criticize him.

RABKIN: There is an element of truth in much of this critique, and that is why the play is so disturbing. It's very easy to attack the villain, the Other. Here Shawn recognizes the undeniable logic of Dan and Lemon's reasoning. But he's also saying there are crucial leaps that are irrational, and negate morality—a twisted process by which the ordinary, somewhat "decent individual" is forced inexorably into the position of monster. That is the valuable part of the play.

I accept your judgment that the minute you begin to probe the overall intellectual structure of the play it begins to unravel. It does *not* distinguish between the act of necessary self-defense and the act of wantonness. Is every violent act immoral? Well, the fight against Hitler produced violent reactions that few of us would condemn as immoral. Shawn puts his finger on a certain kind of logic and sensibility that leads to the inconceivable. He catches that in the logic of the two major characters and that is why his focus is on them and *not* on the liberal response to evil.

MARRANCA: What you're outlining also bothered me as an argument in the play. It's not exactly clear in terms of morality whether Shawn is distinguishing between a person of action and a person reflecting on acts. In other words, Dan's argument is that a person attains a certain stature through action. It's somewhat faulty because action and reflection represent two different realms of society and they're both necessary. Dan's argument rests on the fact that Kissinger was a man of action and the rest of us, the rest of the liberals, talk and criticize.

RABKIN: You're right. We vicariously identify with the hero, the one who *acts*. That point, however, was ambiguously presented by the two casts at the Public Theatre: how *literally* are we to take Dan's adventures? The physical presences of Linda Hunt and Pamela Reed created different emotional profiles in the play. Hunt is powerful but idiosyncratic physically: her reported affairs with Mindy and her professor seemed vicarious within the context of her physical presence. Reed's physical and emotional profile was such that you could believe her. It's ambiguous in the text to what extent Aunt Dan acts on her "amoral" premises, which lead to the immoral. The amoral for Shawn is the world of sexuality, and the world of the bedroom is connected to the world of politics. It's an audacious play in that Shawn deliberately avoids narrative and psychological elements except subtextually and focuses the play upon the rhetoric. These long set speeches are disturbing because on one level he succeeds in what he wanted to do: to force the audience to accept a certain kind of complicity. Aunt Dan, on one level, is a crazy, eccentric Auntie Mame who says all these wild and crazy things that are fantastically attractive to sweet, neurasthenic, sickly Lemon. If the mother were strengthened as a figure, and the liberal alternative presented more strongly, then it would be clearly "them" against "us." We'll instantly identify with the liberal alternative. Shawn succeeds in finding a less conventional attack. I would love to get a reaction to this from your European perspective, Johannes.

BIRRINGER: I think the play is avoiding the complexities of the issues by positing the arguments in a monological way, completely withholding any critical point of view within the play. This strategy, which one might call insidious or irresponsible, collapses everything into a kind of seductive surface where eccentricity comes to look innocent, and innocence eccentric. If the play assumes the audience's complicity, as you have argued, it does so because there is no "liberal alternative" that wouldn't look hypocritical. Shawn's American liberalism admits frankly that it is susceptible to "slightly" inappropriate analogies, and the play becomes dangerously predictable in the sense in which it presents a kind of pragmatized amoralism.

RABKIN: Did you sense an identification with that amoralism?

BIRRINGER: The performance trivializes the issue by making us understand one continuous irony in the play, namely, the monstrous views put forth by two relatively nice women, who seem so innocent in what they're saying although it is outrageous. That quality of outrage gets lost once you see that the play only works in this one mode. I felt really disappointed by the presentation of the issue of Nazism and Kissinger's involvement in the American war machine.

What I would raise as a question since we're talking about the politics of performance is, Can the theater, especially in this country, deal with that question in a public forum, and what are its means? The play shows the difficulties of actually dealing with political questions, especially since a counterpoint or critique was not given in the play itself. I don't know whether it was expected from the audience.

Maybe I can make that comparison to the situation in Frankfurt and the recent controversy over the production of Fassbinder's *Garbage, the City and Death*. It also dealt with the touchy subject of how to address total immorality and total perversion of human values in the past and in a present *influenced* by that past. In Frankfurt, members of the Jewish community prevented the play from being shown. Now, in New York, when I saw *Aunt Dan and Lemon* there was a total passivity in the audience, which in one sense was striking and in another, totally expected, because the play cannot really achieve what it wants to achieve, namely, to create a critical dialogue, or an analysis of the guilt of silent complicity.

RABKIN: But clearly the cultural contexts are so different. Fassbinder's play, whatever one's vision of it and of the political action taken against it, must be viewed within its unique historical circumstances, just as Shawn's play comes out of a culture that was never physically brutalized.

MARRANCA: Paradoxically, Shawn is criticizing the liberal point of view in the play, while relying on a liberal audience to identify with it in the broadest, most old-fashioned sense. To say, which he does in the appendix, that there's a little bit of Hitler's ghost in all of us is a real cliché. It's a spurious point to be constantly told in American dramas about Nazis that we're all Nazis. The critique of Nazism and its philosophy has to go beyond this liberal point of view that there's a little bit of the Nazi in all of us.

BIRRINGER: It's the problem of an anti-liberal humanism play written by a liberal humanist who really doesn't know how to formulate the problem in different ways and whose irony depends on a naive belief in a moral consensus. Shawn's idea of moral corruptibility or complacency, at the same time, seems tied to a history of American political commonplaces that is unaware of its own ideology of innocence or "compassion," as Lemon calls it. (The kind of "compassion" that makes the Reagan administration support "freedom fighters" in Central America and elsewhere.)

RABKIN: I find it no small achievement that Shawn tried within the sense of his culture and the values he shares with the culture to see how monstrous inhumanism can emerge out of individuals who are not themselves monsters and inhuman.

MARRANCA: But the dynamics show that that is precisely the weakness of the liberal humanist critique, because Shawn is caught up in the same dynamic he's criticizing. Let me mention one other point: Irene Fornes mentioned something interesting with regard to this play. She was disturbed by the fact that he gave the reactionary speeches to women. She thought that Shawn, since he was an actor in the play, was hiding behind another character rather than giving these speeches to his own character. What if Wally Shawn were Lemon? Is it a way a playwright hides an unpopular point of view? It's more difficult for a playwright to come right out and say something in a very direct way than it is to couch it in irony or metaphor, giving the speeches to others. That's why his appendix is also so ambiguous. What is Shawn actually saying about morality? On the one hand, applauding a turning away from morality, how it traps us in guilt; on the other hand, in the last paragraph he's saying, "Well, the world isn't all evil."

RABKIN: He would probably acknowledge that this is the dilemma of the liberal in the present day, in that no clear alternatives seem to be viable. As a consequence, one has to try to understand.

Let's return to the Fassbinder play, where similar questions are raised in a radically different context. Let's, for the moment, defer the social implications of the protests against it to focus on the play itself. It is a very, very powerful play, there's no denying that. But it is also a profoundly ambiguous play in that its explicit politics on slum landlordism and property—its inception was real-estate speculation and political corruption in Frankfurt after the war—are constantly at war with an intense sense of the impossibility of the human condition.

Obviously, Fassbinder identifies, as Brecht does, with the outcasts, the marginals, as a means of critiquing capitalist society at large. But also as in Brecht, there is a tension between social critique and an existential pessimism about the human condition. In Fassbinder the balance is further skewed by a scream of *angst* that recognizes *every* character in the play as simultaneously victim and victimizer. There are *no* alternative positive models that suggest the possibility of change, and the play as a political critique is totally overwhelmed by a vision of thanatopia. If there is an anti-Brechtian act of identification at work in this Brechtian play, it's certainly Fassbinder's with Roma B, who asks for her own death and is granted it.

BIRRINGER: I think it is written from an entirely different perspective, the perspective of suffering due to the perceived impossibility of changing the oppression and exploitation of human beings in particular social and political conditions. For Fassbinder the condition of minorities did not change in postwar Germany. That experience of suffering is totally lacking in *Aunt Dan and Lemon*, where the two leading female characters are looking from the outside on something they explain in ludicrously perverse ways. Think of Roma B in Fassbinder's play: she can't get out of the position of being exploited, and she finds understanding and affection from precisely the one character, a rich Jew involved in real-estate manipulation, who became the protagonist in the Frankfurt controversy.

MARRANCA: You said that the Rich Jew is the protagonist. I might add that Fassbinder's German publisher has requested that in future editions of the volume, we change "The Rich Jew" to "A, the Rich Jew" in the cast list. I suppose that means he won't be a type. Do you think that the Rich Jew is the main character in the play, and if so, why?

BIRRINGER: Yes, I would argue that in terms of the representation of social contradictions in the play. It is written of course from within the German situation of remembering guilt and not being able to get out of the self-entrapment of that guilt.

In Fassbinder's perspective it is a way of capitalizing on existing corruption and human degradation produced by the system, where Jewishness becomes almost a metaphor for a complex of guilt, oppression, and self-oppression. In other words, both the characters who are non-Jewish as well as the Rich Jew are part of the same system, which instrumentalizes guilt and the mechanisms that lead to the production of evil.

RABKIN: Fassbinder has always worked with traditions of provocation, in this play primarily overt sexuality and obscenity, the intensity of its violent imagery and sadomasochism. The act of labeling a character "Rich Jew" is to some extent comparable to what The Wooster Group did in using blackface in *Route 1 & 9*: a similar act of provocation against the subject of the unspeakable.

Though I abhor the tradition of censorship, I cannot accept an absolute standard of total freedom of expression regardless of social context. History, German history in particular, shows us that there may be times limits have to be drawn. Whether in the present German context this was the place to draw the line I am not sure. But bad boy Fassbinder will say the unsayable, denying the *cordon sanitaire* created around certain subject matter by German guilt about the tradition of anti-Semitism.

What Fassbinder says is that each human being will use what he or she has to victimize others; in this case the Jew uses German guilt and his connections with the Establishment as a means of maintaining his economic power. On the other hand, he is also a sympathetically ambiguous character who sees with a depth and perception that other characters do not.

MARRANCA: Let me raise an alternative point. I think that the play is more virulently anti-woman. Obviously, that doesn't have the same kind of political imagery or impact in Germany as the representation of a Jew does. But if you look at the imagery of the play, it is more violently anti-woman, as much of Fassbinder's work is. For example, the play takes place on the moon, which is a female image. Also the image of the city is a spider; if you extend that imagery, the female spider devours the male in the act of copulation. The whole urban image is around the notion of this spiderlike web of filth and corruption. Also, Roma is hated by both her father and her mother, she's abused physically by Franz, and Oscar is openly anti-woman. The female image is the image for pollution in this play, not the Jew.

RABKIN: But Fassbinder, in his own sexual ambivalence, more often than not *identifies* with female victimization at the same time that he portrays a world in which the female—but not only the female—is brutalized. Shall we extend this question to similar images of victimization in male-female relations in Pina Bausch, whose appearances at the Brooklyn Academy's Next Wave Festival were obviously one of the highlights of the fall? There are many who have reacted negatively to the intensity of Bausch's symbols of victimization, feeling that she goes beyond the traditional feminist critique to indulge and indeed exploit the victimization of women. How do you react to that, Bonnie?

MARRANCA: I see her work as an elaboration and an extension of much of the Judson aesthetic, except what is different about it is the exploration of male and female social and sexual relations. Her theater is perhaps more important for German theater than it is for American. What's important about it for German theater is the influence and move toward spectacle in a theater that has a very strong literary tradition.

But from its feminist point of view her work is really quite extraordinarily different in the context of dance. Her dancers are choreographed as obscene, awkward, ugly women. So it's a direct attack on the notion of the beautiful female dancing body. Also within the context of feminist theory, Bausch reverses the notion of the "gaze." She refuses to let the female be the object gazed upon and instead turns around the entire dance ensemble to gaze at the audience. It's a rather simple flip of the equation, but within the context of her work it's developed politically, in the use of the body in performance and in terms of the imagery. One of her strong pieces, *Kontakthof*, which is very Brechtian, also uses this fertile tradition that Fassbinder draws on. But in both situations there is a sense, which you don't have in *Aunt Dan and Lemon*, of a very strong social *Gestus*. The entire world created in the German pieces—Bausch and Fassbinder—has a political, social, aesthetic philosophy that is integrated, even though there might be contradictions within it. Now some people say that if a man did what Bausch does he would be criticized for being sexist. That's interesting and perhaps partly true: maybe only a woman could get away with this kind of choreography. How do you feel about that?

RABKIN: You're quite right that there is a tremendous energy in both Fassbinder and Bausch, and in the other figures, like Reinhild Hoffmann and Suzanne Linke, who appeared at the Next Wave Festival, a reconnection with Weimar energy. It's a unique historical situation of having to leap back beyond the Nazi period to reestablish strong links with the past. Bausch's evening of Brecht-Weill, *Don't Be Afraid* and *The Seven Deadly Sins*, was enormously effective in establishing a sense of continuity within her own concerns, with her own subtexts—with the Weimar tradition.

But there are contradictions in Bausch's work that I'm trying to resolve: tensions between form and formlessness, between gimmickry and stunning visual innovation, between intensity and repetitiveness in her fundamental obsession with the battle of the sexes. My feeling, and I know others don't agree, is that when there is a strong coherent structure at work, as in *Kontakthof* or *Cafe Müller*—and despite her sometimes surrender to theatrical effect—her work is powerful and important.

But to get back to your point of the continuation of the Judson aesthetic, some dance critics dislike her work because they feel that it denies the body by using it in ways that destroy its capacity for making formal aesthetic gestures.

MARRANCA: Bausch and Fassbinder are doing the same thing, in one sense. They're addressing taboos in language: Fassbinder's dealing with literary language and imagery, and Bausch with taboos in body language. Brecht is the ideal mechanism for this kind of aesthetic because of the sense of *Gestus* in which the body represents an entire political world. As far as my own interest in Bausch's work, it remains at this formal, feminist theoretical level, which is interesting at this point in dance. It doesn't seem to be coincidental that we should have now a dance theater that deals with sexuality, representation, and social relations between men and women.

BIRRINGER: I disagree with the notion that both in Fassbinder's play and in Pina Bausch's work there is a recognizable exploitation or use of anti-woman or anti-man or anti-Semitic positions. We're not at all dealing with essentialist or racist categories in their work, but rather with the mechanism, perhaps I should say the violence of the mechanism, in which femaleness or Jewishness or maleness appear (i.e., come to be represented). Pina Bausch's work is quite clear in the association between maleness and machismo and the kind of sexist attitudes we identify with male aggression. But it's demonstrated as part of the ideological and social construction of behavior, the "training" of roles that become second nature. Through the Brechtian model it can be shown, in the way certain patterns of behavior are written into the body and the way victimization surfaces in those patterns of behavior. It's not a matter of exploitation but a matter of *demonstrating* it to an extent that it becomes almost unbearable, especially in America, where, as you say, it's unacceptable to show the ugliness entrenched in social behavior.

MARRANCA: I don't think it's a particularly American attitude. Let me just go back a second. I didn't say that she was exploitative. Neither do I think of Fassbinder that way. I do not consider *Garbage, the City and Death* as an anti-Semitic play.

RABKIN: To label it an anti-Semitic play is not the same as to say that it is a deliberate provocation in its utilizing of traditional anti-Semitic elements. We have to recognize that Fassbinder consciously utilizes elements of the anti-Semitic tradition because figures on a stage are exemplary. It's naive to assume that someone with Fassbinder's intelligence didn't know what he was doing.

MARRANCA: That's what people said about The Wooster Group too—that they're an avant-garde group, how could they be racist? Now we've come to the base of how to consider representation. We're back to the Platonic argument that because representation in performance is twice removed from reality it seems inadequate as a clear political philosophy

RABKIN: We also come into conflict with the intentionalist question. Let's extend this into the Foreman-Acker collaboration The Birth of the Poet. If we were just presented with Garbage, the City and Death, and if we had no knowledge of who Pina Bausch is, would our apprehension of their work be transformed? What would our interpretation of Kathy Acker's text be if we discovered that it was a man who wrote it instead of a woman?

MARRANCA: People have said the same thing about that play as they did about Bausch: if a man did that, it would be considered sexist. We're dealing with the same thing in terms of the image of a Jew in German literature. Historically, certain imagery is potent, and there's just no way to get around that.

RABKIN: The contextual element cannot be eliminated. Representation doesn't exist in a void; it exists within the series of apprehensions that a reader or an audience brings to it. Anyone who sets up a totally formalist aesthetic is not really facing this reality.

MARRANCA: This gets back to what we started out with—the issue of liberal humanism. We seem to be in a period where there are several hot issues: we're thinking about cultural images, the politics of representation, sexuality, and, hopefully, not overpoliticizing art. More and more we are dealing with taboos of different kinds of imagery that we didn't see on the stage fifteen years ago. If you think of the ways we talked and wrote about Richard Foreman in 1970, it's almost astounding that nobody wrote about his use of the body. Now it's inconceivable to think about Foreman's work without dealing with it in terms of sexuality.

RABKIN: Let's talk about The Birth of the Poet, because this is a very interesting and problematic work, one of the few works in recent memory in the American theater that has created the kind of scandal Fassbinder's play represents in Germany. Even the very "hip" Next Wave audience was booing, hissing, walking out in droves. Without discussing the sociology of that at the moment, we have to admit we saw a disturbing, malformed kind of event. In my view, the text Kathy Acker produced could not have received a less informed production. The Cunningham-Cage model that prevails in so many Next Wave productions—each element going off on its own independently—is exactly *not* the kind of model that can deal with a text as supercharged and as powerful as *The Birth of the Poet*.

MARRANCA: Is that because it was theater, or do you think the model works better for dance?

RABKIN: The model is most successful in work that assumes a kind of Brechtian distance, work that is cool, in which elements can establish a dialectical relation. Here you have a text that is so hot, so eruptive, that any kind of balance becomes almost impossible unless there really is a strong theatrical welding of all production elements. But it seems to me that Kathy Acker is onto something that connects with the themes we've been talking about. Let me read one passage from the typescript of the text: "The implosion of the world of unbearable passion is the destruction of human meaning. The only possible world for humans now is the realm of ornament, pure nonrepresentation. All languages are finally ornaments or nonrepresentation is the word of God but even God the Father being a religious centralization must be abandoned before we who are abandoned, who are politically powerless can speak." It's these elements that led Erika Munk to defend the play from a feminist point of view, saying that it represented women's throwing their desire back in the face of male phallocratic power. It led Elinor Fuchs to say in conversation that she felt this play signaled the eruption of nonrepresentation in theater, a breakthrough that implodes language as power.

MARRANCA: Interestingly, it's dealing with the same issues as Fassbinder's play—death, pollution, racial issues, and sex, in an urban environment.

RABKIN: One finds that in reading the text, not from the BAM production. Yet even as a written text the play is so contradictory, so ambivalent, so ultimately incoherent as to negate the effectiveness of its undeniable power. I don't find here what I do in Fassbinder's play, a critical intelligence that knows what it's doing, shaping and controlling its provocative events and images. The play is a garbled scream of rage and pain in which I find a complicity with, as well as an attack upon, victimization. It asserts that language is nonrepresentational but is intensely aware of the power of the representation of obscenity. The text is schizophrenic: meaning is always partially created by the reader or spectator; but in this case you have to work overtime.

BIRRINGER: It is a total self-contradiction in the premise that language or action in the theater could be nonrepresentational or could implode in the sense that she's implying. In Bausch's work you can see clearly through what is represented: the connection between sexual conflict and political conflict and the relations of power. In *The Birth of the Poet* the whole question of ornamentation really diluted that and played into a postmodern interest in surfaces, incoherence and indeterminacy of surfaces that is rather regressive.

The production was very incoherent, especially in the interplay between the staging, libretto, and stage designs [by David Salle], which made no sense at all and seemed to conflict with the taboo-breaking and deliberate obscenity of the text.

MARRANCA: That play is such a direct link to Foreman's own work. I have the feeling that—looking back at his Rhoda cycle—if Rhoda wrote, she would be writing like Kathy Acker. Acker is doing some of the same things as Pina Bausch: a woman who's dealing with obscenity. Certainly no woman has ever used language like this on the stage, and that is deliberately provocative. Some works have a topicality in a certain historical period—Acker, like Bausch, is dealing with the representation of the female body, not only linguistically but also physically as a body, and she's denying the traditional contemplation of the beautiful female body as the object of contemplation, of the sublime, of the aesthetic. Again, it's getting away from the idea of the gaze, which has become a dominant rhetorical point, if you could call it that, of feminist theory. That is directly connected to how we see spectacle.

Aside from that, we've accepted this kind of literary tradition—if I can separate the performance from the text for a moment—with Pasolini, Burroughs, Celine. She is working within and playing with that very male tradition of philosophical eroticism and obscenity. These factors are startling regardless of the ultimate satisfaction of the text as a closed form.

RABKIN: I don't disagree, but why should many who look at works by men that advance new images of the female be surprised by the fact that a male is going to have a male gaze? The other problem suggested by Kathy Acker is the danger of ghettoization, sometimes operative at the time of the rise of the black aesthetic. Does the fact that Kathy Acker as a *woman* utilizes this language negate the inadequacies and difficulties within the text itself? There is a danger in that. Ultimately, while recognizing contextual diversity, we still need to work with some standards of universality that allow us to make aesthetic judgments, standards that go beyond the biographical and biological.

MARRANCA: Let's go back to the point of universality. That is the same thing as saying that a work is complete, and whether one's point of view is reactionary, or deconstructionist, or humanist, or formalist, the work remains the same. There is a difference between work that is created in different historical periods, by men or women, or marginal groups. What's interesting in Acker's work is that, like a number of different kinds of new work—Heiner Müller's, for example—in our time we're seeing the history of sexuality connected to the history of the world. Now, I'm not making extravagant claims for her work, but simply pointing out elements that for me in 1986 are interesting to think about, regardless of the lack of success of the production.

RABKIN: I suppose it's a question of difference of perception. I fear the tendency to evaluate the social significance of the artistic act rather than the actual aesthetic result. I didn't mean to advance a universalist aesthetic theory; but it's still necessary to recognize that we *do* have aesthetic models that we apply within our own contextual realities.

MARRANCA: I'm a little surprised at your reaction because of your long-time interest in the Theater of the Ridiculous tradition. I see *The Birth of the Poet* connected to that and a step beyond it. Twenty years ago the Theater of the Ridiculous dealt with many of the same taboos, if you think of early Tavel or Vaccaro. Don't you see this as part of the Ridiculous tradition?

RABKIN: Yes, in its time the Ridiculous Theater very definitely challenged traditional models of representation, but I don't think every work of the Ridiculous tradition demanded equal aesthetic respect.

MARRANCA: I'm not thinking about this production in terms of success. I simply wanted to suggest the idea that the Ridiculous has turned into the Punk aesthetic.

RABKIN: To that extent, the Ridiculous was a politically revolutionary movement that has been subsumed by all kinds of other changes, in pop and high culture.

BIRRINGER: I think we should ask the question whether we are currently in a phase of rethinking representation. The biggest problem was that even if Kathy Acker's text was coming from a new voice—we're also talking about the increasing work now done by women artists— did it materialize in the production? That is to say, since Richard Foreman was directing it, what happened to the libretto? Why were there so many quotations of surrealist staging techniques, and why in a sense was the staging going backwards?

RABKIN: There were problems of sensibility, judgment, and autonomy. The problems that surfaced in the production were also found in other work Foreman has done this past season in staging texts other than his own. In the case of Vaclav Havel's *Largo Desolato*, perhaps someone said, "Well, Richard's world is a world of paranoia, often a world of fear, a world in which buzzers interrupt," and this seemed a perfect kind of metaphor to impose upon the Havel text.

The evidence of both the Acker and Havel productions is that the playwright's and the director's sensibilities did not really mesh, and as a consequence both productions went off in contradictory, unsatisfying directions.

BIRRINGER: The superficially paranoic staging for Havel does not really come to grips with the play itself, because that play is dealing with the utter normality of the terror in Czechoslovakia, which is a different matter. The premise of *The Birth of the Poet* was that we are at a point *after* the catastrophe, after the explosion, so to speak. Set in New York after the nuclear blast, the play showed that something has happened by that time, namely, that we have lost a certain meaningfulness.

RABKIN: Let us note that there *is* a connection of this theme to Richard's perceptions as expressed in his works from *Egyptology* onward through *Miss Universal Happiness* to *Africanus Instructus*, a movement from the purely phenomenological, intermixed with his own vision of the body/mind dichotomy, to the quasi-political. Images of terrorists, revolution, and the Third World have increasingly intruded in his work, as well as an element of social apocalypse, a common theme in many of the works we've been considering. It's certainly in the Acker text and in Schechner's *The Prometheus Project*, which, interestingly enough, have the exact same structure and admixture of sexual violence and nuclear holocaust.

In the case of the Havel play, I absolutely agree with you, Johannes, the absurdism of reality—the paranoic, the hysterical, the hallucinatory—are all part of the fabric of everyday life. Terror is interiorized. To exteriorize it into gestures, and Rhoda-like crouches and walking the walls is to ask for the exact kind of reaction that it got—laughter, which *defuses* terror.

BIRRINGER: Do you think that the whole question of the language might be an important one, if we think, for example, of the ten or so years of a theater of images? Think of Wilson and that kind of theater, which virtually excluded the use of textual language. We're now seeing an increasing interest in using language, in revising myths and representations. For example, Schechner was deliberately going back to revise a myth by conjoining the Prometheus myth and the Io myth.

RABKIN: That is exactly one of the problems that both Foreman and Wilson face as they move more in the direction of dramatic text: they have to face something they never faced before—the performer as actor. In creating their theatrical vocabularies they developed a very specific kind of technique in which acting was negated, in which amateurism, the ordinary individual's deadpan reading of lines, was substituted. Now all of a sudden they're dealing with dramatic texts, in the case of Wilson's *Golden Windows*, perhaps not a coherent narrative text but still much more verbal than anything he had tackled to that point.

MARRANCA: One thing in regard to *Golden Windows* that was interesting to see was the use of David Warrilow. Suddenly his performance, and our knowledge of him as a performer, brought Wilson's text into the world of Beckett, and this was a revelation. However, Wilson mixed nonactors and actors, so it wasn't totally carried through. I feel that his work would benefit by using real actors, and I understand from people who saw *Golden Windows* in Munich that the result created a very different effect because of the use of well-known actors.

BIRRINGER: That raises the question whether we can really speak of a return of the actor if Wilson employs technology to the extent that the text is distributed through amplification and an audio system, in spite of the presence of the actor. Often I have trouble connecting the voice with the body of the performer, and that creates a different sense of what happens.

RABKIN: Certainly in both *Golden Windows* and *Alcestis* the multi-separated voices were used, but, nonetheless, there still were actors speaking live dialogue. It was interesting to note the intersection of the various texts in *Golden Windows* — the visual text with the shifting perspective of the house, the aural text of the separated voices coming on the soundtrack, plus the verbal text that was emanating from the actors. But if you look at the verbal text, you see that it functions in much the same way in *Golden Windows* that it has in other Wilson pieces.

Wilson and Foreman have always used language to deliberately cut loose its signifiers. But now, all of a sudden, in the presence of the performers we begin to feel the desire to impose a kind of signification upon what is spoken. The failure of *Golden Windows* was a failure of the dramatic text because the language does not function in a way consonant with the whole chamber structure as expressed visually and aurally. The very banality of the language, which Wilson has always played with, in this case becomes an obtrusive element working counter to the integration of the multiple texts in the piece.

MARRANCA: I feel Wilson could be an extraordinary artist and that we would see the real connection between Craig and Appia and the theater of images in our own time if he could work with writing as writing, if he could devote time to thinking about the text in an all-encompassing sense of his performance work.

RABKIN: *Alcestis* was very interesting in that regard because the main body of it was a coherent if not absolutely faithful reading of the Euripides play. Even in the prologue by Heiner Müller, interspersed through the main body of the play proper, and in the Kyogen epilogue there was a coherent structure of signification. Nonetheless one felt, how are we to read those actors' performances? Wilson himself did not seem to know how to deal with actors as actors—whether to deal with them in his traditional way as presences, part of the landscape, or to engage them within the context of a narrative.

BIRRINGER: One of the biggest provocations in the German productions of Wilson's work in Munich and Cologne was that he used very well-known character actors, who were turned into carriers of nonsensical, banal, everyday speech. That shocked people a lot because they could not identify emotionally with what was said. The question is whether we can go back to actually using actors in that kind of work, which seems so much more interested in the scenography of the performance as a whole.

RABKIN: Obviously, the actor has always been the primary figure of representational theater, whereas the radical experimentation of the past twenty years has, at least partially, reduced him or her to a performer who is one part of the total scenic representation: neither visuals, aurals, nor actors are privileged. If Foreman and Wilson are going to use the actor in more traditional ways, then they are going to have to rethink the meaning of acting and performance.

MARRANCA: In the last few years we've seen a return to myth, to the proscenium, to the actor, and to classics and texts. Clearly we're in a kind of transitional period.

RABKIN: The reemergence of mythology is an interesting question, as Johannes was saying before.

BIRRINGER: It means a return to narrative, doesn't it? If you deal with myth that presents problems, you need to confront the *construction* of the myth.

RABKIN: Particularly in *Alcestis* you felt that what was missing was what Lee Breuer was able to find in *The Gospel at Colonus*—some modern receptacle for the tragic "spirit," whatever it may be. Breuer found it by connecting with the vital black gospel tradition. But in *Alcestis*, here was a classic myth with no new objective correlative, and that weakened the mythic dimension. Let's extend the discussion to Schechner's *Prometheus*. Schechner had the same aims as Kathy Acker: to intersect nuclear holocaust, sexual violence, and victimization. The problem for me was an overly schematic use of the myth and its modern equivalences, which dissipated the energy coming from the imagery and the performance. I'm sure we will respond to the work from our different male and female gazes. The part that worked for me from the point of view of performance was the Annie Sprinkle pornography-show segment, except for its very end, when there's the obvious point of stopping—one, two, three —and glaring at the audience as if to say, "What *are* you looking at, you people?" You could see that coming. Nonetheless, it created the kind of disturbance that on one level Kathy Acker was able to set in motion— at least for males, because pornography is a male genre and most males have had experience with it at some time in their lives. So observing pornography, *not* in the enclosed worlds of all-male bonding, but within the context of an art occasion with women present, was genuinely unsettling, more provocative than sitting back and saying, "Yes, I agree with you; yes, victimization and rape and sexual violence are terrible."

MARRANCA: Schechner operates on the same assumption that Shawn does, which is the Aristotelian humanistic tradition of audience identification, that certain point of view that we're all the same, that we all have a little bit of the pornographer or Hitler in us. On the other hand, Kathy Acker was working totally in an anti-humanist tradition. She does not operate under the same assumptions.

The problem with the Annie Sprinkle porno section is that it isn't very compelling to have a female stripper, which is a kind of cliché, undressing and talking to an audience that is then supposed to feel that they're voyeurs because they let this happen very passively. What surprised me was the way she could move among the audience, get men to touch parts of her body or put their heads in her breasts.

RABKIN: That was a bravura gesture. I disagree—I felt embarrassed the night I saw it.

MARRANCA: But you know, that makes me think that men must be very comfortable with the female body, that even this stranger could come up in the audience and get any kind of reaction. The representation of women onstage or in film is always done from the point of view of male psychology. The men in the audience obviously were quite comfortable with this poetic perception of her body. I think it would be far more provocative if it were a male there and to see if the same thing would happen, whether men could touch other men. Whether they could perhaps get the women to have the same physical response.

RABKIN: I agree with you that he used a male erotic model here, it's just that *my* male reading of the show sensed a general male embarrassment that nonetheless led, like in stag fraternity-house circumstances, to a certain kind of macho pose of knowledgeability.

MARRANCA: Did you hear of anyone refusing to participate in her seduction?

BIRRINGER: Everyone was quite willing the night I was there.

MARRANCA: I didn't hear of any controversy. I would have been curious to see if women staged a protest or if men refused to engage her. Schechner was dealing only with clichés, he did not deal with the representation of women or pornography in any way that contradicted or criticized the cultural production of imagery.

BIRRINGER: Maybe it wasn't thought through, although he actually used the positioning of the striptease in direct relationship to the positioning of an audience vis-à-vis aestheticized images of destruction. In the first section, he showed in very fast movement hundreds of images—slide projections—that were taken after the bomb was dropped on Hiroshima. I saw this as an attack upon the idea that you can actually watch these images, from an aesthetic distance, and feel secure. In other words, to let Annie Sprinkle walk out into the audience had something to do with physical rupture: we could no longer sit back and gaze at pornography or "beautiful," slow-motion imagery of Hiroshima. This is the kind of slow-motion, anesthetized situation we have in Wilson, when for four hours you see extraordinarily stunning images that go past your eyes. Schechner tried to break down that aesthetic flow.

MARRANCA: I think his work was devoid of strong political content for the opposite reasons that Bausch's and Acker's work was much more compelling in the use of images or sexuality.

RABKIN: He's coming from where he's coming from, and it's his gaze, and within the context of what he devised he tried to create some kind of bridge from this underground world that *does* exist and to have it enter the world of other images of destruction.

MARRANCA: What I find problematical is the same attitude that's problematical in Schechner's writing: after he exposes these so-called everyday performance situations, there is no critique of them; it's a purely descriptive act that accepts performance at face value.

RABKIN: You don't think there was a critique within the performance context?

MARRANCA: Then we're assuming that the critique is always coming from the audience. Perhaps we assume too much. Is it necessary to assume that when things are not politically clear in a performance the audience must make the judgment? I suppose I'm more drawn now to work that seems to have a very connected and clear politics of form, a morality of form, rather than opaque or weak narrative structures that leave the issue of values to the spectator.

BIRRINGER: It has to do with what Roland Barthes has called the "responsibility of forms" that an artist uses. It is precisely because Wilson has no political or historical consciousness that his recent work seems stuck in the visually beautiful but mystifying landscapes that he builds, in the same way in which Sam Shepard repeats his obsession with the empty mythos of the American family.

RABKIN: Schechner is a heterosexual male and has a heterosexual male gaze. The kind of critique that you want to see is a critique that will come from women who are the recipients of that gaze. Nonetheless, I think there is something to be said for the exposure of the gaze and the investigation of it as a beginning.

MARRANCA: I wouldn't deny that at all. I think it's Schechner's most intellectual piece, and he certainly showed a great leap into using more of his own theoretical work and other ideas about performance and technology. I'm simply critical about the pornography aspect and the issue of voyeurism. Back to Johannes's point about Shepard, audiences and critics have made the assumptions that he's criticizing male my-thology. What if we were to ask if Shepard is a reactionary? People have said of *Aunt Dan and Lemon* that Shawn's play is reactionary, that he's a reactionary; they've said that Fassbinder's anti-Semitic. But no one has raised the issue with Shepard. Is he a redneck or is he a reactionary? Nobody has dealt with the issue, which is a central issue of the play, that a husband has beaten his wife—he didn't just step on her toe—and she's brain-damaged.

RABKIN: I don't go to a work of art, Bonnie, for ideological correctness. That's not what I want in my perception of it.

MARRANCA: I'm not proposing that. I'm simply saying that you should look at the politics of a work.

RABKIN: But you seem to be imposing the requirement of a correct political position, a political grid that you place upon the work of art. It is obvious that if certain works manifest values that one finds totally ab-horrent, then that is going to drastically affect one's investigation of it.

The question that you raise in reference to *A Lie of the Mind*, the question of brain damage, is not a disturbing question to me, because I don't read it, first of all, within the context of a realistic play in which a sympathetic character one identifies with commits some kind of heinous act that is then, by whatever means, morally justified. I don't see that model operative at all in this play. I see a play in which *all* the characters are brain-damaged, battered travesties of the pioneer spirit. I see a play that in all its imagery—particularly in its final image of the fire in the snow perceived across half a nation—says, don't take this too literally.

MARRANCA: I'm not posing any model, I'm simply posing questions. It is strange that in all the reviews I've read, written, incidentally, by men, they have concentrated on the father-son relationship, and several re-viewers picked out the image of blowing the ashes from the father's cre-mated body in the little tin. No one has dealt with an issue that seems to me to be important in the play, which is the relationship of the hus-band and wife and the issue of wife beating. Secondly, if you look at the last scene of the play, in my view it was staged with the husband down-stage, virtually center, in a very sympathetic position physically. Sympathy went toward this man rather than dealing with the issue of violence. Now, I'm not saying that Shepard *has* to do that, but if we transfer our thoughts about Fassbinder and whether this play is anti-Semitic or whether he is, and whether *Route 1 & 9* is racist, why don't we think about Shepard's work and its philosophical view? I'm not posing a corrective or saying that he should have a program, but we assume certain things about artists because they're a little bit experimental, and perhaps we shouldn't.

RABKIN: Everybody's noted, you have yourself noted in essays about Shepard, that he has always had a problematic relationship to women in his plays, which have for the most part dealt with a world of male bonding. Particularly in his early plays women have *very* insignificant roles. But it is certainly also true that since *Fool for Love* there has been some attempt to deal with male-female relations in a way that Shepard has not done in the past, and it's even more strongly so in *A Lie of the Mind*. We definitely find in that play a continuity from *Fool for Love* in that the interrelations of the family and its mutual cannibalization are contrasted with some indistinct vision of possible redemption through love. Now, admittedly, this is a redemption that is built upon the character of a man who has beaten his wife practically to death. Obviously, the element of subjectivity we all bring to various works prevents me from responding as intensely as you, Bonnie, to the images of wife beating and victimization that you cannot eradicate from your reading of the rest of the play.

MARRANCA: I think you're reducing my entire comment to a women's issue. It's very clear that we see different things, we see different things even as men or women, but no one here is talking about censorship. However, I am suggesting we look at a work in larger, more demanding ways rather than being overly attached to the notion of artistic effort.

I always look at work formally—but what is the morality of this form, the system of values it outlines? The critical response to *A Lie of the Mind* is more interesting for what is not spoken of. What are the taboos in terms of the work? What are the assumptions?

BIRRINGER: Maybe within the world that Shepard creates there is a politics of sentimentality that doesn't confront the final collapse of moral values, but dreams about final redemption. I'm sure most people prefer the dream, and that's why they don't really react to the sexual frustration and the content of violence when it is directed against Jake's wife.

RABKIN: But I don't think Shepard denies it, he faces it. He is honest to that extent. He doesn't try to mitigate it; it's a submerged violence he makes overt.

MARRANCA: I agree, he's a very honest artist. To quote Irene Fornes again, she made an interesting comment one time in *PAJ* which is that she found in response to audience discussion of her plays that men in the audience responded to only the male characters and women responded to both male and female characters. Just to be provocative, I raise the issue again: if there's such a discrepancy between the way we see things, what is the nature of our looking?

RABKIN: The issues you raise, particularly in connection with all the other issues, are enormously significant, and we have to pursue them.

MARRANCA: I simply think that whoever people are is in their writing. I don't see a separation anymore between, say, the world of the play and the world of the author. Now, I'm not speaking of autobiographical elements, but of philosophies, vision, and human values. Pirandello's fascism was in his work, as Chekhov's humanism was in his structure of writing.

RABKIN: But why should we expect otherwise? I find it almost impossible to read Celine because of the virulence of his anti-Semitism; it is impossible for me to consider Wagner from a totally aesthetic point of view. One has to acknowledge that from the start. That doesn't mean to some extent we can't stand back—it would be foolish to say that Wagner is an insignificant artist. Nonetheless, insofar as we're functioning critically and trying to relate our aesthetic judgments to larger moral, ethical, and political judgments, we have to acknowledge the premises from which we're coming and examine them.

BIRRINGER: Would you say, then, that it's possible to argue there is a logic of the material itself, that there are limitations to the kind of material Shepard treats, going back again and again into the American family and obsessed males in their relationships with their fathers and battered women? That is a limitation I don't see, for example, in a piece that was written, so to speak, from the outside about America as a dreamland. I'm referring now to *Dreamland Burns* by the Squat Theatre. It opens up the problematic in a very different way: a group that has just arrived here looks at what is happening to them.

RABKIN: Yes, there are similarities in apocalyptic imagery between *A Lie of the Mind* and *Dreamland Burns*. Think of Squat's development since they arrived on these shores ten years ago. *Pig Child Fire* was overtly a work of the European avant-garde, very Artaudian, deliberately provocative and similar in certain strategies to the work of Kantor. But gradually there is a thematic transition in their work. The most fascinating element in their early work was the strategic use of their Twenty-third Street Theatre to create a theater of the street, where everything that was happening outside was visible to the audience inside. This device lost its provocation in successive pieces but nonetheless remained effective. Thematically, their work was interesting because of its enormous ambivalence toward the American experience. As a band of Hungarian hippies who were kicked out of their country as subversive, obviously they relished the enormous freedom now available to them. On the other hand, immersion in a plethora of media imagery, in the wildness and violence that is the dark side of the freedom of the West, set up a fascinating tension in their work. On one hand, they reveled in their new freedom; on the other, they were overwhelmed with technology, media—America as a huge baby with television eyes in their piece *Mr. Dead and Mrs. Free*.

The interesting thing about *Dreamland Burns* for Squat is the transition it represents in their work, in a sense coming out of the movie *Stranger Than Paradise*, with Eszter Balint, Stefan's daughter, all of a sudden emerging as Squat's very own home-grown movie star who is an American! She fits and yet she doesn't fit *as* an American, and *Dreamland Burns* is their most American piece, the least apocalyptic despite its apocalyptic title and elements: its opening fire, its shower of objects dropping down, collapsing, but by the standards of the earlier pieces— where shish-kabob skewers were being stabbed into groins and people gave blow jobs and were shot—what struck me was how the coolness of postmodern America has filtered in without totally transforming their sensibility. Through the figure of Eszter as the new urban woman the hippie clan that escaped from Hungary has entered its second generation.

BIRRINGER: But it shows a coolness and ironic thrust toward images of America produced by the American "consciousness industry" that are at the opposite end of the sentimental gesture of the miraculous fire in the snow—the concluding image of A *Lie of the Mind,* which connects the two families.

RABKIN: Shepard likes to end with these ambiguous images, but I don't think it's a completely sentimental image, Johannes. It breaks the realistic convention: the mother in California burns the house, the other mother in Montana sees it. It both universalizes the fact of destruction and suggests the possibility of redemption, the miracle of resurrection. On one level this play is a Western: the California people are the homesteaders and the Montana people are the cattlemen, the hunters. Shepard plays, as always, with mythic American forms, even affirmations: the patriotic ritual of folding the flag, the kiss after all these years. But he also points out that the fire in the snow casts severe doubt on a possible rekindling of the American spirit. The brain damage is something that cannot be overcome. That's the ambiguity in Shepard—the lies of the mind—one can hope that they can be overcome, but ultimately they can't. At least one can hope for the miracle.

MARRANCA: Except that his wife is now a kind of Blanche duBois and totally demented.

RABKIN: But there is a kind of recovery within a structure that is comic as well as mythic.

BIRRINGER: But it's a very strange comic sense. It's as though the wife who is almost beaten to death recovers only to be seen to be married again, to the brother of the one who has beat her.

RABKIN: I think we have to see that for all these losers, no one is going to escape.

MARRANCA: And to see it in the context of all that we've been talking about. In every single case, in almost all the plays we're talking about, we're dealing with female characters who are coming to represent these points of view, starting with the reactionary point of view in *Aunt Dan and Lemon*. The interesting thing is, we still come down to the point that the female body is the scene of this politic, whatever it is. Bausch and Acker, whose sense of sexuality is very different, have confronted this issue. In the work of Shepard and Schechner we are simply given the same old tired images and psychology.

RABKIN: Nonetheless, I think that within the legacy of the limitations created by one's gender, people like Schechner and Shepard are trying to, shall we say, deepen their gaze—perhaps from your point of view insufficiently, but I think honestly.

MARRANCA: If you recall, ten or fifteen years ago the way people wrote or spoke about work was much more formalistic or structural. We've seen in recent years a real return to issues of representation and the body, how technology is used, the politics of taste . . . I think that we've moved from that highly formalistic phase when we were trying to establish a new stage language for theater, and now we're moving much more as the theater itself is, to narrative, to interest in writing and all different kinds of textuality.

RABKIN: Let us move from what you said to the subject of to what extent the development of technology has altered the way representation is achieved on the stage. At present, there's an intense recognition of the conflict between the physical "presence" of the actor and his or her mechanically reproduced screen or video image; an example is *Dreamland Burns*. All of a sudden you realize in that work that a number of figures speaking to you are molded mannequins, with moving faces projected on their sculpted faces. Their utter immobility strikes you, and you recognize that you're dealing with a deceptive image, which is interacting with and problematizing the representation of live actors. We found the same issue explored in *Deep Sleep* by John Jesurun at La Mama.

BIRRINGER: The immobilization of the body was for me very strong in the way in which Wilson uses the human body as a figure in the larger architectural landscapes he creates, contrary to the privileging of the body, let's say, in dance or in some of the pieces we've discussed. It seems that there might be an important strand in the experimental arts, in the work of John Jesurun or the recent Squat piece, where the whole question of technological reproduction or imaging and the emplacement of bodies as projections can no longer be comfortably assumed in the theater, where real bodies or objects used to be considered more real than their images. I think Jesurun in particular addressed the crucial question of postmodern culture: what is the reality of reality? We have trouble knowing on which side we are—whether we are in the screen projected or on this side of the screen. Jesurun's piece was rather striking in making that the focus point of the performance, that struggle *not* to become a projection.

RABKIN: What bothers me in a lot of the current mixed-media pieces is their absence of a sense of history, their intimation that the mere juxtaposition of different technologies is an act of great aesthetic daring, when in fact one can go back sixty years to the era of Meyerhold and Piscator and find the same kind of technological experimentation. In Piscator's famous *Good Soldier Schweik* production, screen-drawn Georg Grosz caricatures became animated on the stage. Film, almost from its outset, has played with its form self-reflexively. And one need hardly note that the problematic intersection of aesthetic and social reality is something that has been observed since Pirandello. So I'm bothered by the assumption that some technological quantum leap has just occurred.

BIRRINGER: But our historical conditions are radically different from those of the early avant-garde. I don't think it's a matter of self-reflexivity any longer. We live in a culture oversaturated with mass-produced images, technological practices, prefabricated consumption —our bodies fragmented in so many different pieces of reified techniques. I see this as an almost total depletion of human reality.

RABKIN: I would like to find in the new works that use diverse technologies a recognition of the way in which technology has changed. But in *Deep Sleep* I'm confronted by a technique of discontinuity and disjunction that has been used by experimental theatrical artists since the era of the dadaists and surrealists. How indeed *is* new technology altering perceptions? Once I had grasped, in the first few seconds, the familiar metaphor of *Deep Sleep*, its levels of performance, narrative text, and technological interaction were insufficient to hold my attention.

MARRANCA: One of the things that's become clear throughout the discussion is a kind of anxiousness to move on. To move beyond the forms that are disseminating now in theater and to be more aware of the links between experiments in the twentieth century, knowing what we know historically and seeing ourselves poised in an era where people are being influenced thematically by new configurations in the world and new technologies. It seems we're at some sort of cutting edge.

I think what will happen in this country is that we'll move away from formalism to more critical forms. The rest of the century will be a kind of critique of modernism and modernist form, positing new ways of perceiving the human being in the world.

RABKIN: The tradition of the new is such that we constantly insist that, as in Lewis Carroll, they run as fast as they can to stay in the same place. If someone like Kantor comes along with a new piece, *Let the Artists Die*, which uses the same vocabulary and themes of his previous works, we say, "We've seen this already. We don't need this anymore." If, on the other hand, as in the recent work of Foreman and Wilson, there's an attempt to move into new territory, we, including ourselves here today, say, "Wait a minute. They don't know how to deal with actors, there's a problem of sensibility, stick to what you can do." So as we as critics uphold the standards that are meaningful to us in trying to make informed and knowledgeable judgments about the work we see, we should never forget the burden of the tradition of the new as artists try to move off into unexplored worlds, and allow them the opportunity to fail.

BIRRINGER: It is possible to see how the current conditions of our culture will determine the kinds of material or "immaterial" realities artists deal with. What we don't know is the extent to which we are already "beyond" the history and the forms of modernism, or beyond history, as they say in Europe. We don't know to what extent mass-produced images have already invaded our imaginary, evacuating all individual ethical substance or psychical interiority. We need to confront this invasion in order to continue to be able to differentiate, to make distinctions—in a political sense—between ethical and ideological questions raised by art. The danger of the problem of implosion we spoke of earlier in respect to *The Birth of the Poet* is that all of this becomes a closed circuit, as in Laurie Anderson's work (cf. *Home of the Brave*, live performance art

having finally moved directly onto the screen), where you cannot possibly make any distinctions between aesthetic, technological, and social
reality anymore because it has become meaningless. The whole question of the construction of sexual difference and of political violence
seems to be something the theater will have to deal with in the future,
as long as we still have theater.

(1986)

Theater and the University at the End of the Twentieth Century

Theater and History

In the twentieth century the reform of arts education was inspired by avant-garde ideals, the magnificent examples being the Bauhaus in Germany and, with the invaluable contribution of its exiles from the Nazis, Black Mountain College in North Carolina. The struggle to imagine new artistic forms that would engender new social values was the very foundation of these educational experiments. Now the topography of our own era is becoming more detailed decade by decade, allowing ever new insights into the configuration of artists, artworks, and ideas that has defined modernity. As the still-emerging histories of the arts take shape, it is apparent that the schools of modernism, which transformed artistic, political, and cultural values in the twentieth century, are what we consider our tradition. The worlds within the words *modernism* and *avant-garde* have been contested in recent discussions of the arts, so precisely for their highly charged and inexhaustible resonance and their formulation of the modern intellectual heritage, I continue to use them here.

It is not my intention to address all of the arts or the entire history of theater. My comments are limited to the twentieth-century context, the area I have focused on in my own teaching of the last decade and to which, since the founding of *PAJ*, I have devoted nineteen years of research and publication. I believe that the twentieth century should be at the center of any arts curriculum, because its artistic contributions in matters of form, style, and organizing principle shape contemporary art and popular culture, its critique, and, increasingly, the construction of its history. Emphasis on the twentieth century is a pragmatic choice as well, since America lacks a classical repertoire to engage in dialogue and reinvention. It was in the postwar period that American experiments in the arts became so influential here and abroad, particularly in painting and performance. Yet, while a rich and expansive scholarship in art history exists, theater has still to develop a comprehensive history of performance ideas. I am not the first to lament that theater lacks a definable epistemology. What body of knowledge should an educated theater artist or intellectual know?

At its very core theater study lacks sustained intellectual rigor and breadth. Theater departments, though they may seem to be "modern," actually offer in the course of study only a cluster of the best-known canonical plays from around the turn of the century and the early decades, with Williams, Miller, Beckett, perhaps Genet, and Pinter at mid-century, and the trendy American and British plays of recent years. Most programs are organized around historical periods, genres, styles, and master artists, with huge gaps in essential areas of study. The list of subjects regularly *not* taught (unless by chance there is a faculty member with a special interest in any of them) is long and all-encompassing: to start with, modernist movements between the wars (futurism, expressionism, dada, surrealism, Bauhaus, constructivism), Piscator and other radical political theater, Russian plays after Chekhov, Eastern European theater, Scandinavian drama after Ibsen and Strindberg, any Italian artist other than Pirandello, any Spanish-language author other than Lorca, the German drama tradition, the history of avant-garde performance, American theater history, the history of directing, concepts in stage design, the history of acting theories, comparative world drama, Oriental aesthetics in Western theater, dramatic and theatrical theory. An evolving history of ideas about theater might embrace the disparate views of, for example, Aristotle and Plato, St. Augustine, Diderot, Rousseau, Wagner, and Zeami or the concepts informing the *Natya Sastra*, medievalism, epic drama, theatricalism, poor theater, semiotics, theater anthropology.

The overemphasis on drama and the indifference to staging practices and multimedia in the curriculum are frequently the result of the traditional interrelationship on some campuses between the theater and English departments. Therefore, if the teaching of nonpractical training courses is initiated in the English department, the British-American dramatic heritage is highlighted rather than drama or staging in European and non-Western theater cultures. Likewise, theater courses in classics and language departments also focus on dramatic literature rather than on theatrical technique.

But theater departments are marked by their own exclusions. They give no significant attention to the visual arts or to dance history or to music theater and opera (in which so many Western directors have worked in the last two decades, with Americans making genuine formal contributions). Nor is there any attempt to organize knowledge in art world crossovers such as body art, installations, and video. Yet, the art world has become increasingly theatrical, and many artists here and abroad are working in multimedia forms that combine image, text, music, and movement. In fact, the most adventurous theater students are more interested in such cutting-edge forms and experiments rather than in conventional play study and production. Such transformations are also supported by the shrinkage of the world dramatic repertoire, due in part to the absence of writers of stature comparable to those in the first three-quarters of the century and the increasing irrelevance of drama, especially for younger audiences, as a focal point of cultural life in America, Europe, and parts of Asia. In New York, Paris, Warsaw, Berlin, Calcutta, Moscow, Milan, Copenhagen, and Budapest the loss of theatrical energy and the lack of a new theatrical vocabulary at this end of the twentieth century is, sadly, an issue of genuine concern.

Theater has not at all confronted the provocation of the enormous changes in the intellectual and cultural environment in a world of new technologies and previously unimagined possibilities of experiencing time and space and text. Where is the impact of the new physics and sciences in the theater of today? Where are the new conceptions of character, language, and sound? Where is the new imagery? As we prepare to enter the twenty-first century, theater needs to become more visionary and not to attempt to compete with other media but simply to create its own contemporary vocabulary. In this age of information, theater has something of infinitely more nuance to offer: knowledge. It is the only cultural space in which felt speech and concentrated listening and looking is preserved and which in each historical period takes as its subject the representation of the self. In this realm one can discover qualities that are increasingly disappearing from contemporary experience, such as privacy and intimacy and spiritual feeling.

The Theater Program

Theater study no longer embodies any sense of its own reason to exist or to engage metaphysical issues in its magisterial heart. What should one read or stage? More imploringly, why? Virtually the entire history of theater is organized around a few predictable plays of the most-read authors of classic and traditional drama, with little movement outside a narrow range of their *œuvres*. Regional theaters are just as short-sighted in their choices of plays. The new play anthologies offering historical surveys inevitably include the same works of the same authors and only an added nod to current successes or obligatory political choices. This cautious orientation may have been more suitable for a postwar curriculum set on making theater a respectable form of study, but it is hopelessly out of date given the last half-century of experimentation in the arts and the shift away from the dramatic heritage, not to mention the tiredness with which the overly familiar repertoire is greeted. Whether they acknowledge it or not, theater departments in general are training students for little more than the largely moribund institutions of mainstream regional theater, even to the point that their theater buildings imitate regional theater architecture.

It is no wonder that programs in theater, unlike those in other disciplines, such as art, in which study can include a critique of the museum, cultural politics, and the economics of the marketplace, do not elaborate any critique of the theater world. To some extent the revered history of American theater has always been the history of successful plays and personalities. The history of the form, its institutions, and critical debate has no explicit place in the curriculum. Film, literature, anthropology, communications, and media studies, to name only a few departments, all now have a well-established critical discourse on the history and nature of their epistemological framework, the development of institutions, audiences/readers, and work processes in these fields, while theater lags far behind in such analysis, a champion of the status quo.

Not only is the nature of production not questioned but there is a proliferation, even an excess, of productions in big theater programs in this country, the vast majority of them of poor quality. Now, I am not advocating doing away with university productions: most theater students go to school to gain practical theater experience, not to train as scholars or professional critics. But they seem to lack any contextualization within the course offerings of a given semester. The first question one might ask is, What should be the relationship of school productions to the theater curriculum?

Students who once might have devoted themselves to scholarship as critics or historians are now most often found in the dramaturgy divisions of the departments, preparing to enter the new service economy of theater. Departments and, consequently, students lack a clear sense of the dramaturg's real artistic value and purpose in the American theater. After all the years of dramaturg training, surely one of the disappointments in the field is that there has not been any substantial dramaturgical scholarship published on theater productions. This is not surprising, since dramaturgs are not well trained in the literature of the theater, and have little exposure to high-quality theater. Once inside the theater bureaucracies, dramaturgs are frequently pressed into service to fundraise and write publicity material. Even many of them have begun to doubt the efficacy of the profession. How can a dramaturg be creative in theaters, professional or academic, most of which apparently have no overriding principles determining what they produce and a mere few weeks in which to do it?

Theater training is drowning in overprofessionalization, while it ignores the demands of either the conservatory or a true intellectual environment. There is little time for students to study, conduct research, and try out new ideas, to learn the history of theater, even to attend arts events on campus, with so much attention given to writing plays, directing, designing, acting, and rehearsing. I propose that in the course of a single semester theater programs try dividing the semester in half: work on productions in the first half and leave the other half completely free for students to pursue deep, exacting critical and historical studies. This way they might learn more about the artistry of the theater and waste less time working on bad productions. It is impossible for students to have this necessary intellectual exploration if they are always in production or preparing to be. They are students, not artists. They should have a chance to learn, to fail, maybe even to dream.

Responsibility for the state of theater education rests with department chairs and faculty committees, who do not give high priority to the nonworkshop training aspect of the curriculum except when they must react to current trends and political pressures. The move to open up the curriculum to world culture is merely empty rhetoric and despicable cynicism if the only change is the addition of a course in Black drama or African drama or Hispanic drama. Strikingly, the changes in the former communist world have gone unnoticed in universities even as they exalt the values of cultural diversity. There are so many creative ways to give students a great sweep of theatrical achievement over continents and centuries rather than unnecessarily making one region or ethnic group or style compete against another, which only reinforces the theater's provinciality. An expanded framework of study doesn't require the addition of numerous courses, only intellectual commitment and a concentrated plan of study that sets the acquisition of knowledge as its goal. What I find most disconcerting in the university is the haphazard, paltry selection of course offerings that reflects no agreed-upon sense of what students should know in order to function in the theater at a level of excellence. That should come before faculty interests and specialties and university politics.

Now more than ever, if universities are truly serious about broadening the scope of higher education, theater departments should reorganize the curriculum around theater history, world drama and performance theory, and interdisciplinary and multimedia studies. Ironically, the intellectual slippage in theater departments has occurred exactly at this moment of profound transformation in world culture, when other fields have already incorporated the vocabulary of performance, and, most disconcertingly, in the midst of serious discussions of historical and critical understanding that are recharting the boundaries of academic disciplines.

Most theater students are trained to propagate the bureaucratic "nonprofit" (in every sense of the word) system. Others plan to make movies or television shows or soap operas. Then there are those faculty who have taken so political a position that one would think the classroom was a revolutionary cell preparing potential cultural activists for civil war. How can all these different interests and performance requirements coexist in a single program, and why should they? I see little, if

any, determination in programs or among students to evaluate or structurally change the theater system, as other generations have done. The
idea of an adversarial culture in any collective sense is nonexistent.
There is not much experimentation, and, sad to say, students may refuse
to direct or act in another student's play if it is too unconventional or
provocative. How can they open themselves up to work that is at first
reading inaccessible? Very little artistic attention is devoted to introducing students to the variety of acting or directing or writing styles that
would prepare them for any challenge and versatility. In the classroom
and on the university stage they are seldom exposed to world theatrical
styles that do not conform to American psychological realism.

Programs extol the values of "difference" without truly doing anything to create an environment in which difference, whether in style,
language, technique, or perception, may flourish. Students need to be
taught the practical and critical skills if they are to learn how to understand and evaluate theater as a multiplicity of art vocabularies, starting
with productions in their own departments. Quality, not quantity, is
what counts. Postproduction critiques can veer from free-for-all opin-
ions that leave students frustrated and embittered to the opposite, a
controlled discussion that proceeds like a sensitivity-training session, in
which nothing but safe consensus is allowed to unfold. Often this condition is exacerbated by the fact that theater on the campus is regarded
as a form of community relations or entertainment for the university
population, which has always regarded theater departments as lacking
in intellectual stature. With this early, public scrutiny, the exigencies
of university protocol and civic standards, and the presence of review-
ers from the local press, students can hardly feel free to take great risks.
Nor do their departments want them to do anything that might alienate
audiences, university officials, or funding sources.

There is no evidence that the current climate of theater study honestly encourages experimentation, radical innovation, and criticism of
the American theater system or theater training itself. Not one theater
school in the entire country has the courage and commitment to set up
a program devoted to the visionary pursuit of the new frontiers of performance thinking, and not to the open market economy. Surely there
must be enough students waiting for such a center of learning. Programs like to glorify their eclecticism, but that claim only makes it all

the more difficult to see what they really stand for or if, in fact, they operate at all by any discernible artistic values. What so strikingly exemplifies university theater study nationwide is its lack of vision. In fact, it is appalling that so many faculty who teach theater do not regularly attend theater locally or travel to see it elsewhere. How can they be given the responsibility for the training of artists? Students too are afflicted at an early age with this theater malaise: a major topic of discussion today is the lack of interest theater inspires even in those in the profession. The culture of banality that passes for theater in this country now pervades every branch of its thinking and practice. It needs desperately to be addressed, especially at this cultural moment, when ignorant, loud voices question the place of art in society.

The Responsibility of Students

Students who strive to be artists must become more responsible for their own learning process. They cannot wait for theater programs or university bureaucracies to organize their creative lives, though of course they can demand more of them. They must undertake their own interdisciplinary research with students and faculty in departments other than their own. They must take it upon themselves to experiment, to be daring, to find alternatives to the mainstream system of production and distribution, to found new work spaces, to free themselves of the grant mentality, to work outside of institutions, to cultivate an attitude of inquiry.

Students should learn to value all the resources available to them on campus, because they will never again have so much material readily accessible in one place and at no cost. Unlike anywhere in the world, American universities have extraordinary slide collections and music and film archives for student use on campus, as well as innumerable volumes of books and periodicals in open library stacks. Students must be inspired to educate themselves. How is it possible to convey to them all the sacrifice and self-education and humility it takes to be a true artist? Being an artist is a way of life, not a career. Never for one moment should students accept the lie that everything has been done, that there is nothing new. That is the lazy way out of the striving for excellence.

The Curriculum and the Contemporary

In recent years the obsession with the contemporary in the study of theater has been alarming in that it is becoming too journalistic, and topical, like the professional theater itself. At a time when the world is globally interconnected, theater is more and more localized and insular. Theater ought to be able to distinguish itself from a television talk show or magazine feature in its quality of thought and manner of composition, its psychological range, and the expectations of audiences. But this is no longer the case, as contemporary culture itself mistakes self-expression for art, and exhibitionism for authenticity.

On the whole, theater has become either more entertainment-oriented, or dogmatically political, or splintered into subgroups, in all cases less concerned with art. One of the recurring topics of discussion in the theater, art, and dance worlds in the last decade has been the vast difference in artistic quality, the lack of complexity and imagination in new work, and audience desire for accessible entertainment compared with a period even as recent as the late seventies. I have no doubt that the general lack of artistic vision in the theater of the last dozen or so years, aside from the inescapable influence of an impoverished American culture, is related directly to the superficiality of university arts training and the complicity of the university in trading intellectual standards for a vocational-training mentality. The crisis state of the theater has also been generated by the ascendancy of hype and publicity in place of intelligent critical thinking and taste and the overbearing politicization of the arts that now pervade institutions and individuals in all sectors of the arts and education.

Besides the impact of careerism in the schools, the trend of pursuing what's hot and what's news is due in part to the proliferation on campus of contemporary playwrights and directors who tend to teach their own work and interests rather than take a historical view of the field. The presence of working professionals on campus has many good results to recommend it, namely, its influence on aesthetic standards and work ethics, but in its sycophantic manifestations it reflects a courting of celebrities to help give programs more publicity and greater fund-raising capability. At the extreme, it substitutes for the now vanishing species of the good, old-fashioned professor with a vast knowledge of the theatrical repertoire who could really make students understand a work inside out and in relation to the history of theater and to the world. Unfortunately, many of the "artists" on campus reflect their own dubious achievement and even less knowledge of the theatrical heritage. They also take the place of permanent faculty, who should define a department by providing continuity and commitment in a serious course of study over several years. But in the last decade or more, professors of dramatic literature and history have become fewer and fewer as more faculty lines and visitors have been devoted to teaching practical courses such as playwriting, acting, and directing. Regrettably, now students are taught very little theater history and a severely limited scope of world drama and performance through the centuries. American theater itself is sketchily represented.

A course in contemporary performance might feature Laurie Anderson, Eric Bogosian, Karen Finley, and Spalding Gray but for the most part no one who came to national prominence before the 1980s. What counts now is media coverage. Writers who have become known in the last several years are taught in courses on contemporary drama, especially if they fit the sex, gender, race, and culture categories, but, shockingly, absent from the curriculum are the dramatists of so recent a period as the sixties, such as Rochelle Owens, Ronald Tavel, Adrienne Kennedy, Kenneth Bernard, Tom Eyen, Megan Terry, Rosalyn Drexler, Ed Bullins, Paul Foster, H. M. Koutoukas, and Jean-Claude van Itallie, to name only a few, who could be analyzed within a similar context and at the same time provide focus and continuity to the study of American drama. Increasingly, audiences and critics have taken note of contemporary writers who have a special feel for language, citing Mac Wellman, Eric Overmyer, and Suzan-Lori Parks. Why not connect them to the long poetic tradition in American drama? One can introduce students to the plays of Gertrude Stein, now, half a century after her death, slowly entering theater schools, and to those of Wallace Stevens, Djuna Barnes, William Carlos Williams, Frank O'Hara, Kenneth Koch, John Ashbery, V. R. Lang, Michael McClure, Robert Lowell, Paul Goodman, and Lawrence Ferlinghetti, for a start.

With regard to collective work, The Wooster Group may find its way into the curriculum because it is still visible and active, but students are taught next to nothing about The Living Theatre, Judson Poets' Theatre, The Free Southern Theatre, The Open Theatre, Jerzy Grotowski, The Performance Group, The San Francisco Mime Troupe, The Ridiculous Theatrical Company, Mabou Mines, or The Ontological-Hysteric Theatre. I am surprised that Robert Wilson's work is so little studied and frequently absent even from design classes. Since most schools offer no history of American drama or theater, students can not trace the development of the Provincetown Playhouse, The Group Theatre, the WPA, the poets' theaters of the fifties, Caffe Cino, or La Mama and the Public. Therefore, they have no context in which to understand the development of theater and cultural politics in this country nor the struggle of American artists to make a life in the theater.

The shame of the American theater is that in the last twenty-five years more work of vanguard American artists has been seen by European audiences than by American audiences. To counter the financial demands in the nonprofit sector and commercial venues, universities might have made more of an effort to invite these individual artists and groups to present their work on campus or organized regional festivals and theater meetings so that students could be exposed to the new ideas in performance and writing. Such theater might have had a chance to gain expanding audiences instead of being forever marginalized in the "nonprofit" sector as the "avant-garde," with all the preconceived notions these descriptions can confer in public perception. By middle age, European avant-garde artists are at the center of the dominant theatrical culture, but here they remain in the same spaces, juggling the same puny resources for decades on end. Besides stifling their growth, it compartmentalizes both theaters and audiences, on the basis of economics, not artistic invention. This lack of connectedness and continuity with the accomplishments and concerns of successive generations creates a frightening climate of obsolescence and disposability in all theatrical effort, as well as the more blatant disregard for historical and cultural consciousness.

Limited attention to the classics also informs the difficulty of comprehending the new plays that rewrite or allude to them. Popular culture has almost totally replaced the classics as a reference point. Though it can be an extraordinarily energizing force (and I do not intend to set in conflict high and low culture), there are simply times when Marilyn

Monroe does not have the same mythic resonance as a Helen of Troy. How, for example, will students understand Charles L. Mee Jr.'s *Orestes* or Heiner Müller's HAMLETMACHINE, if they don't know who Electra is? To acquire the requisite theater comprehension, students need a firm grounding in genres such as tragedy, comedy, and the well-made play, as well as a grasp of styles that include melodrama, romanticism, tragicomedy, expressionism, and the traditions of popular entertainments and folk forms, such as historical pageants, burlesque, minstrelsy, and storytelling. What is also necessary is at least a working knowledge of non-Western traditions such as Noh, Kabuki, Bunraku, Kathakali, and African ritual, which are so prominent in the twentieth-century repertoire. Only by knowing how to differentiate dramatic structures and theatrical styles can students even begin to understand how contemporary theater reworks this heritage in the continual process of critical thought that informs the highest theatrical endeavor.

Theater people are only deluding themselves when they become infatuated with media coverage and "making it." The worth of an artist is measured in decades, not years, and ultimately by his or her inspiration of other artists and contribution to the discourse and history of art. It may not have much to do with media attention, as the case of many an artist demonstrates. How can schools hope to train artists, when they give so little thought to the cultivation of artistic values? How can students know against which standards they are to be measured if they lack knowledge of the wonder and variousness of theatrical life? Students might become more passionate about their art, and learn what it means to be part of an artistic heritage, if they could be made to appreciate the great world achievements in theatrical thought of more than two thousand years. Nothing is more valuable for artists than to be educated in art.

Contemporary work should not take the place of a more engaged, intensive study of the past. Besides, contemporary work is now well represented in numerous theater periodicals, in play anthologies, and on occasion on video or television or in the live performances that can be seen increasingly around the country on campuses and at local spaces. Students can seek out these performers and writers on their own, and should, if they are serious about being in the theater. It is time for theater programs to assume their responsibility to offer in-depth study of American theater and its artists, the ideas that have shaped them, and the works they have created. Similarly, students need to be familiar with European theater and history if they are to have any understanding of modernity, the concept of the avant-garde, and the sociopolitical issues of the century, which are part of an ongoing contemporary dialogue. From this grounding in their own heritage they can move on with some sense of reference to the rest of the world, increasing their knowledge through prolonged study and intellectual commitment. Knowing who you are begins at home.

Theater and Theory

Much of the current transformation in the university has coalesced around the issue of identity. In the last decade or so, theater study has become overly politicized by the agendas of feminist theory, queer theory, and cultural studies that many faculty members have brought to the arts and humanities, and where that isn't the case, it is often intellectually shallow and irrelevant. The resurgence of interest in Brecht has led to the extension of his theatrical ideas on narrative acting as a way of constructing a social text that challenges the conventional gaze, especially in feminist- and queer theory strategies of the self-conscious "performance of gender" as cultural subversion. Likewise, the increased attention to Artaud has meant that his themes of presence/absence and the "body without organs," evidenced by French theory and philosophy especially, have found their way into advanced literature and theater courses. But I am not convinced that students have studied the primary works of these seminal thinkers thoroughly enough before learning their application in theory. There is all too often a tendency now to study theories instead of, or isolated from, the original works they address, though this is probably more true of English departments than of theater departments, where critical material has less of a place and cultural studies have not had the same impact. Moreover, owing to the empirical nature of their training, theater students are not often enough encouraged to read critical, literary, and philosophical essays.

Unfortunately, in any department it is the faculty members with ideological interests who have become the most vocal proponents of curriculum change, with the result that theater study is tied to theory, for which students are intellectually unprepared. They haven't sufficiently explored the history of the field and its influential currents of thought to be able to adopt critical, independent views. I've yet to meet students who can even define postmodernism. How can they, since they haven't learned what modernism is? For some, being postmodern simply means being against the Stanislavsky system or conventional realism or just being contemporary. Unquestioning acceptance of the idea of postmodern theater displaces informed, historical thinking. Since the achievements of theatrical modernism and the avant-garde demonstrate that the techniques and values claimed for postmodern theater had already described the vocabulary of European theater experiments before World War II, the very use of the term *postmodern* in reference to theater surely must be one of the great intellectual hoaxes of our time. Still, the number of general books on postmodernism that exclude any discussion of theater, while affirming that performance is a defining concept in postmodern theory, is by now countless.

If theater scholars had had any input in the making of the theory of postmodernism, the discourse would probably have been very different. Instead, in the rush to empower themselves, theater scholars and critics adopted a critical position, long after it had saturated the fields of architecture, film, literature, and dance, that only served to justify a great deal of bad or incoherent current work. Anything that had no center or no point of view or was structured by pastiche was simply thought to be postmodern. Any avant-garde artist of the decades up through the seventies then had to be considered an ur-postmodernist. In the post-postmodern era critics have moved on to other theories. But that is a mixed blessing.

If at first the new theories, like any addition to the history of human thought, generated an alternative to received ideas, their spread on campuses has by now fostered a dogmatic corruption of the educational process and critical writing. Professional writers and artists find them intolerable, but those who are promoting theories aren't really interested in art. Why struggle with irresolvable contradictions in artists and artworks or difficult, even inaccessible structures of thought that defy categorization? Why celebrate individual imaginative expression, when a theory can explain everything that, as they say, is socially constructed anyway? Theories have become coveted status labels of an elite consumer class, institutionalizing in publishing and academia their own economy, language, and power systems. Held together by collages of set phrases and vocabulary, the largely unreadable writings generated by this self-serving society have in our time truly led to the triumph of the essay as "ready-made."

Already one can see the revisionist, politicized histories of performance before the eighties constructed around contemporary theories about the body, culture, race, and feminism, which now interpret every gesture as a social intervention. This view is not supported by the artists' own writings and the primary or critical avant-garde performance documents of the period in the visual arts, dance, film, and theater (with the exception of some phases of The Living Theatre, The Bread and Puppet Theatre, The Performance Group, and guerrilla theater groups of the sixties), which position themselves in terms of art discourse, technique, style, and popular culture. A cursory glance at the available historical material on, for example, Black Mountain, Cage, Cunningham, happenings, Fluxus, Judson Dance Theatre, Judson Poets' Theatre, and La Mama as they were chronicled by the avant-garde critics of the time, such as Jill Johnston, Susan Sontag, Jonas Mekas, Michael Kirby, Michael Smith, or Gregory Battcock, who edited several influential anthologies of artists' and critics' writings, shows that the arts were not written about in a political context. The arts vocabularies of the decades before the eighties emphasized issues such as consciousness, energy, process, repetition, structure, task, space, presence, and perception: most of the discussion focused on how a work was put together. In fact, the arts in New York have a history of critical debate on the issue of expressionism versus formalism, particularly as it concerns performance.

I can also speak from firsthand experience, since *Performing Arts Journal* was founded in 1976 and seven issues of our second periodical, *Performance Art* (later called LIVE) were published between 1979 and 1982. The essays and interviews that appeared in these publications did not address political issues, but artistic, formal ones. Likewise, one of the respected, opinion-shaping newspapers at that time featuring extensive coverage of the burgeoning downtown arts scene, the *Soho Weekly News*, for which I wrote about theater from 1975 to 1977, reflected no serious political thinking on the arts beyond the prevalent theme of what was then thought of as the politics of consciousness. Except for generalized ideas about the arts changing society, performance (in both the theater and art worlds) as it was written and talked about never evolved a coherent political discourse even remotely comparable to the programmatic criticism in the arts today. The rhetoric of the Vietnam War era, when all cultural life in America was politicized, affected the artists too, but only temporarily. In fact, after the war the styles of performance reverted to the characteristic though expanding avant-garde vocabularies of the New York School, as the notoriety of Robert Wilson, Richard Foreman, The Wooster Group, Mabou Mines, Meredith Monk, Laurie Anderson, the many new dance companies, and emerging genres of performance art and video art confirm.

What is occurring now in contemporary scholarship is the revisionism and rewriting in the vocabulary of the new cultural politics, which reads every personal act as political, every artistic act as cultural subversion, an essentially apolitical bohemian, formalist, conceptual, Zen, utopian avant-garde performance world of the postwar period up through the seventies and early eighties. Paradoxically, its two major influences, John Cage and Marcel Duchamp, though revolutionary, were not political artists. The recent attention given to Fluxus, for example, reflects this new politicized scholarship. Another, different result of today's disregard for historical context in criticism and the curriculum is reflected in the commentary on contemporary performance by women. Can anyone honestly engage issues in feminist performance who knows Karen Finley and a handful of current performers but nothing of the pioneering work of Carolee Schneemann or Yoko Ono?

Moreover, because the nature of performance is ephemeral, and reviews, essays, interviews, artists' notes, and documentation in the form of photographs and video are all that remain, there is a particular danger in reading, perhaps even distorting, the history of performance through contemporary theories and political ideologies. It is all too easy for the young student or scholar to quote fashionable vocabulary for his or her subject without having to do any independent, critical thinking. Already students in art and theater departments in the United States and abroad are producing dissertations and theses on feminist performances they have never seen, analyzed through current feminist theory. To be honest, I am not sure that anyone should write about a contemporary

performer he or she has not seen, except in the most rigorous historical reconstruction and scholarly project, as has been the case with the
best theater scholarship. Certainly, serious analysis should not be based
on contemporary theoretical works alone, whose ready-to-wear vocabularies are made to fit any work by women. Regrettably, students no
longer receive sufficient training in research, its protocol and methodology, and the development of bibliography. More and stricter attention
should be paid to writing and research, not only to maintain a level of
scholarly standards in the field but also to develop the wide-ranging currents of thought required to address complex art issues in contemporary
culture.

Performance/Art/Theater

In one sense, the absence of its own recognizable epistemology accounts for the widespread appropriation of the idea of performance in
the humanities and social sciences, frequently in the most naive, unin-
formed manner. The lack of substantial input from theatrical theory by
theater intellectuals in such discussion is lamentable, especially since
contemporary thinking has pushed the condition of performance to the
forefront of any understanding of art, culture, and politics. The significant shifts in thinking that have occurred only begin to draw attention
to themselves in the substitution of the word *performative* for *theatrical*.

In the last twenty years much of what in nonmainstream work used
to be delineated as theater is now called performance, and what was
once described as acting is also now defined as performance. One of
the distinguishing features of this transformation in theater has been
the gradual shift away from dramatic action and the creation of character (acting) toward more self-conscious use of autobiographical material
by performers who make no attempt to act out roles, but prefer to construct their own texts or actions (performing) rather than stage another
author's work. Solo performance affirms this choice, as do certain collective works of groups. The art world has always disdained theater's
attempts to create illusion and character in a staged drama, preferring
instead real time and space and the use of the body of the artist as conceptual medium. This activity was thought of as performance art until

the last dozen or so years, when *art* was dropped, ostensibly to do away with any elitist or aesthetic connotations. The same change occurred in video art.

What this redefinition actually signaled was the art world's move closer to the concerns and techniques associated with theater. Nevertheless, for at least two decades now, visual artists, composers, and others whose work reflects art world aesthetics have ceased to use the word *theater* (except in the pejorative sense) to describe their performance activity, though it was in common usage in art discourse of the fifties and sixties, as the writings of John Cage and Allan Kaprow demonstrate. All through the eighties the art world was coming closer to the idea of the theatrical in performance, photography, installations; the theater world was de-theatricalizing, moving away from the prominence of directors or groups to emphasize the solo performer instead.

Now the performance umbrella covers everything from the most rigorous avant-garde work to offbeat, middlebrow entertainment, from body art to stand-up comedy, from solos to ensemble theater productions, with the result that there are no longer agreed-upon critical standards or art values for addressing any work. These distinctions have become more fluid and imprecise, even irrelevant, in the context of contemporary art and culture as the vocabulary of performance is used increasingly to interpret all kinds of human expression, artistic or otherwise. Today performance has come to designate a way of being in the world, a lifestyle or form of social activism.

How is one to sort out the various meanings generated by the concept of performance? Neither public nor academic discourse differentiates with any degree of refinement between performance as an ontology and performance as gestural attitude, performance in social space and performance on the stage. The two crucial distinctions I am articulating here are these: between being and acting out and between social role-playing and performing a role on a stage. These differences are conflated under the rubric "performance" now that society itself is viewed foremost as an arena of spectacle. *Performance*, then, is used interchangeably to describe actors playing characters or avant-garde performance situations, everyday human behavior and ritual or social action conceived as a performance act. Contemporary critical discourse, especially in the university by those performing Marxism, celebrates it as a form of social intervention, cultural transgression, or political strategy. What is lacking in all centers of discussion is analysis of the performing self as social text within any philosophical, metaphysical, or ethical perspective. The freedom, even euphoria, of self-willed performance actions may be inherent in democracy, but it was essential to the cultivation of fascism as well. Twentieth-century history has shown that societies are drawn to theatrical expression at moments of profound identity crisis and myth-making.

The term *performance* increasingly characterizes the individual drive toward self-realization, regardless of its impact in the public realm. Perhaps this is one explanation for so much autobiographical solo performance in the last decade. It was inevitable that the genre would move toward theater; solo performance had to acknowledge the necessity of spectatorship if it was to be legitimized as a political form. But the idea of a performance culture may not be so appealing if it is discovered that the obsession with individuality and the breakdown in American civic society are mirrored in the narcissistic solo performer/citizen. In somewhat of a historical paradox, the often scorned actor is now the symbolic figure of liberation, though this is not quite what Rousseau had in mind as the celebration of citizenship. The great freedom everyone can agree upon in America is the freedom to make yourself up, to be self-made. Intriguingly, the cultural turn that joins the aesthetic realm to the public realm has made representation into a rights issue, every body into a legislative body.

The cultural/political outcome of this development is as yet unclear, but surely society has moved beyond the *theatrum mundi* metaphor. Because in many ways performance is so new, and still evolving, a concept in the history of ideas, it lacks the conceptual framework in which the profound philosophical and political dimensions of its vocabulary can be evaluated and understood. Today's crucial task is to elaborate performance in relation to being, not merely acting out, to distinguish the nature of spectatorship in society and in theater and, finally, to examine the interactions between public and private space, reality and fiction, ethics and relativism.

Theater and the Visual Arts:
The Two Histories of Performance

As performance becomes more central to the contemporary curriculum, it only highlights one of the most problematic issues in the field today: the existence of two different histories of avant-garde performance, one in the theater, the other in the visual arts. A fundamental task confronting performance scholars is to integrate these two histories into a comprehensible epistemology. The next step would be to link the history of performance to the history of ideas. Theater and the visual arts share a common heritage in European modernist and avant-garde performance, beginning with symbolism, then diverge after World War II, with the visual arts tracing a lineage from Cage/Cunningham, happenings, Fluxus, the Judson Dance Theatre, body art, and conceptual art and the theater tracing its own in The Living Theatre, The Open Theatre, The Performance Group, The Ontological-Hysteric Theatre, Robert Wilson, Mabou Mines, and The Wooster Group until both histories converge again in eighties solo performance. (I've followed this heritage in major, influential avant-garde artists and groups in New York, since they represent the longest continuous line of American performance, with roots in the entire century. The decade of the eighties saw the end of this dominant modernist trajectory in the turn toward political theater performance and away from formalism and avant-garde aesthetics, though this shift can be traced in the black and feminist theaters of the seventies, rooted as they were more in drama than in performance concerns. A comprehensive history of California performance, which followed another development, is yet to be written.)

Much of the lightweight feel of performance study, when it is not dependent on a theoretical apparatus, is a result of the absence of any unified history of performance in the twentieth century. While there is a substantial body of historical scholarship and critical writing on theater, the visual arts never developed performance critics at the intellectual level and autonomy of its best art critics or the most knowledgeable theater critics. Instead, the visual arts interest in performance emphasized documentation, the individual act and process more than criticism, communication, and evaluation, so that what evolved was a great deal of self-promotion and mythology rather than critical analysis. A necessary project for the rest of the century is the construction of a history of American avant-garde performance (interweaving theater and art) of the last fifty years and the recuperation of artists, movements, and styles that elaborate a narrative joining America, Europe, and Japan, whose artists have historically shared formal concerns.

The study of performance needs a history to give it legitimacy and grounding in the world of scholarship, since as both concept and form it seems to be here to stay in the university and in the culture. For the purpose of organizing this history, which is so essential to the field of performance, the art world will have to reevaluate its theater prejudice, and the theater world overcome its lack of art-historical consciousness. Knowledge of the evolution of performance ideas is a prerequisite for any comprehension of modernity. Now, at the end of the century, as so many currents of thought, in numerous fields of the humanities, arts, and social sciences, open themselves to the paradigm of performance, it may be worth exploring whether performance holds the philosophical key to an understanding of contemporary life, if not of the century itself.

It is important that the curriculum be reconceived as truly interdisciplinary, which means that performance cannot be taught separately from the histories of the visual arts, theater, dance, music, film, and video. It also needs to assume a transcultural approach, elaborating concepts of performance occurring simultaneously in different countries around the world. Universities, in their specialization and isolation of departments devoted to arts training, are out of touch with the true needs of students, depriving them of the full expression of advanced studies and the exchange of resources and ideas a place of learning can offer. Since so many students in the arts and humanities plan to write, paint, or perform, the universities ought to take a long, honest look at their training of artists.

At the forefront of artistic training and practice, the avant-garde has always been defined by its cosmopolitanism and interest in other cultures and continents, the erasure of boundaries between the arts and between high and popular culture, the willingness to address taboo subject matter and search for new kinds of knowledge. What has also been true, though often forgotten, is how well the historical avant-garde knew its artistic and cultural past, which was continually drawn from as a living archive of texts and images. It is in this courageous gesture of reconfiguring traditional and experimental forms, the past and the future, that a new ecology of the arts in the university can emerge and point the way to a vision of arts education for the twenty-first century.

Theater and the World

There have been moments in the classroom when I wondered why notions of art and culture that I had taken for granted seemed remote from the way students understood them. Then one day I realized that many students have no concept of a culture, a heritage, a society. They could only conceive of life in a subculture, grassroots activism, and a sense of community mingling artistic feelings with the politics of the personal, which is why they doubt the possibility of universal experience. Students seemed to accept a certain marginalization as much as I took for granted a rightful integration into cultural life through professional work and affiliation. Surely students feel this way because they have little or no opportunity to acquire an organized perspective of their chosen field, of history and the world of ideas, nor to engage an intellectual legacy. They have been robbed of this world book of knowledge by the chaotic, politicized nature of study in the university throughout the eighties and nineties, which has bred a culture of fear and despair and self-hatred and divisiveness. Even the brightest of students are frustrated by their lack of conceptual tools to grasp the inner language of art, to know how to situate their insights in the world of the imagination and the culture of human feeling, and to be certain when impassioned disagreement is more beneficial than consensus. University study can no longer be counted on to give coherent shape to the world or to establish a shared history of thought and action. The magnitude of this loss of memory cannot be ignored.

Even if it takes one class at a time, one person at a time, what must be restored to students is a sense of belonging to the world, of partaking in its history, of continuing its intellectual struggles, and of confronting with awe the extraordinary beauty and terror of the human imagination that is its life. The conditions are ripe for an intellectual and spiritual renewal, but the search for new artistic values that are also new cultural values comes from within. Education is that journey, and life itself the play of thought.

(1995)

Private Landscapes

Garden/Theater

When the eighty-year-old Marcus Terentius Varro sat down in 37 B.C. to write *De re rustica* as a guide to husbandry for his wife, he pointed out that fifty Greek sources on the subject already existed, if she needed further assistance. That husbandly gesture hardly seems likely to occur again, so vast has the literature in the field grown in the intervening two thousand years. Besides, too few people, much less a statesman/landowner, have time to write the six hundred or so books Varro produced in his lifetime.

But more to the point, what the Greeks and Romans left as a foundation of thought demonstrates how expansive a range of topics such treatises encompassed then: the care of fruits, crops, vines, animals; religion, history, myth; ecology, philosophy, aesthetics. The concept of cultivation described a way of being in the world, with the result that the same word made civilization a synonym for husbandry. To cultivate both the land and the mind were regarded as activities of a responsible life, and so for centuries the idea has come down to us that the measure of civilization is the attitude of a people toward their land. Regrettably, in our time a misguided sense of progress has separated one kind of knowledge from another: the mind from the body, humanities from science, agriculture from ecology, philosophy from action, the individual from a common good.

Likewise, natural history is often isolated from our understanding of the history of the world. History books are filled with exclusions, among them the place of nature in human consciousness. They tell instead of wars, the lives of kings and queens and statesmen, of exploration and invention, the creation and destruction of cities and cultures. Few tales are told of any other species than the human one. How simple it would be to include with our other histories those of plants and animals in the world, their habits and habitats. How many know the names of the plants in their neighborhood, or the birds and butterflies that frequent them? If naming is the greater part of possession, we live as strangers in paradise.

Research on *American Garden Writing* led me to the conclusion that there is a theme larger than the one I initially envisioned in the way Americans thought and wrote about plants and worked in their gardens. The evolution of gardens and gardeners is inseparable from patterns in American society. That the lives of plants follow the same developments as the lives of people is not surprising, because they share the same cultural and economic circumstances. Horticulture, like art, commerce, or technology, is one more historical portrait of a nation, in any given time and place.

So close to recent times, American gardeners have struggled to name, to plant, to study the species of a New World. Out of this effort has emerged a rich heritage of horticultural documentation that extends from the seventeenth century to the present. If the notion of a garden belongs to the history of ideas, then garden writing, like other literary genres, offers its own perspective of the American imagination.

We search for answers to the great questions in books and ancient wisdom, even in statistical data, the new oracle, when, quite simply, there are times in history when knowledge grows on trees. Since the beginning of time philosophers and writers and craftsmen have made the symbol of the tree part of the poetic life of civilizations. My own favorite arboreal fantasy is depicted in Italo Calvino's joyful novel *The Baron in the Trees*, in which a young aristocrat in protest against society goes up into the tall trees of northern Italy one day and never comes down again. From his leafy home the baron as an old man writes a "Project for the Constitution of an Ideal State in the Trees." Alas, we are not so fortunate in our time, having neither leaders who can imagine such a life nor the network of trees to support us.

Those who, like myself, woke up early the morning of October 4 last fall [1987] to the white sound of cracking branches witnessed a stormier scene in the relations between people and trees. The unseasonal wind and snow blasts that sent trees toppling throughout the Hudson Valley, then moved on to stun English parks and gardens from the deep green sleep of time, showed that nature has no thought of us. We are the spectators, the setting. I wonder if the orioles, perennial boarders in an old silver maple, will come back to a Catskill tree whose unwitting new airiness has transformed its shape. As somebody once said, we don't live in the first chapter of Genesis. If I will never see Capability Brown's now damaged landscapes, I can console myself with poppies left in Etruscan tombs.

Now as I sit and write these words from the center of a city, snow is falling outside and I wait anxiously for spring to come again. Fantasies are easily packed in snowflakes. Yet bare trees bring their own semaphoric calm to the glow of urban skies. I know that flowers need their privacy to go underground for a time of sexual frenzy unknown to us mortals who envy their abandon. When I look out the window, the ground acts as a blank mask, a sheet of ice melting into a sheet of paper, on which I project my thoughts of how to write about ephemerality.

I judge a garden by the gardener who cares for it, the one who invests space with daydreams. What is a garden but a species of desire? How well I know the downward gaze into the face of the earth, the feeling of a luxurious body in good, dark soil that slips through the fingers in the rush to return to its dirty delirium. Each gardener creates an ideal world of miniature thoughts that drift languidly into each other like flowers on a dry afternoon. Here silence has the rhythm of wishes.

Gardens have that special resistance beautiful things offer to our understanding. Some days I think it is enough to watch a hummingbird wander into the sweet tunnel of a trumpet vine climbing up a summer sky. Maybe gardening is a form of worship.

Strangely enough, I feel at home in this ephemerality of time because I have spent many years experiencing it in the theater as a theater critic. I still feel the same sense of melancholy in a winter garden or an empty theater. Even more of a coincidence, thirty years ago another theater critic, Joseph Wood Krutch, edited a collection of garden writing, his *Gardener's World*, featuring selections from around the world and through the ages. Really it is not so difficult to move from a theater to a garden. Each creates a world in a space that celebrates pure presence, and the fabulous confusion of nature and artifice, which is to say, reality and illusion. At least one half of gardening is dreaming yourself into a new setting.

For me it started with a house in the country and a new landscape, then learning the names of plants, buying them, too many, dividing them for friends, getting their surplus, looking at catalogues and going to nurseries, buying more plants, now old garden books, eventually finding myself in a garden too big to care for unless I quit my job. This, I think, is the general pattern of a gardener's life in its beginning stages.

It is very rare for anyone except professionals in the field or retired people to have the luxury of doing nothing but gardening. This book is filled with contributions by gardeners who were also historians, explorers, statesmen, editors, architects, scientists, novelists, preachers, entrepreneurs. Little by little they discovered the world as a garden. At that point everything changes, and suddenly one's whole life becomes the life of a person who gardens.

The next step, if one is a writer, is to find a way to turn gardening into a book project, so you can explore gardening as writing, at last unable in any season to give up the pleasures of manual labor.

(1988)

Originally published as the preface to *American Garden Writing*, a collection of writings from the seventeenth century to the present on landscape, gardening, agriculture, plant hunting, culture, and natural history.

A Hudson Valley Life

|||||||| The most beloved writers through the ages and throughout the world reflect in their work one of the basic truths of humankind: the realization that in local knowledge begins self-knowledge. Here is the starting point for what used to be thought of as worldliness, now transformed into global consciousness. Whichever expression one chooses, the essential premise, in large measure, still points to an understanding of what it means to live on this planet, with its galaxies of grief and pleasure. But what exactly is "local knowledge," and how does one attain this state of presumed comfort and wisdom?

For most of the history of human presence on earth, experience of this kind was rather the natural rhythm of daily life, because one simply had to know as much as possible about the land and the sky and the sea and folkways as a matter of sheer survival. Human history has reached a point at which technological transformations have so reordered the perception of space and time and human relations that many people spend much of their lives in a physical and cultural world they do not truly know in their bones, much less in their neighborhoods. It is like learning only parts of the language one speaks, not knowing the names of important objects.

Learning the language of a country is a life's work, enraptured by the many themes of this language that find expression in the manner of speaking and writing that defines a particular place and time and people. Besides, there are many narratives in the life of a country, region, or town, by turn historical, social, ecological, and cultural. What kind of struggles did a people fight, were their houses made of stone, which bird songs awakened them, did they love honor?

Social history and natural history are bound together in the composition of the world we inhabit, like leaves in a solemn book that reminds us it comes from a sturdy tree. Broadly speaking, if we are to contemplate the true nature of a place, the cultural system cannot justly be separated from the ecosystem in the life of a society. Now we have learned to tell time by the trees.

In the Western heritage Herodotus, the father of history, made geography an aspect of the description of momentous events. But in our era of overspecialization the strands of human affairs have become disengaged, not intertwined, erasing geography from the understanding of history, agriculture from the context of culture, the humanities from science. Through this process of erosion the transmission of knowledge becomes more and more restricted by a kind of forced zoning regulation, while the universe of knowledge itself is continually enriched. In the most profound analysis, a society is ultimately judged by the connections its people make between the urgent themes of their world. There is a good deal of truth and subtlety in Emerson's view that "no man can write anything who does not think that what he writes is for the time the history of the world."

Here again is that irreducible leap from the local to the global perspective. For what is the sense of place if not the beginning of a world-view of things. Can one rightly think of place, which is history, without thinking of nature, the natural history of habitats? It is not possible, I have found, to write of the Hudson Valley without writing of nature. More than a region, it is a topography of the spirit.

Some landscapes are known by foot, others by horseback or boat, many more by automobile. Regions themselves are usually defined by dialect, cuisine, by music or dance, by furniture, costume, and art forms. The more than five million current inhabitants of the Hudson Valley have not been joined over the centuries by any of these cultural inflections, not in the nearly four hundred years of European settlement nor in the millennia-old tribal ways of vanquished Indians. One cannot construct a continuous "Hudson Valley culture" out of these themes. No, the people of the Hudson Valley are unified by one earthly fact: geography. They are joined, spectacularly, by the shared presence of the Hudson River, which spills a 315-mile watery trail through New York State, from its headquarters at Lake Tear of the Clouds in the Adirondacks to the end of Manhattan Island, where it moves out toward the Atlantic Ocean. Perhaps as many as sixty-five million years ago what Henry Hudson called the "great River of the Mountains" began to slice a valley through the Catskill Mountains to the east and the Taconic Mountains to the west.

The stretch of the Hudson most celebrated is the 150 or so miles from Manhattan to Albany, where towering Palisades, elegant mountain passes of the Highlands, and the soft figuration of the Catskills beyond the western shore create a blue-green haze of reflected grandeur and winding calm. East and west the shores play with images of each other, and again north and south, in continual, forced double perspective. The Janus-faced riverbanks, like opposite pages of an open book radiating diverse people's histories and the history of the landscape, remind us that Janus, the god of passageways, is another name for Chaos. This, the name of our contemporary condition—let's call it another version of the persistent American theme, urban versus rural life (corruption versus innocence).

Nowhere in the Hudson Valley is this duality more certain than in the land between the boundary lines of Manhattan and Albany, which once was New Netherland and is now New York. The word *New* is significant in every sense. The Hudson Valley was the "New World," whose profundity of natural resources Adriaen Van der Donck, its early historian, proclaimed to would-be Dutch settlers. Here Crèvecoeur was sure he had found democracy's "New Man," who would eventually influence his own French compatriots. And the Swede Peter Kalm discovered new species to populate the plant kingdoms of old Europe.

The Hudson River itself was never a passive scenic partner, but an active participant in new currents of thought in the American mind. Along its waters the people made a revolution to shake off British colonialism; many of its residents—Robert R. Livingston, Robert Morris, John Jay, DeWitt Clinton, Alexander Hamilton, Martin Van Buren, Franklin D. Roosevelt—were statesmen who helped to make a country. The Hudson was the surface on which innovative modes of transportation played—the steamboat and the Erie Canal, and then the railroad that ran along its shores. In small river towns and growing cities the

Industrial Revolution moved people and forests and mountains in the surge toward prosperity. The very landscape captured the American imagination in some of the country's earliest travel writing and nature writing set in the Valley, which also became, in the national period, a center for painting, tourism, architecture, and horticulture whose influence radiated throughout the country and across the Atlantic.

Ideas flowed to and from New York City as surely as the Catskills sent its cool, clear, refreshing waters there, making it a world capital of culture and finance and a gateway to new possibilities for those who would call it home. From everywhere they came. Multiculturalism defined New York from the very start. When the English took the colony from the Dutch in 1664, at least eighteen languages were already spoken around what is now Manhattan, which at the time had a European-descended population of fewer than two thousand.

The Hudson Valley region embraces a heritage that has fed every tributary of American enlightenment. That is what it means to be a landscape rather than merely scenery, a world not a setting. But it is past history alone that has cast emblematic shadows over its velvet hillsides. In the twentieth century the Hudson Valley has not been a frequent theme in the American cultural consciousness. More than a century ago the West superseded it as the symbol of wilderness and spirituality. American myth has always looked to the landscape for its sense of poetry and identification, and in times of trouble for solace. Even today the population swells westward.

There were other cultural changes that would draw attention away from the region, those occurring from the third quarter of the nineteenth century to the decades before World War II, such as the decline of the Hudson River school of painting, whose canvases by Thomas Cole, Asher B. Durand, and Frederic E. Church had symbolized national themes for tourists and natives. The lack of a sustained *belles lettres* tradition, originated by the likes of Washington Irving, James Fenimore Cooper, James Kirke Paulding, Nathaniel P. Willis, and William Cullen Bryant, surfacing only sporadically at opposite ends of the century, between the publication of Henry James's *American Scene* and T. Coraghessan Boyle's *World's End*, has been an overwhelming factor in the loss of the image of Hudson Valley life in the literary imagination. There are, of course, Edith Wharton's *Hudson River Brack-*

eted, Maxwell Anderson's *High Tor*, John Gardner's *Nickel Mountain*, William Kennedy's more urban novels of Albany, to name a random sampling of twentieth-century works set in the Valley. But no modern novelist, poet, or essayist has made so prominent and permanent a literary home in Hudson Valley country themes that his or her work is identified with the region, as writers have done elsewhere in the country. To this day, a century and a half later, Edgar Allan Poe's picturesque tale "Landor's Cottage" remains unsurpassed in its exquisite portrait of the mid-Hudson landscape.

The overwhelming attraction of the Valley has always been more visual than literary, though a school of painting is now long gone. The untimely death in the 1850s of young Andrew Jackson Downing, whose indigenous architectural style gave its name to the Wharton novel, was a great loss to horticultural and architectural life here. His partner Calvert Vaux remained a few years more at Newburgh to design homes before bringing his feeling for the region's romantic landscape to the creation of Central Park and Brooklyn's Prospect Park, which he conceived with Frederick Law Olmsted.

Even with the region's great beauty and variety of nature, the absence of any local nature writer of national reputation since the death of John Burroughs in 1921 is unsettling to discover. Unlike New England, for example, the Hudson Valley has not developed an ongoing tradition of nature writing or travel writing, a puzzling situation given the proximity of such a magnificent landscape close to New York, with its substantial population of writers. Indeed, a comprehensive cultural history of the Hudson Valley has yet to be written.

Here is a place where history is marked indelibly in the landscape. Ancient Indian arrowheads jostle with bottle caps in the dirty silence beneath wild meadows, old country barns are mirrored in satellite dishes, the ghosts of dying main streets haunt shopping malls, which push profligacy and prophylactics. Everywhere the incongruent images pile up: meat and potatoes and Tex-Mex, dumpsites and country seats, prison farms and golf courses, high tech and migrant workers, and here and there an occasional glimpse of "Hudson River Bracketed" through the urban detritus, ironically framing the alternating scene of wealth and welfare that winds its way through towns up and down the Valley. Endangered species of bald eagle and the short-nose sturgeon glide over and around the magenta nuisance of bountiful loosestrife, and the shad runs through toxic waste. Fireflies light up backyards like stage sets, the gypsy moths pitch their tents in our trees. Welcome to the New World! Scientists are just coming around to tell us there is no balance or order in nature, no original scene to which we can return, as if we hadn't suspected that all along. Americans have always been busy "peopling solitudes," to use Tocqueville's majestic turn of phrase. Isn't it time to rethink the myth of country life? The great-estates nostalgia of the Hudson Valley shrouds its stubborn pentimenti and disordered sublime.

Already by the middle of the nineteenth century mid-Hudson life was contrasted with the brutalities of New York City streets. In the 1850s the dandy Willis wrote about declining pastoralism in the face of what we now call "development," which changed the look of the land in the antebellum years. Farms have continually been going out of business, about 93,000 acres' worth in the Hudson Valley—more than 13 percent of the farmland—between 1982 and 1987. Even with all the farmland remaining, 700,000 or so acres, it is sometimes easier to find fresh vegetables in the middle of Manhattan than in a small rural town upstate. Still, many of these towns have all the amenities associated with the contemporary good life: environmental awareness, artists and arts organizations, imported foods, historic restoration, service industries, ethnic restaurants, waste recycling . . . the list goes on and on. Now that IBM is the Valley's largest private employer, it is becoming increasingly difficult to define the borders between urban and rural life.

In a rather strange reversal of history, the twentieth century has brought to the region its own "ruins," the absence of which was much lamented by the romantic travelers of a hundred and fifty years ago. But our ruins do not evoke the passion of medieval or Renaissance poetry, only the industrial and agricultural attrition of modern life. Kindly neglect, failing economy, disregard for historic buildings, lack of civic responsibility, and wanton destruction are often to blame. I believe in what the landscape historian J. B. Jackson calls "the necessity for ruins." Our landscape is littered with these sorrows of architecture, but history is not a theme park.

I rarely take the Thompson Street hill down past the old cemetery to the center of Catskill without looking up at the distant hills where the Catskill Mountain House once grandly presided over the aesthet-

ics of the picturesque, before it was torched into a burning forgetfulness
nearly three decades ago by the New York State Conservation Department. The absence of the Mountain House is not merely the loss of a
building but the end of its life as a metaphor that would have aged in
the pages of our histories of culture, social life, and ecology, an image
in which generations would continue to define who they are. When we
neglect or destroy the things of our world, we silence chapters of our
history, and without history society is bereft of the sense of itself as a
people. The urge for history, or more simply, rootedness and connection, grows more compelling as a source of nourishment in our world
of computer menus and sound bites and fast food. Tasting the deep, sat-
isfying aromas of one's own small world takes a little time.

What makes a Hudson Valley life different from any other life? It begins with knowing where you live. For me, local knowledge is the smell
of a wet woods, the color of autumn, patterns of traffic and deer damage; it's stores opening and closing in town, the revival of Kingston and
Athens, the hard work of turning clay into garden soil; it's following the
year-to-year population of cicadas and Japanese beetles, measuring the
violence of sudden storms and the sour tears of acid rain. But most important, it is to hear the first song of the oriole who nests each year in the
silver maple, signaling the start of summertime, and then to follow little
by little the buttery glaze of evening light that sweeps across my lawn.

The history of a place is written in the landscape as surely as in its
books, and memory acts as a kind of dormant seed. Hudson Valley history, from its earliest entry into literature, has been depicted in a dreamy
disremembering, the sleeping and waking theme that Irving introduced
in his story of Rip Van Winkle. A century and a half later there was
another awakening, this time less a literary than an ecological quake—
the Storm King controversy, which threatened to disrupt the sanctity of
the Hudson Highlands with a hydroelectric plant Consolidated Edison
planned to build there. The legal issues that grew out of the protests by
local residents influenced environmental law and put Hudson Valley
conservation ethics at the forefront of a new ecological activism.

Today there is a third awakening in the New York state legislature's
creation of the Hudson River Valley Greenway Council, which has proposed a Hudson River Trail on both sides of the river from the Mohawk
to Battery Park. Such a plan, involving twelve counties and eighty-two

units of local government, would surely generate a new social organization of cities, towns, and countrysides, sound land-use policies, joint public and private responsibilities, long-range planning by regional and local governments. The scope of this vision is unprecedented in a place where community independence has always superseded regional cooperation. Plans for the Catskill Interpretive Center have slowed since Governor Mario Cuomo's support of it a few years ago in his State of the State address. Earlier, Governor Nelson Rockefeller's Hudson Valley Commission (1966–74) proved ineffectual in the long run, failing to meet the environmental challenge of the region's future. The Greenway Council plan, on the other hand, matches desire with vision and timeliness, complementing the Department of State's recent inventory of ten sites designated by the Coastal Resources Management Division as "scenic areas" of statewide significance, thus acknowledging their need for special protection. More recently, parts of Dutchess and Columbia counties have been declared the Hudson River National Historic Landmark District.

Up and down the Hudson, environmental groups, local residents, and planning commissions are joining together to accept the stewardship of the Hudson Valley's natural resources and to encourage greater public awareness of environmental issues. This is in contrast to the necessarily more local and site-specific battles Scenic Hudson fought in the 1960s and 1970s on behalf of Storm King Mountain. Now everyone is getting involved.

More than anything else a new environmental ethos will bring the Hudson Valley into the twenty-first century, as a humanistic model for the people of the region, as a gift to themselves. A large population reflecting diverse interests and pleasures can perhaps come together to create a contemporary Hudson Valley culture in new spatial and cultural configurations of the very landscape in which they live, work, raise their children, and, at the end of the day, dream. When all else is done, it is in their plans for the future that societies distinguish themselves.

To be sure, the future is always rooted in a usable past. Knowledge of the world begins where each of us lives—in our body, in our town, in our country. Literature too is a home, the repository of memory in which fact, myth, and fantasy cohabit to engender the various histories by which an age measures its presence in time. Like any writer surveying a surrounding world, I looked to old books to describe the place where I live. In nearly four hundred years of this "decayed litera- ture" that Thoreau claimed makes the best soil, I found a gathering of travelers, artists, inventors, writers, statesmen, scientists, and historians. Here is what they wrote of a place, and of people who have dwelled there.

(1990)

Originally published as the preface to *Hudson Valley Lives*, a reader on the Hudson Valley region of New York State, spanning the seventeenth century to the present, with selections on literature, history, travel, art and architecture, culture, and ecology.

Ecologies of Theater I I

Continental Drift

The Century Turning
(International Events)

Image World

In the subway someone was playing "Rudolph the Red-Nosed Reindeer" on a steel drum. On the F-train a black man peddled *Street News*, "America's Motivational Non-Profit Newspaper," a new monthly sold by the homeless. I got off at the stop not far from Park Avenue, where a man at curbside was making a video of the apartment buildings, looking uptown, talking into a microphone, "Some of these apartments rent for three to four thousand dollars a month."

I walked on to the Whitney to see the "Image World: Art and Media Culture" show. Big color blowups of the homeless plastered the sides of the ticket counter. In one photograph a black man was selling Italian silk ties. *Ticket Booth* courtesy of artist Dennis Adams. On the fourth floor a "walltext" alerted, "Those looking to art as a refuge from the outside world will not find comfort here. This is work that challenges our expectations—about the limits and definitions of art forms and the institutional authority of the media. In the hands of artists these media have become new perceptual instruments which have transformed how we see the world around us."

Several of Jenny Holzer's cast aluminum plaques were dispersed about the gallery rooms. One read, USE WHAT IS DOMINANT IN A CULTURE TO CHANGE IT QUICKLY. Jeff Koons arranged himself in an *Art in America* ad that looked like a scene from a David Lynch film. Cindy Sherman's untitled film stills quoted the history of the image. Appropriation strategies have their limits.

197

I prefer the open-ended generosity of Nam June Paik's *Fin de Siecle II* (1989), a video installation of approximately three hundred television sets arranged like an electronic wall hanging that dominated the show, due as much to its ideas as to its size. This work is what it is, supremely situated in its medium, without signaling messages or education programs with good intentions.

The center panels of the installation were organized around three images, representing pop culture, technology, and art history: namely, David Bowie, a digital computer creation of a Bauhaus-style figure, and analogic computerized images of a female nude. Music by Philip Glass, Bowie, and Kraftwerk was easily recognizable. So was the iconography of the twentieth century, which supplied images for all the television sets at the borders of the installation: the airplane, the city, the film, the car, the TV, the video camera. Montage as a form of tourism. Joseph Beuys and Merce Cunningham made cameo appearances, homage to the old masters.

Fin de Siecle II, however, was not about seeing but about glimpsing. One might say that it expressed an overall new romanticism: sensual but not sexual. The cubism of form was joined to the surrealism of image content. The last great visual ethnography, surrealism's longevity is a marvel, even more so with the capabilities of technology. On one level consciousness is the memory of images.

Paik's installation grasps modernism as a philosophical position, assured of its faith in technology as liberal politics. Historically, modernism was profoundly committed to spiritual and social change, with the promise of technology the center of that vision. As we now know, it led in two directions: to democracy *and* fascism. But modernism was always deeply rooted in Judeo-Christian tradition, and, not surprisingly, one of the earliest dadaists, Hugo Ball, ended his life writing religious works once he had lost his faith in art. In our own time we can see the reversals of modernism in the difference between Kafka's castle and Havel's. And now in Europe the concept of the mass has shifted from the sociological to the liturgical, with sidewalk shrines and honored martyrs a natural part of the cultural landscape.

What modernism eventually brought to the twentieth century was a popular (youth) culture—not a culture based on tradition (old forms of song, folk dances, festivals, ritual, and the like), but one of speed, tech-

nology, dynamism, and innovation. Internationalism replaced ethno-
centrism, and the roundness of myth and ritual was supplanted by the
angular, nervous edge of modernity. Modernism was urban, not rural;
cosmopolitan, not local. The measure of Paik's range is that one can
find implied in his television sets the visual, metaphorical cues for the
leap in our century from the Bauhaus to Bladerunner.

Overall, Paik's vision pushes the ideal of modernism and its liberal
component, cosmopolitanism (which is always a crime in conservative states), to its global implications. His work is anti-nationalistic, the
new ethical ideal. From the point of view of modernism, perception
has evolved from the abstraction of nineteenth-century symbolism, the
first modernist, international movement—the movement that first emphasized the sign—to today's apprehension of imagery *as a form of experience*. If aesthetics were to be charted geographically, the trajectory
would be from France to Prague, that is, from symbolism to semiotics.
Is it so surprising that the Czechs would rattle their keys in Wenceslas
Square?

If cosmopolitanism, even in its crudest dream state, can be juxtaposed with the travel of images (i.e., the representation of new models of
behavior), totalitarianism seems now to be linked more to the power of
a single voice, that is, to rhetoric. The European democratic revolutions
of 1989 owe their success in some measure to the performance realm of
television. This is the triumph of "the world as picture," in the Heideg-
gerian sense. It is also the triumph of performance (mimesis) as a potentially ontological act, the self imagining the self in a new world of being.
"If television falls, the revolution falls," warned the announcer from
Studio 4 of Free Rumanian television. The ascendancy of the image
over rhetoric is the beginning of modernity for Rumania. Ironically, it
was Rumania that gave modernism one of its first media artists, Tristan
Tzara. Then suddenly one day a man who proclaimed himself genius of
the Carpathians began taking over the media with his own lampisteries,
wallowing in the labyrinth that is the word, the image, and the world.

The Role of Natural History

Ceausescu bragged that Rumania would be changed "when pears grow
on poplar trees." The agronomy students decided to risk everything for

the sake of appearances. They cut out the shapes of pears and hung them on trees.

Spectacle of the Revolution

Hey, what's all this to me!? (the flippant title describes an equally care-free philosophical attitude) was more or less an anthology of scenes of war and revolution—French, Chinese, Islamic, Bolshevik, with dancers representing at various times World War II allies, the PLO, Soviet troops, and the Women's Detachment of the Red Army. But the scene that stirred French audiences most of all showed Danton, Robes-pierre, and Marat in a nursing home, where they sat and watched a televised bicentennial celebration featuring "The Golden Guillotine Awards." Japanese tourists came by to take souvenir snapshots. Com-pagnie Maguy Marin's *Hey, what's all this to me!?* made a spectacle of the French Revolution.

Marin's work (in collaboration with Denis Mariotte) appeared at the same time that historians were debating Simon Schama's revisionist his-tory *Citizens*, which in its examination of violence and revolution draws a line from the Terror to Stalinism. As if to underscore not only the uni-versality of violent political struggle but also its necessity as liberation, the last section of *Hey, what's all this to me!?* turned dark and strangely disquieting in its representation of a futuristic society. In a factory per-formers and puppets played out a *danse macabre* as severed heads rolled along a conveyor belt in a relentless procession of stylized slaughter, so that it was no longer possible to separate the killers from the killed. The conveyor belt became just as indiscriminate a piece of technology as the guillotine in the revolutionary moment. This time there was no black humor, only the terrifying color of efficiency.

In any year Compagnie Maguy Marin's demythologizing spectacle might pass as just an expensive, spiffy rock musical on a subject cer-tain to put French audiences on opposite sides of the barricade. But in 1989, two hundred years after the French Revolution, fifty after the end of World War II, and a remarkable year itself by any comparison with the landmarks of world history, this work suggests deeper political im-plications, the more so coming as it does as a product of European ex-perience. In fact, it is a work that could only have originated in Europe, and especially in France, with its embrace of spectacle and revolution, often at the same time. But all the more uncanny is that *Hey, what's all this to me!?*, with its continental politics and cultural signs, seems now so much a part of postcommunist Europe. Though it came too soon to include the new, nonviolent (except in Rumania) models of revolution proposed there, the linkage of theatricality and politics is just as significant. In the difference between Marin's take on the French Revolution and Ariane Mnouchkine's own in the earlier 1789 one can read the political disturbances in European intellectual life.

German Tradition

While Germans were dancing under a full moon on top of the Berlin Wall, Heiner Müller, who already lived East and West, came to New York to perform in *The Man in the Elevator*, a music theater piece he had created with composer Heiner Goebbels. He would read parts of his text in German from a desk in the performance space. "It was not easy to come here. I feel dizzy," he said. Then he smoked his cigar.

The Man in the Elevator—it already appears on compact disk—is a section from Müller's longer dramatic text THE TASK, which takes the French Revolution as its starting point. In a brief, "contemporary" scene that leaps across centuries, a worker becomes disoriented in a corporate headquarters on his way to see the "Boss" and finds himself in a Latin American country. "Who would believe that I came to Peru from an elevator. . . ." It is his long monologue, distributed between two voices besides Müller's, in both English and German, that serves as the basis of the piece.

The music itself crossed borders: of jazz, rock, and Brazilian pop. Though this conception brought a certain world-beat sophistication to the work, the overall staging drew from the gestic approach that has proved so dominant and suggestive a theatrical style in Germany. The combination of gestic voice and jazz arrangements made a truculent mix, because the black musical tradition's own historical connection to attitudinizing speech (exemplified fiercely now in the proliferation of rap music) is itself situated in ideas about narration. And Müller is not a writer of melodies, but of rhythms. Jazz brought a scratchy political surface to his commentary on colonialism and big business.

One can look back from Müller through the long German epic theater tradition, from the revolutionary montage of Büchner to Brecht's *Lehrstück* and Handke's *Sprechstück*, the latter two radical reconceptions of performance/speech. And in the visual realm, in a scene in which performers sat before terminals or used their instruments as pure percussion, the "stock" expressionist scene in the bank or financial market was casually quoted for a computer age.

The panorama of German theater with its century of leftist politics that transformed the drama in each new generation, came through this work. In 1953, when the East Berlin workers were rising up on Stalin Allee, Brecht stayed in his theater to rehearse a play. At this latest uprising Müller was in a theater performing his text about revolution. He would return home four days later to rehearse simultaneous productions of *Hamlet* and his own HAMLETMACHINE, a text built around the role of the intellectual in society, placed in the frame of the 1956 Hungarian revolution.

Brecht's successor, a man who could walk through a wall: what theater will he create for a new Germany? And how will Brecht play in the brave new world of Eastern Europe. "Unhappy is the land that needs a hero," he once wrote.

The World Is Round

In my field of modern cosmology, the first principle is called the "Cosmological Principle." It says that the universe has no center, that it has the same properties throughout. Every place in the universe has, in this sense, equal rights. How can the human race that has evolved in a universe of such fundamental equality, fail to strive for a society without violence or terror? And how can we not seek to try to build a world in which the rights due every human being from birth are respected?

May the blessings of the universe be upon us. . . .

—A message from Fang Lizhi, American Embassy, Beijing

A Woman and a Song

Mercedes Sosa fills an entire space with happiness the way only a singer can. (Watching the crowds of tens of thousands in the squares of Europe, country by Eastern country, one can understand the power of the mass and the voice that leads the mass. How quickly chants spread through a crowd, so that many voices become one voice.) Ironically, only a singer ever faces alone so large an audience, the one among the many, in quite the same way. That sense of audacity is not present in any other non-political experience. No wonder totalitarian societies banish their artists and intellectuals first. They know the power of the voice in the word.

For Sosa it once was exile from Argentina. And so her concerts in New York play for largely Latin American audiences the theme of an exile's return, but also the return of speech. The attachment to art and artists by an entire country is all the more powerful at extraordinary moments in their history, when it crosses generations, regions, and classes and ordinary people mourn lost emotions as if they were ruins. Song is the first art to return from exile to the people, speech the first public act to come back.

It is more difficult than one would imagine to understand a singer in another language, because songs live for the nonspeaker only in rhythm, in phrasing, in texture. They remain separate from the world of the word, which embodies the nuances of social relations, and we do not yet have a history of the world in rhythms. So one simply listens carefully, observes silently, studies the performer. Spectatorship has its quiet pleasures, even those seen from a distance. Like a tourist, one experiences all sensations as if for the first time. (Art is a foreign country.) I could hear the gratitude of the audience for this large woman, no, this mountain of sound, who meant so much to Latin Americans as a deep, rich symbol of their cultural and new political life. They surely experienced in their hearts a kind of serenity known only to people who together have felt great fear.

Sosa took her audience through a range of sadness, then joyous celebration. She brought them the fresh breath of purified air, which is what beautiful singing is. *Gracias a la vida*, she sang to them, as if she had created the words to give thanks for such a gift at such a time.

We Americans don't experience art as a people, a nation, with the urgency of collective need that grave moments in history seem to demand. Here singers have celebrity status but not symbolic value. Though we have sincere folk singers, we have no Sosa, no Wolf Biermann, no Victor Jara, no Vladimir Vysotsky, no Karel Kryl around whom forbidden thoughts could be organized. Our political destiny has carried us to artists by another path. Or have we simply made of them entertainers. And this politics, in the end, is the difference between culture and entertainment.

The Death of Beckett

More than any other modern playwright, Beckett imagined the endgame of human existence in our half-century. He is perhaps the last of the universal playwrights in this post-drama age, with its shrinking international repertoire. Increasingly drama will become as culture-bound as most languages, a kind of local knowledge, and only those writers, like Havel and Fugard, who are emblematic of a political system will travel easily to foreign lands.

On December 20, 1989, two days before Beckett's death, the New York lawyer and human-rights activist Martin Garbus carried to Havel in Prague a signed manuscript copy of *Catastrophe*, which Beckett had dedicated to him in 1982, when he was in prison. The plays of both Havel and Beckett were banned in Czechoslovakia then, and a poster circulating at the time featuring a gagged Beckett carried the caption, "If Samuel Beckett had been born in Czechoslovakia, we'd still be waiting for Godot."

Now, in 1989, nine days after receiving the manuscript inscribed to him, Vaclav Havel becomes president of Czechoslovakia. Outside the Civic Forum office in Wenceslas Square new posters announce, "Godot is here."

Representation, a Rights Issue

Television carried the Central European revolutions to people all over the globe. In this way, representation (whether political or theatrical), one of the most dominant themes of the twentieth century, positioned itself within the framework of rights, as symbolic potential. Wherever the media charts the struggles of people attempting to stage their own lives—in Europe, the Soviet Union, the Middle East, Asia—the idea that society works itself out in the popular realm of spectacle has become an increasingly powerful social force. Less apparent until now was the extent to which the realm of representation has helped to create the political and personal desire for individuals in large groups to play their historical dramas before global viewer-critics who would be influenced by them, as a matter of political taste. Human beings have a greater sense of their own bodies as legislative bodies, of their actions as performance acts. Contrary to the pattern of mass movements in the period between the two world wars, now the social structure is organized around the ideals of individual choice rather than of collective necessity: the one instead of the mass. What we witnessed in 1989 was the triumph of representation as a rights issue, which, by its very nature, extends to the individual the freedom to insert him- or herself as a subject into history. Here one can begin to explore *performance ethics* as an aspect of philosophical inquiry.

The Role of Natural History

In the middle of the night Havel hid his manuscripts in the trunk of a tree behind his farmhouse in northern Bohemia. (It was the best place to keep a secret, and besides, hasn't there always been a tradition of closet drama?) A strange, compelling beauty joins Havel's primitivism and his utter grasp of the realness of security police. In the European landscape forests have always held a mythic power, not only in the private dreams of nationhood but in their sense of place in wartime, as a hideout for resistance fighters. How resonant an image: an author returning his manuscript to its material origin—the tree, with its inborn knowledge of good and evil—for safekeeping. Here is Havel the bohemian in a wood, building a nest for his plays, butterflies in his stomach, hands covered in silent bark.

Christmas

I dreamed I saw a snowman on top of a tank in Timisoara. Women in ugly rubber boots were sweeping death from the squares of Bucharest, cheered on by old palaces burning with joy. Each of them had 2.2 pounds of meat, 10 eggs, 1.1 pounds of cheese, 2 pounds of sugar, and 1 lightbulb to symbolize their powerlessness, donated by an eminent strategist of happiness. Leonard Bernstein was conducting Beethoven's Ninth at the Schauspielhaus near Unter den Linden while couples were kissing by the Brandenburg Gate. Havel was about to become the next president of Czechoslovakia as hundreds of thousands were jingling keys in the square of good King Wenceslas. The bells were ringing at St. Basil's.

I dreamed I was back in the American Embassy in Moscow where cafeteria workers were selling a color poster of Soviet tanks that taunted, "Visit us before we visit you." Do you have any half-and-half I asked. Are you kidding a woman laughed. Outside of the Theatre for Young Audiences, I heard the sound of the earth rumbling as if sidewalks were folding crowds of people into giant sandwiches. Someone said it was only a rehearsal for the November 7 parade. Giant pictures of Marx, Engels, and Lenin decorated the metro stop at Kievskaya. All over the city women were searching for soap to wash off Estée Lauder.

Later in New York I told Heiner Müller that we have never heard the sounds of tanks in our streets. He laughed oddly as if I'd said I was a virgin. The only tanks we have are think tanks. They were playing a movie that took place in Panama. Noriega was holed up in the Vatican Embassy in a room with a broken television. Fatigued troops blasted rock music outside his window. It was the first funky mass ever celebrated by the Papal Nuncio in the history of the world. Helicopters flailed their heavy metal arms in semaphoric time to No Place to Run and a young soldier shouted good morning, Panama. Operation Just Cause and the Dignity Battalions fought it out under a Reebok sign while the Maximum Leader was doing voodoo. Sweaty men in tank tops ran through the streets with refrigerators on their backs. From the Holy See a Polish pope gave his holiday greeting in fifty-three languages via satellite. An electrician was lighting up Poland. Soon airplanes started unloading coffins wrapped in stars and stripes and the taps of sorrowful shoes and trumpets. In Bucharest boxes were filled with young students and disemboweled women and strong men who wanted to sing carols, lined up in a bare room like opened gifts in the shapes of people. Then all of a sudden there were daisies in the snow. A young artist said in disbelief that it had been almost impossible in recent years to get hold of the color white.

(1990)

Thinking about Interculturalism

I

When Saddam Hussein declared at the start of this new year that there would be no end to what might become "the theater of our operations," no one could have imagined the extent to which war as spectacle would dominate the lives of cultures and continents, on a scale of global spectatorship unprecedented in human history. Before the Gulf War started, we had barely settled down from the euphoria of watching on television the revolutions that brought enormous political and cultural transformation to Eastern and Central Europe.

That part of Europe had been so fixed for decades in its icy grimace many had forgotten that Europe was not an undifferentiated entity but a world of diverse cultures, encompassing Anglo-Saxon, Latin, Arabic, Teutonic, Slavic, Nordic, Celtic, Gypsy, and Semitic peoples, to choose only a sampling of those who historically have created the idea of Europe. Looking toward the Soviet Union, part Europe, part Asia, we have stopped counting by now the number of ethnic populations who want to break away from Kremlin centralization. Increasingly, there are items in the press on ancestral homes long forgotten in contemporary history books: Moldavia, Transylvania, Swabia, Bosnia-Herzegovina, Slovenia, Nagorno-Karabakh. When last did we speak of Bohemia? Long-suppressed ethnic rivalries and dangerous nationalist tendencies are producing rising tensions in countries experiencing the first taste of freedom in the postwar era. The world is opening up to us and closing in on itself at the same time, as people and places alternately exalt local, regional, and global affiliations. If strong ethnic identification is aligned to progressive politics in the United States, in many other parts of the world it is feared as reactionary. All around us the old divisions of political life are being challenged.

In Latin America, several countries are slowly moving toward democracy after years of military rule, and in South Africa the promise of an end to apartheid can at last be envisioned. In Korea, in Japan, in Singapore, and in India the expansion of new economies is modernizing the lives of many Asians. Some brave Chinese people tried to make a democratic revolution, but they did not succeed in toppling the old men in their palaces. While everyone was looking in another direction, toward the Middle East, they put Wang Dan on trial. And the Soviets quickly moved their tanks into Latvia, cutting down the young filmmaker who was documenting their brutality. But there is no place to hide in the world any longer. Everyone is watching.

As we look toward 1992 the European countries are preparing to unite in a new European Community, which will surely change the nature of North American–European relations. Europe, the old world, the longest link in the political, cultural, and economic chain that has bound the United States to the Continent, and it to us, for over five centuries, is about to reorganize itself as a new world.

Nearly five hundred years ago America was called the New World. Its ways and wonders were studied, classified, traded, and marveled at for centuries, influencing people all the world over in the natural and human sciences, economics, art, politics, philosophy, and history. St. Jean de Crèvecoeur, equally at home on his colonial farm in the lower Hudson Valley and in the high-heeled Parisian circles of the *philosophes*, thought he had discovered here the New Man. His independent American wife was, of course, a new woman.

On the eve of the Revolution, in Crèvecoeur's world there were foreign peoples, chiefly from Great Britain, Holland, Sweden, France, Belgium, Germany, Switzerland, Africa, and the Caribbean, living in the English colony. Less than a century earlier, downriver near the Dutch-ruled Manhattan, among the European-descended population, which numbered fewer than two thousand, nearly eighteen languages were spoken. Farther west, in territories that would remain for some time un-united with the new states, the language of Spain ruled.

America, now a nation with an immigrant population of 40 percent, more than any other country in modern times, is again reconstituting the idea of the New Man: *homo multiculturans*. America has always been a culture of more ethnic diversity than any other in the West, and, singularly, it has been for centuries the land where people have come to escape their own histories and cultures even as they cling fiercely to those values and symbols left behind. There is more than a little truth in William Gass's contention that the only history America can have is a geographical one.

In the last two decades especially, the flow of refugees moving over the surface of the globe, now thought to number about fifteen million, has focused attention on cultures everywhere, forcing each country to address its own questions of identity and definition. At no time in memory have more people throughout the world publicly argued changing beliefs in nationalism, internationalism, ethnicity, and culture, in the face of global interdependence in economic, military, cultural, and environmental spheres. Against this background, the conflict in the Gulf signals a new definition of *world war*.

We began 1991 sitting around the television, which circles the globe like Rumor, watching a war in Iraq, the alleged home of the Garden of Eden. This Mesopotamian region was the cradle of civilization, where the arts and sciences, mathematics, and religion grew and spread around the earth, intermingling Near Eastern, Mediterranean, and African cultures at the beginning of the exchange of ideas and skills between peoples. The epic *Gilgamesh*, one of the earliest stories written down, told of the people of this land. It was a story of war between men, and the destruction of the landscape. *Gilgamesh* was the text behind Homer's text. One world inside another world, the future in the ancient past.

In almost every intersection of cultures, everywhere there are worlds within worlds. In the world of contemporary performance, what I shall call the "discourse of interculturalism," and by that I mean its evolving affiliations and themes, has positioned itself to reflect these crosscurrents as a strategic mode of inquiry. This is my subject.

II

What is interculturalism? The writings that cluster around the world of this word alternately address theory, technique, politics, aesthetics, theatrical production, critical writing. Interculturalism is linked to worldview, practice, and theory/criticism, that is, to the mental attitude that precedes performance, the performance process, and the theoretical writing that accompanies performance. A fairly recent addition to theatrical vocabulary, interculturalism, then, is a state of mind, as much as a way of working.

Our plan for this anthology [*Interculturalism and Performance: Writings from* PAJ] proceeded from a genuine desire to explore the issue of interculturalism within the history of performance ideas and to articulate themes that may have been overlooked in previous writing on the subject. As editors, Gautam Dasgupta and I hoped to situate this subject in a broader frame than the social-sciences approach that has characterized intercultural writings of the last decade or so. We wanted to include discussion of the idea of interculturalism within the scope of the literary essay and in the context of different traditions of theater. Our intention was to expand the theme beyond the East-West polemic, to treat Europe and America as intercultural spaces; to reflect on the historical avant-garde and neglected topics such as the dramatic text, music, video, the new urban cultures. Our editorial design was to encourage a historical perspective, by giving a diverse, often contradictory group of people the opportunity to address interculturalism as both theory and practice, in a personal, speculative manner. Overall, we set out to construct a *critique of interculturalism* in the polyvocal views of contributors from around the world.

We proceeded to commission several essays for the special double issue of *Performing Arts Journal* 33/34 from which to begin an investigation of what people in the theater thought, wrote, and practiced around the idea of interculturalism as they understood it. We also solicited new contributions to address specific themes, and to these essays we added selections culled from fifteen years of issues of *PAJ* and from the books we have published to date. Together, the selections make up *Interculturalism and Performance.*

For me editing became a way of analyzing the major concepts of interculturalism as it has evolved thematically in theater discussions over the last decade or two. Increasingly, I began to question what was written about interculturalism and, especially, what was not written about. The discourse of interculturalism, in its specific rhetorical inflections, raises a number of profound concerns about the nature of representation, which I would like to pursue in this preface. By *rhetorical inflections* I mean the variety of attachments and oppositions, spoken and unspoken, to which interculturalism as a philosophical position has become aligned over the years. These include theater anthropology, social sciences, postmodernism, multiculturalism, cultural studies, grassroots politics, people's theater, new historicism, the East-West axis.

It is chiefly the discourse—the voices—circling about intercultural themes, the kind of thinking the subject has engendered, that engages me, rather than specific works. In fact, a proliferation of theoretical apparatus rather than exemplary works characterizes this school of thought, which is rooted more in academic writing than in the voices or manifestoes of artists, as was the case, say, with surrealism. Interculturalism, though, may be more method or critical perspective than style.

Ironically, no recent theater work, the form which by nature takes as its subject *representation*, has generated as much controversy around the notion of interculturalism as did the 1988 publication of Salman Rushdie's novel *The Satanic Verses*. The Ayatollah Khomeini condemned the novel and called for the execution of Rushdie as an enemy of Islam. Did he not *misrepresent* Islam? Rushdie's book succeeded brilliantly, not only as it leaped into the history of the satiric comic novel but in the author's deeply committed mastery of conveying his own imaginative life between two cultures (an Indian-born Muslim living in England) in its pages. Here he blended the texts and textures of Asian and Western culture, dreams, history, geography. Rushdie created a new way of writing the English language, setting postcolonial India and Thatcherite Britain in Bakhtin's explosive dialogical tension.

There is no such worldly creation to which one can point in theater (except, and in a different artistic direction, the unrealized CIVIL *wars* project of Robert Wilson), but the work that has focused the most debate around what theater people define as intercultural issues is *The Mahabharata* of Peter Brook, also an Englishman. Less known here are the stunning orientalized productions of France's Ariane Mnouchkine. That some of the most suggestive work comes out of the intersection of British (or French) culture and that of a former colony is in no small measure a decisive factor in the discussion. For one cannot put on interculturalism like an imported shirt or a new gestural vocabulary. American interculturalism has not grown out of the experience of colonialism, but from this country's own geography and changing demographics.

Though American links with India are very recent, and not extensive, India figures prominently in the writings on interculturalism, beginning with the early influence of Grotowski and continuing today in the work of Eugenio Barba and Richard Schechner. Notwithstanding, contemporary Indian sensibility has filtered into intellectual life here in recent years through the novel rather than the theater, in the writings of such authors, among several others, as Rushdie, Bharati Mukherjee, Amitav Ghosh, Vikram Seth, Ruth Prawer Jhabvala, and, earlier, V. S. Naipaul. A few decades ago Indian music influenced (at the same time that it did the Beatles) American avant-garde composers, of whom Philip Glass is the most prominent. In the world of performance, "India" exists largely in theoretical writings or as a model for performance discipline. Its classical dance and musical forms are known and performed here, though not contemporary Indian drama.

My own view is that the far greater impact of Japan on the history of American performance has not been fully acknowledged in the discourse of interculturalism. Since before World War II and continuing into the present (from Michio Ito to the contemporary fascination with Kabuki, Noh, and Bunraku), Japanese aesthetics, design, and philosophy have had an enormous effect on avant-garde performance, centered historically in New York. Japanese influence, whether aesthetic or Buddhist, extends from Martha Graham to the Cunningham-Cage collaborative model, to Fluxus, to the Judson school, to individuals such as Nam June Paik, Yoko Ono, and Allan Kaprow, who inspired the beginnings of video and performance art, and continuing up to the work of many of the experimental directors working today: Lee Breuer, Peter Sellars, Elizabeth LeCompte, Meredith Monk, Ping Chong, Robert Wilson, and puppeteers Julie Taymor and Theodora Skipitares. These artists declare their attachment to the highly stylized, refined sensibility of traditional Japanese aesthetics in many ways: the approach to narrative, the construction of theatrical space and time, conceptual use of puppets, separation of body and voice, and the general development of formalistic vocabularies attuned to rhythm, composition, silence, and abstraction. Weaving its way through the visual arts, multimedia, dance, and theater, Japanese aesthetics joined with European modernism to create the New York School of avant-garde performance in the post-war era.

Interculturalism as theatrical practice divides itself into two distinct lines, and I believe it will continue to do so more often in the years to come. Those artists inclined toward formal experimentation and abstraction as a performance mode will draw closer to Japanese aesthetics. Others who declare themselves for a politically engaged, popular theater will emphasize Latin American, Indian, Southeast Asian, and African affiliations. Artists of both persuasions will take it for granted that their work reflects social commitment.

The politics of this alignment is reasonably clear. The discourse of interculturalism as it has evolved in this country orients itself around the notion of "people's theatre," in reaction to Western theater convention and the more formalist, literary impulses of modernism. Generally, this theater demonstrates a less formal separation of performer and audience, independence from the dramatic text of a single author, and disinterest in the work as an aesthetic object to be viewed. The more stylized, abstract theater experimentation proposes a clear demarcation between performer, audience, and spectator decorum and links itself stylistically to modernist movements. In this latter sense, there is no attempt to represent the Orient, just as decades earlier Brecht did not aim, in his own stylized work that drew upon Chinese acting technique, to create "Orientalness."

In New York it was mainly the groups prominent in the '60s, such as The Living Theatre, The Open Theatre (in earlier years influenced also by Japanese philosophy), and The Performance Group, which concerned themselves with the autobiography of performance, social criticism, and at times audience participation.

As we move into the decade of the '90s, avant-garde performance (coming from the directions of both theater and visual arts), intercultural or otherwise, is beginning to seem more similar to the '60s counterculture events or street (people's) theater than to the formalist, at times high-tech modernist stance of artists who dominated thinking about theater two decades ago. They include, for example, Mabou Mines, The Ontological-Hysteric Theatre of Richard Foreman, and Robert Wilson, whose work exemplified what I had called the theater of images.

(In attempting to articulate themes that address American intercultural practice, I am aware that the perspective outlined above is shaped by my own local setting—New York—turned toward the East Coast–Europe–Orient axis, which has had the most impact on performance theory and production here. On the other hand, the geographical setting of the West Coast reflects an intercultural practice shaped more decisively by Chicano culture, which has not yet been sufficiently integrated into the discourse of interculturalism. This would be a necessary step in the development of a truly intercultural national consciousness.)

It is interesting to note that if interculturalism is any proper gauge, there is a certain anti-modernist attitude in the reevaluation of the European legacy and a search for the "authentic," real experience elsewhere than in Western culture. That was certainly the case in the promotion of the recent Los Angeles festival, which made a point of distancing itself from both New York and European performance. I note this in the sense that cultural historian Jackson Lears used to characterize a strong tendency in American culture to react against modernity. As he contends, at the end of the nineteenth century American artists and intellectuals, in shrugging off the "overcivilized" rationalist values and aesthetics of European culture and the effects of new technologies, looked instead toward Oriental culture, the primitive, religion, and myth, in search of the *therapeutic*. Lears's view of this turn-of-the-century turbulence offers a tempting analogy for contemporary life and artistic practice.

III

If we were to pursue the idea of interculturalism as a kind of people's theater to its logical end point, we would confront a situation in which boundaries between actor, spectator, and spectacle blur and disentangle. It would feature only participants. Here is the precise intersection of theater and anthropology, the staging ground of Grotowski, who, as Polish critic Konstanty Puzyna has pointed out, was the first contemporary theater artist to link the fields of study. Grotowski, of course, was extending the project of Artaud, who looked East in search of the sacred and the mythic. The mythopoeic impulse plays a dominant role in the history of twentieth-century performance, challenged only by the Brechtian model. The essential antinomy of the twentieth-century theater evolves from Brecht and Artaud: the world as text/the world as spectacle.

The performance trajectory Grotowski's example describes represents a profound shift from the conventional acceptance of the dramatic text in performance as revelation to the emphasis on the creative transformation of the participant in a sacred act, from redemption (or catharsis) to the ritualistic celebration of human potential and spirit. As an anti-modernist performance vision, in the context that I have outlined above, it posits a new utopia for our time, founded on the *fin de siècle* turn toward physical and spiritual discipline that has framed the twentieth century.

Grotowski is the most extreme example of the contemporary urge to turn away from spectacle, spectatorship, and, by extension, aesthetics. Two decades ago Grotowski spoke of the end of such words as *theater*, *performance*, *spectator*, and *actor*. His emphasis on the holistic life (with consciousness as its supreme state) and his search for a universal human language in sacred, ritual experience intersect with the problematics of New Age philosophy. Grotowski's view of human nature, his universalist ideal — "man precedes difference," he contends — bypasses the contemporary cultural politics of difference and its disenchantment with humanism's claims to universality. His world is no longer that of art or theater, but one of a theaterless society. It is like Rousseau's in one respect: social science is set in conflict with theater (representation). However, while Rousseau was interested in the *public* individual, Grotowski is concerned now with *private*, exclusive circles of initiates, suggestive of earlier spiritual and artistic movements, beginning with symbolism.

In a 1985 essay, "*PAJ*, A Personal History," I suggested that a critique of theater anthropology should begin with Rousseau, the first to link theater and anthropology in the modern sense, a point to which I'd like to return. Rousseau, of course, is notorious for his attack on theater in *Letter to d'Alembert*, in which he extols a new vision of society that forbids theater (plays). Instead, from the perspective of a social scientist he imagines the *polis* as public festival, comprising only participants making a spectacle of themselves, in democratic harmony. "Let the spectators become an entertainment to themselves; make them actors themselves; do it so that each sees and loves himself in the others so that all will be better united." But Rousseau's ecstatic vision was directed toward generating "patriotic charm" as a form of citizenship to preserve the paternalistic authority of the state in tandem with the moral authority of the family. His body politic was intended to dramatize the values of the republican constitution—a profoundly conservative pageantry.

Generally speaking, theater anthropology shares an obvious infatuation with social contracts (or social structures). I am troubled by the anthropological view of performance as "social drama" because of the implications in the notion of social order on which such drama is founded. The communal or ritual performer is not, by definition, a critical, dissenting participant in the social drama.

What I find problematic in this aspect of intercultural discourse—the valorization of the social pact, or public festival—is the disappearance of boundaries between actor, spectator, and text, in effect, the denial of spectatorship. One result of this denial is a Nietzschean, ritualistic play of mass spectacle and quasi-religious experience that carried into Artaud, then to Grotowski, and finally into the writings on interculturalism (by way of structural anthropology and ethnographic studies), coinciding with contemporary popular currents in psychology. Another outgrowth of this development is the assumption that one can "do" culture.

The notion of social drama has a long, complicated history in the modern world. On a personal level, I continue to return to the visionary work of Pirandello, in whom the dynamics of individuality and group ethos illuminate how frighteningly ambiguous and intertwined are the strategies of performance acts, in both democratic and totalitarian systems of government. In the modern era, the urge toward self-transformation linked itself to the theatrical gesture, then moved on to the realm of ontological act. In this larger philosophical sense, performance as an existential, self-defining act, outside of theatrical activity, projects itself as phenomenological gesture. Pirandello clearly distinguished between performance as an ontological act of individuation and the construction of a role encouraged by the prevailing social structure. Theater anthropology and sociologies of theater need to confront the fundamental political and philosophical issues that complicate the interactions of the individual and the group.

Early, important studies of crowd psychology coincide with the rise of mass movements in the modern era. In our own time, it is fascinating to watch the spectacle of societies in different parts of the world, particularly in the kinds of transformations that have taken place in the

Soviet Union and Eastern Europe and, from another political perspective, in the Middle East. Borders between the democratic and totalitarian political impulse frequently blur, as do theater and spectacle, or politics and religion.

The Eastern European example is provocative in relation to the subject of theater. From all reports, during the stages of social revolution in the Eastern European region, as life in the street became more and more compelling and public speech was encouraged, the audience for theater, up until then the site of political discourse (albeit veiled), dwindled. Audiences, reveling in their new role of citizenship, lost interest in theatrical representation. Acting themselves out, staging their own dramas, became more important. Gradually, however, people began to distinguish between self-dramatization and the representationalism of theater. They realized they were two different realms of experience.

In the allusion to the Greek ideal that underlies the modern revolutionary fervor in imagining the new *polis*, the New Man, and this has been the dream of all avant-garde movements of the twentieth century, there is an important issue that seems to be obscured in current performance theory: *thinking is a kind of spectatorship.* Acts of thought, of contemplation, are related to judging: thinking discerns the differences between things. As Hannah Arendt, from whom we can learn a great deal on the subject of social life, has argued, only the spectator, not the actor, can know and understand the spectacle. Extending her philosophical insight, then, it becomes obvious that a performance world in which epistemology is centered in the body—in doing—only serves to reinforce the mind/body dualism. In the context of performance, this position generates another version of the nature-culture argument.

If consciousness, and the subjunctive expression of becoming as integral to the order of a social community, is one of the valued aspirations of the anthropological approach to performance theory, it is important to remember that consciousness is not the same as thinking. Only thinking, which involves thinking *about* something, is a dialectical process.

The represented drama is the conventional object of thought in theater. Yet the play of single authorship (especially when it is contemporary) is disdained in the discourse of interculturalism, which sets itself in opposition to a theater of dramatic literature, to propose in its place a theater of the actor's body as emblematic of community and repository of knowledge. This strategy has not been seriously questioned in recent critical writing, nor has the obvious power play of directors who undermine the significance of the dramatic text. After all, an *auteur* is an author too. Given our contemporary knowledge of the complexity of textuality, it no longer seems useful to encourage the view that the text only fully comes into meaning in performance or that literary knowledge is dependent on performance knowledge in theatrical production. That intercultural writings have not made a more substantial attempt to bring into the discourse the difficult questions of dramaturgy or to explore their own literary ambiguity is regrettable, especially since interculturalism can be understood more broadly as a form of intertextualism. But what is the crucial issue here—authorship or the place of literature in performance?

Not only the dramatic text of theater but the theater building itself has been called into question in contemporary performance theory. Rather falsely, I believe, there has been an attempt to suggest that the mere act of working in a conventional (institutional) theater puts one in the hands of an "elite" audience forced to be "passive" voyeurs of "consumerist" *objets d'art.* Conversely, as the argument plays itself out, the folksy informality of a theater for a highly particularized, microcommunity actively promotes social change. In reality, both kinds of performance share the same financial support in this country: the National Endowment for the Arts, the Rockefeller Foundation, foreign governments, state arts councils, universities, and so on. Frequently they share the same audiences.

Theoretically, then, the undifferentiated (counterrevolutionary?) audience in the theater judges and consumes the aesthetic object, while the community-conscious theater precludes judgment and, instead, spectators-as-participants are drawn into a shared experience. The outmoded "high" and "low," ruling class versus folk, decadent or sacred opposition that underlies this view, often combining with the rhetoric of postmodernism by way of '60s-style provocation, obfuscates the very important differences between commodity entertainments and artworks, between consumers and audiences, between culture and mass society. It also tends to obliterate differences between popular forms of art and those that do not appeal to popular taste. More importantly, the argument does not take into account the historical circumstances of the spectrum of art forms created at different times and places for many different social groups. (This is true not only of Western performance spaces and traditions but of those in Asia as well. In non-Western art, in addition to distinctions between classical and folk forms and "high" and "low" art, there is also a distinction between religious and secular forms.)

When it obscures these kinds of theatrical differences, when it confuses culture and art and dismisses the contemplative, critical life of the spectator in favor of the audience-as-performer, then interculturalism and theater anthropology, as critical strategies, risk a new kind of philistinism. Much of the already published writing inscribed in the interculturalist perspective, rooted as it is in the various sciences, has developed a scientific profile and a laboratory approach to performance, as well as a documentary attitude toward criticism. What is emphasized is technique and training, social process. The act of judgment or evaluation of the performer or performance in the context of art seems to be discouraged. For my part, I prefer Kantian disinterest to this dubious objectivity. Philosophically speaking, the struggle I have outlined is between materialism and idealism.

Ironically, as certain schools of thought in the arts here look toward other parts of the world for creative inspiration, many in Asia and, most recently, the former Soviet-bloc countries have looked for renewal toward individualistic aspects of Western art and democratic pluralism developed within the humanist tradition. We should not underestimate the value of abstraction—from the art object, the state, the church, the crowd—that has evolved in this cultural tradition. It is the private, individual I, that many people have made revolutions to recover. This abstracted, even alienated subject is worth holding on to, more fiercely than ever, in the face of contemporary ideological pressures.

IV

The social sciences, psychology, and anthropology have had a significant impact in the scholarly discourse on interculturalism; indeed, they have instigated its exploration and expansion in performance theory. But the scientific approach has its limits in dealing with art forms. The sciences are more attentive to process, structure, system, and research methodology than to the moral, ethical, and aesthetic questions raised by human performance and cultural artifact. The scientific approach tends to be concerned with the how of activity rather than the why of it. Perhaps it is time now to open up interculturalism alongside discoveries in literature, philosophy, visual art, history, geography, and architecture. Anthropology, for example, is most interesting when it embraces literary values, as in the recent work of Clifford Geertz and James Clifford and, earlier, Victor Turner. Do we really need to restage the art/science — two cultures — debate in the theater at this late date? Instead, why not bring into the world of performance all textures of creative intelligence?

Since the goals of interculturalism are so deeply linked to the concept of multiculturalism, which is rooted in the new urban cultures, we need to understand the nature of the city in history, following the groundwork of someone like Lewis Mumford or, in our time, Richard Sennett, who, like Mumford, confronts the new life of cities and their cultures. We might also build upon the writings of Walter Benjamin to enlarge the understanding of today's *flâneur*, our *homo performans*, who inhabits cities all over the world.

In essence, writing on interculturalism would make a marvelous leap if it adopted a more cosmopolitan outlook on the galaxies of knowledge in our world. Oddly enough, while touching base quite naturally with new historicism's attention to what Stephen Greenblatt has called "the circulation of social energy," interculturalism is surprisingly ahistorical in its critical approach. It needs to develop a *historical consciousness*, having now made its large contribution to performance theory.

Unfortunately, even as it places culture at the center of its ethos, interculturalism reflects no strongly defined theory of culture. This situation lends a certain paradoxical twist to the writing: the emphasis is more often than not on performance technique, more specifically the aesthetics of form (especially Indian or Balinese), rather than any sense of the historical-cultural-social-religious settings of these forms, past or present. Furthermore, in the turn toward other performance traditions, namely, those of Hindu, Buddhist, and Muslim cultures, there is a certain dissociation from analysis of their social and religious strictures and hierarchies. The intellectual rigor applied to the critique of humanism should, in fairness, extend to other philosophical traditions as well. Not to do so, then, leads to the aestheticization of cultures and the dehistoricization of their forms. Not to "represent" another culture is perfectly acceptable—after all, it is the Brechtian option—but that conflicts with the natural linkage of interculturalism and cultural studies. What, in the larger sense, can we learn from interculturalism: How is it different from other ways of representation, in both theory and practice? Is it truly a new worldview or simply a new name for an evolutionary process? More to the point, what is the difference between the representation of interculturalism and the very thing itself, between "intercultural-ness" and true interculturalism?

The framework of interculturalism would be revitalized if, for example, there were input and debate from several different schools of thought in the field, as in like-minded literary and art criticism, which is more developed polyphonically. As I indicated earlier, one of the main objectives of this anthology is to open up new perspectives on our understanding of the nature and practice of interculturalism and to articulate issues other than those that now define the parameters of its discourse.

If interculturalism as a critical enterprise is to embrace more eclectic themes, European modernism should certainly be a point of departure. For over a century intercultural practice has been linked to avant-garde movements, in particular literary modernism (often overlooked in intercultural writings), beginning with symbolism and its infatuation with Orientalism. Symbolism outlines the beginning of abstraction in Western art, the point at which artists became interested in the concept of the sign, also coinciding with interest in the dance dramas—based on the sign—of Asia. In the history of modernism the influence of Orientalism and the search for spiritual renewal extends from the symbolists to Artaud, the first modern European theater artist to turn away from the West, to Grotowski and Wilson, who represent two different paths of this symbolist legacy at our own turn of the century.

In my view, the importance of the spiritual element in the historical development of virtually every movement in modernism throughout Europe and in the Soviet Union has been erased in much of postmodernism's desire, which carried into interculturalism, to distance itself from modernism. This oversight misconstrues the inseparability of revolutionary politics and avant-garde aesthetics in the evolution of modernist performance. We need to investigate the deep linkages of avant-garde performance, literary modernism, and interculturalism, especially in influential individual theater artists such as Yeats, Strindberg, Meyerhold, Brecht, Artaud; in the attraction of Russian artists to the Islamic art of Central Asia; in *fin-de-siècle* Japonisme; in the major role in experimentation played by cities of the Austro-Hungarian empire, viewed as an intercultural construct; in the movements from symbolism to futurism to constructivism to surrealism in the pre–World War II era.

French culture, owing to its colonial past and its unparalleled role in the spread of avant-garde ideals on the Continent, in the Soviet Union, and in the United States, can be an obvious point of departure for intercultural studies of a historical nature. That would bring together performance ideas and the literary text in an analytical frame. It might also take us closer to Edgar Allan Poe, who was so influential for the French symbolists and the first important American artist for whom Orientalism was an aesthetic strategy. (Perhaps it is not so coincidental that his writing is appearing increasingly in contemporary theater works.)

On the subject of Orientalism, the world of opera too, from Rossini's *Semiramide* to Philip Glass's *Akhnaten*, is poised for inclusion in the discourse of interculturalism. Edward Said's erudite genealogy of "imperial spectacle" attending the Cairo premiere of Verdi's *Aida* provides a fresh opening to theater history and criticism. Opera is an astonishingly resonant field of inquiry: plenty of primary artifacts are available; a history of theatrical theory and an entire performance tradition are in place; the contemporary repertoire offers for reconsideration a dialectical landscape of Asian, Middle Eastern, and African settings of works of numerous European composers. Not the least significant encouragement is the fact that today many of the most innovative directors in the world are working in opera.

If America does not have its own operatic history, there is an intercultural music tradition of more than three centuries. Black music, rooted in the mixing of African rhythms, Protestant hymns, and the European classical forms that fed into the creation of jazz, is at the heart of our popular song. One cannot even begin to catalogue all of the musical exchanges revitalizing pop music, as it creates the world beat. In the intercultural spaces of the South and Southwest especially, old ethnic traditions are coming into the mainstream. Music performance, both popular and avant-garde, should be highlighted more in the interculturalism context because it is so indigenous to American culture and

so dominant a performance mode in our time. But also, and especially significant, its roots are more in artistic expression than in theory.
Theater researchers needn't abandon this subject to ethnomusicology
specialists.

Specialization may not be the best guide to the twenty-first century.
In our world, knowledge is increasingly compartmentalized as subjects
are no longer rooted to their former, natural settings. Through the process of erosion the transmission of ideas is progressively more restricted
by a kind of forced zoning regulation, while the universe of knowledge
itself continually expands. As recently as last year we saw old categories
of thinking collapse in the punctured illusion of the Berlin Wall. Nothing is written in stone. In the time it has taken me to complete this
essay a war has been fought that will transform another great region of
the earth, in ways that we cannot yet begin to grasp. More and more
of the world is revealing itself, forcing us to find untried, creative ways
to apprehend the insistent dreams of cultures and continents. What is
performance, and what are we to it, in this new world being made?

Interculturalism must become more worldly in its pursuit of global
affiliations and dare to cross intellectual frontiers as casually as geographic ones. In the most profound analysis, a society is judged by the
connections its people make between the urgent themes of the world.
The cultivation of worldliness can only deepen and make more radical the interculturalism project, openly welcoming the wandering eye
of the traveler, a philosopher without a system, to the glorious book of
knowledge that is our world, our home.

(1991)

Originally published as the preface to *Interculturalism and Performance:
Writings from PAJ.*

Meredith Monk's Atlas of Sound

New Opera and the American Performance Tradition

|||||||| In the history of modernist performance ideas the representation of the body in space has always been shaped by each theatrical generation's expression of the search for spiritual renewal. This persistent though often overlooked theme of theatrical modernism, extending from its beginnings in symbolism to our own turn of century, is at the center of Meredith Monk's *oeuvre*, nowhere more expansively than in her first full-scale opera conceived for an opera house, *Atlas*. Still, with its eighteen singer-performers and ten orchestra members, and its premiere at the Houston Grand Opera, this is no ordinary work in the genre. In place of the conventional book there is a repertoire of vocal techniques that encompasses glottal effects, ululation, yodeling, speech song, animal sounds, and vocalization. Texture of the voice is more important than text in this opera that dances. The musical line, which overrides any sense of literary line, is inseparable from the line of the body.

Atlas: an opera in three parts evolves as continuous movement, organized in the thematic divisions Personal Climate, Night Travel, Invisible Light. Movement joins with song in a melisma effect that characterizes the opera from the very start, generating highly emotional moments. It opens with a scene of domestic life. On one side of the wide proscenium stage of the Annenberg Center at Philadelphia, where *Atlas* was presented as part of the American Music Theatre Festival, there are two parents in a conventional living-room setting, and at the other side is a young girl in her bedroom, its window looking out to the world, a lighted globe nearby. Pictorially, the opera emphasizes this horizontality as a reflection of its internal linear movement, specifically the work's unfolding as a journey. Warming this space of desire, lit by bright colors and framed by patterned wallpaper, are the restless dreams of thirteen-year-old Alexandra.

She gets up from her bed, cuts a wide span of the torso, in simple stretching, grasping movements that match the open vowels of her vocalizing, "la-la-la. . . ." The emphasis on vowels here and elsewhere in the opera enunciates its theme of travel, to inner and outer worlds. Not unlike their proliferation and effect in Monk's earlier *Recent Ruins*, they open wide to the air, to experience. What is a vowel but a song?

Alexandra's dance is used less to give steps to a character than to create a movement pattern. This is a general principle of *Atlas*; one might call it figuration instead of characterization. As the scene progresses a French horn highlights the mood of travel, and the clarinet adds a certain reedy breeze to it. In contrast, the violin and cello underline the parents' worried duet, the father's anguish registering in his lower aching tones, the mother's in the high-pitched shrills of a wounded animal. In this way, the trio of mother, father, daughter—sometimes at opposite ends of the stage, at other moments close together—is dramatized musically, through major and minor keys covering a wide range of vocal textures. The voice is choreographed, as it were, the expressive content reinforced by Monk's distinctive ostinato.

Some critics have interpreted the first scene as a commentary on the sterility of bourgeois life, but this interpretation distorts Monk's imagery. Scenes of home life and childhood have been an essential thematics in her theatrical narrative over more than two decades; the institutional branch of her artistic company she named "The House." Monk's domestic scenes have always been cast in loving, respectful tones. In *Atlas* the parents appear in three scenes, two in the first section and a third in the second section. They are also given some of the most beautiful melodies in the opera. Nonetheless, the daughter leaves this balmy climate to seek out new worlds; her search is for enlightenment, not love. The interplay of light and dark, harmony and dissonance, wisdom and ignorance filters through *Atlas*, whose intrinsic subject is vision, the art of seeing—but only in the sense of spiritual radiance.

A film (in negative) of a horse running wildly is projected just beyond Alexandra's window, uniting freedom and eros in her fantasy of adventure. The horse's head splits open, and out step two guides for the impending journey, a male and a female dancer: performers as guardian spirits. At times the guides interpose variety acts between parts of the opera in a manner similar to Robert Wilson's "knee plays," but they are more integrated by Monk into the narrative as individuals, dancing their way into the opera, moving it along.

Young Alexandra begins her rite of passage to womanhood. Monk herself now comes on stage to play Alexandra from the ages of twenty-five to forty-five, at first interviewing potential travel companions in an airport. Whether or not they belong to her chosen group depends on the sound of their voices; those who do not belong have a dissonant tone. From time to time a screen high in the corner of the stage projects the biographical facts of a performer to personalize him or her. *Atlas* draws its inspiration from the life of Frenchwoman Alexandra David-Néel (1868–1969), the remarkable seeker of spiritual perfection who traveled through India, Sikkim, Tibet, and Nepal in the first quarter of the century. In remote parts of Tibet she was frequently called *khadoma*, the name given to a reincarnated female spirit—the privilege of such a role not unappreciated by the former opera singer. Like many other *fin-de-siècle* Europeans attracted to theosophy, occultism, and mysticism, David-Néel turned from the West to the Orient for wisdom. The tireless lecturer, writer, and traveler published more than two dozen books on Buddhism and her sacred experiences in Asia. But *Atlas* is much less her story than Monk's own spiritual biography, a personal mythology linking it to her signature works, such as *Quarry* and *Recent Ruins*, and the films *Ellis Island* and *Book of Days*.

Structurally, the narrative of *Atlas* follows closely Joseph Campbell's view of mythological adventure outlined in *The Hero of a Thousand Faces*: separation-initiation-return. Campbell calls this the "nuclear unit of monomyth." Its constancies include wondrous sights, the figure of a guide, visits to unknown regions of the earth, trials and temptations. All of these defining points find their way into Monk's poetics.

The tripartite structure of *Atlas* depicts this journey and transformation, the horizontality of the performance space arranging itself naturally as a zone of myth. Like travel narratives, which are becoming increasingly popular, the journey is spatial, the searching outward for new places; but like the mythic quest, it is temporal, a soul-searching. In her mapping of consciousness, Monk combines the two (site/sight) through music (time) and movement (space). The route is the vocal line, which grows organically from the line of the body. So the voice itself, then, has body. Eventually the journey ends where it begins: at home. In the last scene Alexandra, now sixty, is seated at a table, and on the same bed where she as a girl dreamed of faraway places the other two Alexandras sit quietly. The child-woman is one of Monk's enduring portraits, Atlas demonstrating in a larger context the education of the girlchild, her most persistent motif.

In its own way it is a teaching play of sorts whose ethos is founded on the ideal of community, even the more Jungian world soul. However, though the opera is designed with a series of lessons represented in a frame, accented by the staging of scenes (stage pictures) in squares of the space, it is not Brechtian in its intentions. The performers always inhabit an emotional space that reaches out toward the audience. They don't quote social behavior in any gestic manner; besides, Monk proposes a view of "human nature" as an internal process. If Atlas is epic in its narrative structure, nonetheless it demonstrates that the Brechtian dramaturgical style can open up new possibilities for use in a highly abstract, emotive, and more allegoric theatricality. In this way, it avoids the prosaic psychological plotting of both dramatic realism and conventional opera.

The use of imagery as a narrative strategy retains a strong attraction for Monk and many influential artists of the last three decades who, like her, have deep roots in the dance, visual arts, theater, and music worlds of the '60s and '70s. A key concept of that period, "energy," has evolved in contemporary art into the discovery of spirit and the sacred, a powerful theme in Monk's theater. The polyvocality of her community-based ethos, as it pertains to the musical settings of Atlas, the fullness of the orchestral sound, and the opera's relation to the audience, serves as both structural and political principle.

Alexandra's travels with her explorer-companions take them to many kinds of communities: Western, Middle Eastern, Nordic, Asian; they visit rural and urban landscapes; they experience arctic, forest, desert climates. The scenes, whether warm, cold, dark, or light, flow easily into one another, as in the fluidity of dreamscapes, so parts of stage props and more elaborate design elements appear in one scene and then another, almost as if the staging itself were moved by the feeling of legato.

To illustrate the manner of segue: After overcoming the trials of the ice demons in an arctic bar, the explorers find themselves in a forest, where they walk the tracks of an ancient man's beard, spread out in five directions on the ground. In made-up wordplay Alexandra "translates" for him the questions of her friends, "Has anything changed?" "Can one find love?" Musically, the scene (one of the rare verbal sections) is very moving, culminating in the final moment, after the explorers have all left the stage carrying their tree props, when a lone woman who remains does a brief angular twist away from the old man toward the wings, as if she were uprooted in a great gust of wind. All the while the cello and viola instrumentation subtly incorporates the tango rhythms of the next scene, which is a desert tango set in the Middle East. In a visual pun on the dry passion of the dance, the two guides, dressed in formal attire, dance downstage while tents are set up behind them and performers costumed as camels prance in between. The early part of this scene (it later turns dark and ominous) is a good example of Monk's humor, while also signaling a certain whimsical performance attitude that is identifiably an outgrowth of the New York avant-garde of the last three decades.

Monk's work has a willful naïveté, even utopianism, but that masks a sophistication that can go unremarked. Oftentimes a contemporary attraction to new themes brings into focus aspects of an artist's work that were overlooked in other years due to political or aesthetic preoccupations prevalent then. Monk has had a longstanding interest in the life of cities and world cultures, far in advance of contemporary events. Seeing her work against the background of current concerns, what is immediately striking is, of course, the ecological theme, which in the American context is inseparable from the spiritual theme. Extending from Thoreau, this seems an even more powerful linkage within the perspective of the environmental crisis. Monk's view has always been biocentric, with its dimension of concern for all species of life and the overall survival of the planet. The long scene in the second part of the opera, which takes place in an agricultural community, is in a sense a testimonial highlighting the value of self-sufficient human labor on the land, organized by the rhythms of work songs. In *Atlas*, the concept of culture is implied in its classical meaning: that the measure of a civilization is the attitude of a people toward their land.

Given the thematic composition of *Atlas*, with its attention to *communitas*, self-knowledge, and cosmic harmony, especially the spiritual climate of a place, it is not surprising that the opera should include a contrapuntal response to the peaceful agricultural society portrayed. That moment comes in the frantic gesticulation of a man in a business suit spotted at his desk in glaring yellow and green light, accenting his arms as they cut wildly through space. He conducts the "Possibility of Destruction." Troops in bright orange uniforms march behind him in an industrial setting to the sound of electronic noise, the sky raining white flakes of doom. This condemnation of the combined forces of the military-industrial complex is the harshest note of the opera. Led by the guides, the explorers climb a ladder that takes them out of this social terror and, in fact, out of this world. They join a heavenly choir and observe the earth from above. Here they inhabit a dark blue, socialized space, filling it with an ethereal sound that takes on architectural dimensions, pure sound that calls to mind the religious chanting echoing across the mountain peaks of Asia. The strong tones of the color blue in this opera, whose scenes are rendered in precise color choices, recall the early modernist preoccupation with the coordination of emotional states, sound, and color, the result of the unity creating illumination in the spiritual sense. (Kandinsky believed that blue was the color of spirituality.) Of necessity, it is more sound than song.

Musically, Monk has for a long time now experimented with the rhythms and harmonics of Asian, Middle Eastern, Western, and Eastern European composition; folk, classical, avant-garde, and popular music; chants, animal sounds, children's rhyme. Certainly, she has thrived on the resources of the world beat longer than any well-known artist working in performance. Monk also has the singular distinction of being the only woman from the "downtown" scene to have a commission to create an opera in a leading opera house, a rare enough occurrence for any artist in this country, much less one without academic credentials.

She is of the generation who inherited the musical freedom opened up by Cagean aesthetics and empowered by its reaction to serial music. Monk is frequently placed with the minimalists because she came of age in the milieu of La Monte Young, Terry Riley, Steve Reich, and Philip

Glass, all of whom have been interested in harmony and tonality. But minimalism doesn't describe her music any more than it does theirs; she shows much less interest in structure than in the use of the voice as a lyrical medium, expressing the melodies of world cultures. Monk seems to be striving to create an ethnopoetic atlas of sound.

This transcendentalism, part primitive, part avant-garde, is a defining factor in the American performance tradition. In fact, music theater and avant-garde opera (not only by composers such as Monk, Glass, and Adams but by the directors Sellars and Wilson as well) are increasingly outlining a performance style that may be a way out of the solipsistic impasse of performance art and, at the very least, an alternative to European opera convention. Dance and movement-based performance are slowly coming to the forefront in the American way of making opera, not only in Monk's work of many years but in the Robert Wilson–Philip Glass landmark *Einstein on the Beach*, in the more recent Peter Sellars–John Adams opera choreographed by Mark Morris, *The Death of Klinghoffer*, and in the new Bill T. Jones–Leroy Jenkins opera *The Mother of Three Sons*. Directors and composers who ordinarily might have remained in the theater are turning for inspiration to opera, which is filling in the gap left by the international decline in dramatic literature that transcends local culture and providing an alternative to the dominance of realism on our stages. American artists have always had the luxury not to have to use theatrical forms to preserve the speech of a minor language or small country or the political discourse of an oppressed one; they preferred to create narrative imagery. And, ironically, there is a certain unregulated exploration because theater work is so marginalized and noncommercial in the culture. At another level, this new work reflects today's worldwide yearning for spiritual transformation, because as music it is linked to the notion of the sublime and as dance, to a freedom of spirit that has made dance so prominent a part of American performance style in this century. Perhaps it is not unfair to say that in the realm of inspiration a pragmatic idealism influenced American artists as much as Marxism did European artists, the one generating a new vocabulary of formal experimentation, the other highly theorized political stagings.

What is occurring in this country in the new vision of opera is the elaboration of an American idiom based in imagery and movement that, unlike traditional opera, which has been rooted historically in the dramatic text, draws upon traditions of the New York School, in performance, dance, and the visual arts, and Asian aesthetics, especially Japanese.

The Japanese influence in *Atlas* is striking, not only in Monk's collaboration with Yoshio Yabara, who worked on the scenario and designed the opera's storyboards and costumes and co-designed (with Debby Lee Cohen) the sets. More specifically, it defines the opera's second section, Night Travel, which is performed in the style of Bunraku. A space is created by masking in black the upper and lower parts of the stage; a long, horizontal opening runs the length of the stage. Hooded performers in black pass from one end of the space to the other, manipulating long sticks held upright, each with a miniature airplane, ship, planet, car, or truck at its tip.

Japan has had an extraordinary influence on the New York experimental arts scene, beginning at least in the forties with Martha Graham and spreading in the postwar period in the "downtown" worlds of dance, music, video, performance, and theater. It would be difficult to imagine the New York arts scene without the Japanese influence, whether philosophically, through Zen and its spread by Cage, or aesthetically, in the highly formal theater that has influenced artists from the era of Black Mountain, happenings, Judson, Fluxus, and the more recent decades of the '70s and '80s. In the long view, American transcendentalism seems to have intermingled with Buddhism to forge a distinctive performance style, embodying for the most part a spiritual reverence for space (place) and an abiding interest in the rhythm of consciousness.

Monk's own eclecticism, an aspect of her integrity as an artist, gives definition to her ethics of performance. The interweaving of ethic and formal principles is found, for example, in the use of harmony, of duets, trios, chorus, and the principle of polyvocality; in the international casting of performers, who represent world cultures; in the ideal of transcending the self to envision a larger society; in the geographic settings of the narrative. Geography—the gestalt of a place—is a recurrent theme in the work Monk has produced for more than two decades, not only *Atlas*. Monk treats geography the way Stein, the guiding spirit of American avant-garde performance aesthetics, did: as a field of revelation. And like Stein, whose theater work is more musical than literary, she sets the rhythm of the voice—human breath—at the center of textuality. (This may be Walt Whitman's theatrical legacy, carried into theater by Stein, as much as his gift to poetry.)

The prominence of the voice is nowhere more compelling than in the scene just before the final image of the sixty-year-old Alexandra returning home. This a cappella setting, Invisible Light, is the long last scene of *Atlas*. Here the performers have an out-of-body experience and appear as a chorus (oneness) in black robes, lined up on either side of the stage, perpendicular to the audience, at first bowing and tilting like human bell tones. The repetitive (because eternal) harmonies, at times nasal drone, build to a sound that levels off only when it reaches ecstasy, the kind that accompanies a deep calm.

This energy has a spiritual dynamics, elaborating the symbolist heritage of Monk's vision and, of course, linking it to her choice of Alexandra David-Néel as spiritual double in the opera, a woman whose "aesthetic spiritualism" originated a hundred years ago in the impulses of the symbolist movement. The two women and their enlightenment project interface in the reflection emanating from "atlas," as image and concept, for the family atlas, an obsessive interest of the adolescent David-Néel, now figures on stage in the lighted globe, and it is Monk's appellation for her own spiritual journey in art. Symbolism, with its allegorical imagery and profound faith in nonmaterial reality and the sign, its praise of solitude, and Orientalism, is just as resonant a path for artists now as it was a century ago. What is increasingly clear at this turn of century is symbolism's deep affinity with the poetic side of the theater of images as it has evolved over more than two decades. The only international modernist movement, nonideological in its dreams, symbolism defined an avant-garde style founded in spiritual crisis, in myth rather than history, in the celebration of nature and the senses, in the ideal of universal culture. Its visionary poetics and idealism, joining modernism and medievalism, East and West, art and spirituality in pursuit of ecological consciousness, now quietly breathe in the world's winds of change. In *Atlas*, religiosity accompanies aesthetics, the other face of contemplation, in the heroic quest for beauty. Perhaps this is nothing more or less than the search for form, which is a kind of harmony.

(1992)

The Forest

Robert Wilson and Interculturalism

Natural Selection

"One day I discovered the habits of a porcupine fish," Charles Darwin recorded in his journal while traveling about the world on the *Beagle*. Gilgamesh's Mother relates his curious pleasures in a monologue that precedes Jean-Henri Fabre's lesson on the need for air. Darwin's theory of natural selection finds a playful theatrical allusion in this gathering in *The Forest*, texts and images that have no reason to be together, mating in the same production, wandering in and out of one another's realms. (Theatrical production is always reproduction.) A ballerina walks a lobster, the forest overwhelms a great hall. Even the moon comes down to earth. Words drift through centuries. All life forms cohabit effortlessly in the desert, the city, the forest, the mansion, under ancient or industrial skies. Adaptation is the cornerstone of natural selection.

This theater is one of fortunate hybrids. Here the origin of species is no longer an issue; genre courts possibility, not principle. Animal and human metamorphose, and reptiles, birds, fish, people, and rocks settle into narrative. Words are a form of sedimentation. In this new theatrical enlightenment natural history shares the scene with human history, for an alternative view of culture. Aesthetics is a branch of natural science.

The ecology of theater: Wilson chooses texts and images from the collective ancestry to situate in multiple environments, then documents (stages) their adaptability. The seasons are sensational. His theater has biological perspective. A production is an organism, its very joints called "knee plays." Structure is a body of thought, nature and art inseparable.

Lizard, warrior, sea creature, raven, a Renaissance man, a child called Berlin: the already there is imagined in extraordinary landscapes. Oh, wonderful kind of rapture. Not since surrealism has there been a new visual ethnography.

Linda Alaniz/Martha Swope Associates

History/Memory

Wilson treats history not as a body of fact but as a landscape of experiences. An anthology of images, of texts: knowledge as database. A menu. Food for thought. (There is always a dinner table in the work.) His theater does not make history, only its poetic other side, memory. He lingers in myth, the space between literature and history. Intuition is the way to his encyclopedia, and one must have the watchfulness of an angel in a library. In the great sweep of his search for images in the dreams of cultures, Wilson adds a new chronotope to theater: the archival.

The interplay of history and memory suggests a way to consider the mysterious collaboration of Robert Wilson and Heiner Müller, the mystic and the materialist. Müller wants to be a machine, Wilson is always inventing the wheel. Müller believes in the blood of time, Wilson in the color red. Wilson prefers the cave, Müller the bomb shelter. Wilson loves the moon, Müller the sun. Their work plays out the struggle of the text and the image, or figuration and abstraction, in the art of the twentieth century. In this post-Brechtian world, theater after the final purges from paradise, the collective now only alludes to myth. Symbolism is just an earlier mode of *Gestus*: it depends on the sign of the times. Artaud waits in the shadows with Janus/Chaos, two-faced mask of time. Who better tells the story of the human race?

The Dramaturgy of the Dispersed Text

The cultural displacement of contemporary life finds its double in the lives of texts. These are the dispersed, refugee texts from lost civilizations, those of unknown or forgotten authors, the texts of books languishing on library shelves, texts found in archives, texts exiled into oblivion. They find a home in today's world, preoccupied by restoration.

A Wilson production elaborates distinctions between the "Text" and the "Book." In *The Forest* credit for the text is given to Darryl Pinckney, who wrote several sections, including the knee plays, and Heiner Müller, a portion of whose play *Cement* is used. Pinckney and Müller also collected texts of other writers. The Book is the actual literary document in which texts are arranged and fitted and on which the staging is made. There is also a visual book of lights, costumes, and gestures, research for which is drawn from photography, film, and painting sources. The Book, then, is the basis of the production. Wilson is the only visual artist working in theater in the twentieth century who has a fully developed style conceived over a period of time and embracing every aspect of a work: performance, narrative, design. Once the proscenium arch was thought to reflect the shape of perspective; now, in Wilson's theater, it is the book that shapes the arch.

Wilson's way of making theater, as the act of living and creating in many cultures, finds a parallel in his own displacement, precisely in his artistic emigration from the United States to work in European theaters. He inhabits the cosmopolitan's kind of homelessness, the capacity to live anywhere and nowhere. The natural state of his work is translation. If the idea of the "dispersed" describes the lives of texts, Wilson's own manner of working only stylizes this general condition of literature.

In this collection of texts that shape *The Forest* there is a significant factor at work: the recovery of the dispersed text is not only a way of constructing theatrical narrative but an attitude toward the past as an archive (remembered cultural artifacts). A remarkable hidden order, not mere randomness, characterizes the organization of literary material, as even a few facts drawn from the program and outside research reveal.

Gilgamesh, a Middle Eastern epic dating back to about 2600 B.C. and rewritten by multiple authors over a period of two thousand years, was discovered buried in the ruins of Ashurbanipal's library in Mesopotamia in the middle of the nineteenth century, then deposited in the British Museum. The epic began to be written down only centuries after the invention of writing, on twelve clay tablets. Parts of the text, which has never been completely recovered, were found in other cities besides Nineveh—Ur, Sippar, Uruk, Megiddo, Sultantepe, Ashur—in the languages Sumerian, Akkadian, Hittite. Though *The Forest* is modeled after themes of *Gilgamesh*, it doesn't use the work itself as text material.

Another old text collected for *The Forest* is the *Florentine Codex* (*General History of the Things of New Spain*), the pre-Colombian work originally written in Aztec, with Spanish added later, completed by 1569 by the Spanish missionary Fray Bernardino de Sahagún. Its twelve books were scattered during the Inquisition and found in the 1880s in the Laurentian Library of Florence, where they have remained since the 1790s. This major historical document, whose text is supplemented by visual illustration, may have served as the model for the frescoed ceilings by Buti in the Armory of the Uffizi Gallery.

Two stories by Edgar Allan Poe provide the organizing frame of *The Forest*. "Silence—A Fable," an 1839 work that was originally called "Siope," opens the production. Its Orientalist, stylized setting evokes the ancient world of myth and startling nature, ruled by mysterious forces. In "Shadow—A Parable," from 1835, a fragment of which closes the work, seven men grieve at the ghostly deathbed of a friend during a time of pestilence; outside, the planets cross in an unusual configuration. The actual background was linked to an American cholera epidemic at the time and, coincidentally, the appearance of a comet, which greatly troubled the populace. Poe's tales weave through and around *The Forest*.

(The literary and the visual compel the restless voices of allegory "in the well-remembered and familiar accents of many thousand departed friends," the ending of "Shadow," which concludes *The Forest*. Here one finds resonance in setting this text beside the story of Gilgamesh and Enkidu, perhaps the first story of a great love between two men, and then placing both texts in the context of AIDS. So, too, does one recall that Gilgamesh and Enkidu cut down the cedars of Lebanon to build a city, and the forests are still being cut down to build cities, and the forests are dying . . .)

The only Müller text in the work is the section HERAKLES 2 OR THE HYDRA from his own play *Cement*, which is based on the celebrated Russian novel of 1928 by Gladkov. Herakles had twelve labors, the second in the forest. (By now it should be clear that twelve and seven are recurring numbers in *The Forest*.) The methodology for constructing the visual book follows the same fastidious technique of composition: research culled from books of Oriental art, images from the period of the Industrial Revolution, sources of architecture and painting. Caspar David Friedrich's work suggested backlighting in silhouette for one of the scenes. Perhaps the most intriguing visual source is the book *New and Curious School of Theatrical Dancing* by the Venetian ballet master Gregorio Lambranzi. This recovered text, a manual with fifty engraved plates of dancers, was first published in Nuremberg in 1716, and it was discovered in the British Museum in the first quarter of the twentieth century. The movement, which looks remarkably like postmodern dance, serves as inspiration for the knee plays between the seven acts.

In our world, where time is now told by the rings of trees, the forest of symbols is an archive. Dispersed texts, then, create a mosaic pattern in which the refracted light of ancient suns turns old books into illuminated manuscripts.

Linda Alaniz/Martha Swope Associates

Hands of Time

Splayed fingers on a surface, ravenous fingers, a wrist slightly bent, the palm held sideways, a hand pointed downward, palms turned upside down, arms pointed in opposite directions, one arm at an angle to the body, elbow angled behind the back, an arm a triangle.

Hands are the points of energy in Wilson's work. This is the feeling of portraiture he has brought to the theater (where hands fall down at the sides of the body like defeated lines of dialogue. Or hide under the dining room table, its cloth their shroud). Everything in his theater exists in space. How one looks is what one is. Reality is geometrically beautiful.

These are the most beautiful hands in theater, this theater is hand-made. First it is drawn, then it is staged. Fingers are destiny.

Linda Alaniz/Martha Swope Associates

Economies of Theater

In the world of global trade America is becoming more and more a purchaser of things, less a manufacturer. On the artistic level this situation is reflected in the example of Wilson, who now creates most of his work outside the United States, in countries where the culture industry is heavily subsidized. *The Forest*, then, was experienced in New York as an import, a design from Germany. Many scenes quoted the overall "look" of German theatrical vocabulary, namely, expressionism—the familiar captains of industry, a grid, a cabaret, the Krupp residence, the masklike actors' faces, their language. David Byrne's music alluded to German musical references. The Oriental epic *Gilgamesh* was taken as a starting point for a work that treated the theme of nineteenth-century industrial Germany, for a presentation during the year 1988, when Berlin celebrated its 750th anniversary as a city.

Work is made on the body of a culture, as dance is made on the body of a dancer. Every culture has the self-satisfied feeling of understanding the world, and the world of emotion, through its own artists. Experiences may be "Proustian" in France, "Kafkaesque" in Central Europe, and in the West life itself is more and more described as "Beckettian." But Wilson's success in Europe is due to his Otherness. Aesthetically, he can work anywhere outside his own culture because he lives entirely in artistic process as a form of travel, discovery, sights. His way of working subverts the sense of making and (for audiences) of viewing theater from one's own cultural center. If earlier in this century the avant-garde expressed nationalist tendencies, while at the other end of the spectrum reflecting interculturalism as an avant-garde theme and technique, now at this century's close the intercultural model Wilson presents—work that is literally between cultures—outlines a changing political economy. The worldliness of Wilson points to new possibilities for allegory, in art that lives here and there.

The Fractal Text

Wilson problematizes the issue of rupture, dislocation. His *Forest* is part fable, part fiction, now epic, now science. Genres are temperaments that shout across millennia in long-forgotten grains of the voice. Side by side, underneath, through and on top of each other, words are folded into a promiscuous forest of sounds, echoing the plenitude of species.

This text is *fractal*, chaos theory's word an aesthetic principle. Fractal now a way to tell of, to think about, the surface that is irregular, broken up, nonlinear. The shape of Wilson's book of knowledge: not smooth, casually ornate, crackling with strange attractors. The fractal text is the one without clear definition (border), the text that falls out of a book, an exile from its source. Elastic, punctured, crosshatched by its own inner rhythms of image and sound: pattern inside of pattern, self-similar. At once turbulent and coherent, a self-organizer, infatuated with scale. A theater of process rather than state, of becoming more than being. Pocked with promises of a glance into the texture of infinity. Wilson takes a quantum leap of the theatrical imagination over mountains of well-made play.

He welcomes chaos theory to the theater. A remarkable coincidence: the application of the principle of chaos to a system is *global*, not local. Which is to say that this new knowledge of the way events can be described is unobstructed by borders. Wilson works, theatrically, by the same guidelines: he takes as his laboratory the art and artifacts of the world, measuring them with new technologies of time. His vision is global. A theater of memory, which is a kind of mathematics.

This theatrical model outlines a new (scientific) perspective from which to consider the theme of interculturalism: the intercultural text as fractal.

The Writer, the World

In the year 2000 B.C. an Egyptian scribe lamented: "Would I had phrases that are not known, utterances that are strange, in new language that has not been used, free from repetition, not an utterance which has grown stale, which men of old have spoken."

(1989)

Originally titled "The Forest as Archivo: Robert Wilson and Interculturalism," in "The Interculturalism Issue," *Performing Arts Journal* 33/34.

The Culture of *Perestroika*

As publisher-editors of *PAJ*, Gautam Dasgupta and I visited the Soviet Union in October and November 1988 for an international conference sponsored by the International Theatre Institute in Moscow. During our stay we had an opportunity to join the editor of West Germany's *Theater Heute* magazine, Peter von Becker, for an interview with theater critic Nina Agisheva in her *Pravda* office. Agisheva's comments outline the changes in Russian culture taking place under Gorbachev, with specific reference to the theater.

Attending the ITI Conference were delegates, mainly editors, journalists, and ITI officers, from Western and Eastern Europe, Canada, Scandinavia, America, and, for the first time at such an event, China, to address the topic at hand, "Theatre Art and Mass Media." The event was chaired by Mikhail Shvidkoi, vice president of the ITI Communications Committee and an editor of *Teatr*, the Soviet Union's foremost theater periodical. (Incidentally, our Chinese friends at the conference, in describing the situation there, complained of paper shortages, making it difficult to bring out the 270,000 copies of *Chinese Theatre* each month—and that is only one of China's theater publications. The rest of us, struggling along with audiences in the few to several thousands, had to really stop and think a moment about our intended seminar topic, that is, art and the concept of the "mass.")

During the three days of meetings at the Theatre Union there was a frank exchange on a wide range of topics, given so much urgency in the context of Gorbachev's far-ranging proposals for transforming Soviet policy. The new openness under *perestroika* was sharply contrasted to the strictures in the previous "period of stagnation," as it was termed. Participants in the conference asked what changes in cultural policy had occurred, in what sectors of the arts, and what the new strategies for publication and theatrical production were.

On the first day of our meeting, *Teatr* magazine's editor, Afanasy Salinsky, pinpointed one of the critical issues among theater intellectuals: understanding the difference between theater on the stage and society as cultural spectacle. Gorbachev, it was reported, had recently been quoted in *Der Spiegel* as saying, "Theater is not so interesting compared to all that is happening in society." Shvidkoi, who gave a comprehensive overview of Soviet cultural policy at this time, announced that his magazine had just published an essay entitled "The Theater of Joseph Stalin," and we countered that we were about to publish "The Theatricks of Politics" in the age of Reagan in a forthcoming *PAJ*.

Our meetings were broadened by exchanges outside the conference itself, with colleagues from other parts of Europe. All of us were aware that this was a time of significant shifts in political, economic, cultural, and philosophical attitudes. Gorbachev's policy of *glasnost,* the structural changes in the Eastern European countries, the role of the United States in East-West relations, and the coming erasure of borders, in more ways than one, among the EEC countries in 1992 have contributed to a real feeling of transformation on a global scale. We talked more about culture than about specific works of art.

We, as American theater editors, were mindful of a contingent of theater people who had come to a very different Soviet Union fifty years ago. Harold Clurman, Lee Strasberg, Stella Adler, and many others brought back news of sweeping political visions and artistic revolution as well. Now, once again Americans are traveling to the Soviet Union in large numbers (and Russian artists and administrators are coming here too), but in this postutopian age there are no more illusions, only the great hope of intercultural exchange in the community of artists. The Russians are eager to reenter the world of modern art, to which they have contributed so much — in literature, painting, theater, dance, and, tragically, the lives of many great artists.

In the two weeks that we were in Moscow and Leningrad, we were able to see a dozen productions, a mere sampling of what was available last fall. Among these productions were Aleksandr Galin's Maly Theatre staging by Lev Dodin of *Stars under the Morning Sky*, whose nudity and subject matter concerning Moscow's street sweep of declassé types during the Olympic games signaled a new frankness in the Russian theater; so did the equally naturalistic play critical of contemporary life, *Cemetery*, at the Sovremennik. We attended an extremely well-acted production of Mrozek's *Emigrants* at the Theatre of Man (one of the many studio theaters that have burgeoned in recent years) and a *"perestroika"* version of Mayakovsky's *Bathhouse*, complete with a rock band, on the stage of the Theatre for Young Audiences.

Outstanding among the works we saw were two earlier productions of Yuri Lyubimov's, still playing at the Taganka. His *Mother* (based on Gorky) and the anti-Stalinist play *The House on the Embankment* were especially powerful in their staging of large casts and exquisite timing and use of sound. Also at the Taganka there was Anatoly Efros's *Misanthrope*, given a gimmicky Pirandellian twist, with an oddly out-of-sorts jazz soundtrack.

What would a trip to Moscow be without a production of Chekhov at the Moscow Art Theatre? We saw a good but old-fashioned *Ivanov* there, notable for the link the acting style still kept in its use of caricature types in secondary roles, as attested by the actors' photos from MAT productions since Stanislavsky's time lining the lobby walls.

The performances were supplemented by visits to museums, the most eventful of which was the opportunity to see an exhibit of Soviet art of the twenties and thirties a few days before it was to open at Leningrad's Russian Museum. A director of the museum arranged for us to be escorted privately through the galleries. Most of the paintings were literally on the floor or stacked against walls. We saw works by Puni, Sashin, Malevich, Stepanova, Suetin, Annenkov, Exter, Goncharova, many paintings that had not been seen for fifty or sixty years.

What surprised us most of all was that the cubo-futurist or suprematist vocabulary of the avant-garde abstract art of the teens and twenties still retained its modernist technique, at the same time that it was switching to proletarian and industrial themes and iconography, into the thirties. Then it abruptly stopped, and there was never again any hope for this kind of art and the artists who made it. Only now is this work coming out of hiding.

Later, back in Moscow, we attended a large exhibition of paintings and drawings by the little-known artist Pavel Filonov, who died in the siege of Leningrad. His designs were seen in the brilliant avant-garde productions of his day. Seeing Russian artworks in their own setting made all the more indelible their presence in what we think of as modernism.

It is difficult to convey the immense feeling of sadness one experiences when confronted with the great, gaping craters at the center of Russian culture. The attempt to search out and rebond with this lost heritage has given artists a great deal of hope in *perestroika*. Gorbachev has not yet brought economic change to the Soviet Union, and that may ultimately decide his fate in this country so desperately in need of day-to-day necessities. But as one of our Russian friends said of the intelligentsia, which has tried to keep the culture alive in small groups, among friends, when it was not possible to do so publicly, we can do without bread if we can have our books. His words were no attempt to be romantic or sentimental, but simply and overwhelmingly a reflection of what they had learned they could live without and what they could not.

Interview at *Pravda*

Theater critic Nina Agisheva talks about contemporary theater in the Soviet Union.

Q: Let's begin with some basic information. How long have you been working for *Pravda?*

A: I've been here for fourteen years, since 1974.

Q: How did you come to *Pravda?*

A: I graduated from Moscow University, in the faculty of journalism. Several people from different universities were invited here. It was just a matter of injecting fresh blood into an old organism. Since then we've never had a similar situation here. While studying at the university, for five years I had specialized in theater, so I was invited to the culture department here.

I'd written a dissertation on the theme of modern Russian theater before the Revolution. My interests now are the Silver Age, which is what we call the prerevolutionary theater, and the contemporary theater. To my mind, the prerevolutionary period of Meyerhold is more interesting than after the Revolution. At that time there were many outstanding artists, such as Bely, Blok, Briusov—also many interesting theater ideas.

Q: Earlier you said your arrival signaled the infusion of "new blood." What happened to the "old blood"?

A: Unfortunately, maybe four-fifths still exist here. Three retired on pension, another became ill. But we didn't have any ideological change here. That happened when Abalkin was dismissed from the paper.

Q: He was the very reactionary head. The head of the cultural division?

A: Yes, for about fifteen years, until 1974. It was a long and morose period for culture, even when he left, as we had to publish a lot of articles, despite the fact we were opposed to such information. It was the highest moral deed at that time just to avoid writing in that situation. You're told to write such an article concerning a certain theme. So it's best to avoid it, not to write at all. But we didn't have any possibility to help even one or two theaters.

Q: In the seventies did you write articles that weren't published?

A: A lot. . . . I had written two or three articles that it was impossible to publish even in the time of *perestroika*. When that was started in 1985, it was the same situation. Only the last two years can I boast that I don't have any such articles.

Q: How many staff members are there at the paper? What is the extent of arts coverage?

A: About two hundred. We're used to publishing our material five or six times a week in different sections. As far as theater is concerned, two or three times per month.

Q: So there is no specific theater page?

A: No. We are struggling against this. . . . *Pravda* is authorized to publish a lot of official information.

Q: You said that around 1985 you wrote articles that were not published. What sort of discussion did you have with the editors when they were refused? Why couldn't they be published?

A: I have my own chief editor and didn't have any contact with the paper's editor.

Q: Has there been since *perestroika* a meeting with all the staff members where they could argue and discuss things?

A: We have special short meetings, and here the staff members are involved. Our party congresses are conducted in a new way now . . . Very often the reason [for not publishing a certain article] was just the opinion of a certain boss. For example, everybody knows his opinion of, say, Lyudmila Petruchevskaya, and the opinion of this boss was known to the editor of *Pravda*. He told that to my chief editor, who told me. They are not in the habit of explaining reasons. Unfortunately, that was the style of our life. We used to keep silent about some basic questions. We didn't have any principal exchange of views, and it was difficult, because we used to struggle with the air, not a specific person. It's a very complicated situation. Many people of my generation failed—very talented people—they drank a lot or changed their profession.

Q: Nina, you look like a very brave lady. Now, if there were two productions in the Moscow theater, one social realist but new, perhaps dealing with *perestroika*, and say there was another production that was more formalistic and dealt with Jewish questions or whatever, which would you review?

A: For *Pravda* I would prepare a review for the first production. I would write about the second one in *Moscow News*.

Q: So there is another newspaper that deals with semiofficial culture.

A: *Moscow News* is not semiofficial culture, just official culture. But the majority of people who write may be opposed to it. As for me, I agree with their point of view 99 percent of the time. I'm very grateful to *Pravda* that in all these years of stagnation I was permitted to publish my articles not only in *Pravda* but in *Moscow News*.

Q: These would be articles against *Pravda* policy, and you could still publish them in *Moscow News* and the editors here did not bother you?

A: It's a delicate question. My bosses just pretended that they didn't know about it.

Q: We've been told that there is no more official censorship in the field of art.

A: I cannot say categorically that we don't have censorship at all, because there are a lot of the same people [from the earlier period] who work at the Ministry of Culture, and they try to interfere.

Q: But the theaters do not have to ask to show their work? What about film and literature—can you compare these? Is theater the freest medium now?

A: No. As far as the movies are concerned, it is much better there. In literature it is worse than theater. In one of our biggest film studios, Mosfilm, there are five absolutely independent concerns, and they are free to do anything. They don't have any controls. I can mention a number of extremely good films, but I cannot say the same of theater.

Q: If you were to cite some real taboos for artists that might occur in the coming years, what are they? What is not allowed in theater? I was told that Joseph Brodsky's play *Marbles* has a scene of masturbation and that this scene must be censored. Is sexuality going to remain a forbidden area, and are other areas forbidden?

A: Sex and violence. We are very limited in showing such things. Now, there's a very popular production in Moscow, *Ward 6* [an adaptation of Chekhov's story], staged by Yuri Yeremin. There is a lot of naturalism and physiological details in it. Don't forget about our Russian tradition. Before the revolution we didn't have anything of this kind on our stage.

Q: Is there any significance attached to women working in the theater? By that I mean is there a women's theater, or feminism, or issues that women wish to address as directors or playwrights?

A: Emancipation is not limited by women's fate. During the period of stagnation, women were more able to stand this period than men. Now we have very interesting women playwrights—Lyudmila Petruchevskaya, Lyudmila Rasumovskaya, and Nina Sadur. Despite the fact that they are very different, I think they are the most talented playwrights at the moment. They write about women's fate, but a lot of psychological, moral, and social problems appear connected with it.

I'm not interested in feminism itself. It seems to me it is not up to date. The world is tired of an exclusive showing of emancipation. But at the same time, there are many problems, in our society too, that belong only to women. I like this theme, and I write about it. In a recent issue of *Teatr* I wrote about Petruchevskaya and the problem I've just mentioned.

Q: Is there anybody who is forming a new policy for cultural affairs besides Gorbachev?

A: We don't have the second Lunacharsky . . . you know our administrators in power then [the period of stagnation] used to govern culture too. They failed in different fields of our social life—in agriculture, in the economy, in culture. In such a society, it is difficult to point to a person you are describing. The relationship of the artist and power is very dramatic in any society.

It was a great unhappiness to all of us that for a long time we had treated art itself as just a part of a socioeconomic system. Therefore, in our estimation of art ideological attitudes prevail. There are some moments that we as critics used to call "vulgar tautology." It's a great problem of our art and critics, and only now have we started to step aside from these methods. You know, Gorbachev speaks of the priority of our human values over classes. The subject of art is always human values. All our best artists were involved in this.

Q. Do you have to be a party member to work at *Pravda*?

A: I am a party member. We have some who are not . . . it's not necessary. But the majority are.

Q: I look at your monthly theater calendar for Moscow, with so many productions, and yet you have only two articles a month on theater. You also cover theater in the whole Soviet Union. Who decides what appears in the paper?

A: The problem is that it is not only Moscow. Our country is very big, and there are the republics and theatrical regions—Georgia, the Baltic, Leningrad. These are the most interesting theatrical regions. Naturally, one has to choose between theatrical events. Before *perestroika*, in order to write an article about a performance, it would have to be a political one, such as *We'll Win* by Mikhail Shatrov. Now we write articles about Anatoly Vasiliev's *Six Characters in Search of an Author* [at the Taganka], which wasn't possible before. I can say that concerning the change in attitudes toward art itself, people are starting to recollect that in art we may feel some hope, some magic. Even an esoteric approach.

Q: Are you saying that before *perestroika* it was a mandate of sorts to only review social realist plays, and now you can review more formalist plays?

A: Of course, in many cases we wrote about political performances, but if it was necessary to publish a separate, large article, we used to write about works with a social approach.

Q: Earlier you mentioned Bely and Briusov, who wrote symbolist plays, at the far end of the spectrum from social realism. Could you review those plays then? Were they performed?

A: We've had much discussion about social realism. A majority of very intelligent people think that such a phenomenon doesn't exist at all. There is modernism, realism, existentialism, avant-garde, but there is the view that such a phenomenon as social realism is just artificial. Of course, we can write freely about Andreyev, Briusov, Bely. In principle, we can write of dissidents who've left our country and are still alive. It's easier to write of dead writers.

Q: I was told that before *perestroika*, before the studios became state-supported theaters, for example, The Theatre of Man, it was an underground theater.

A: We cannot say that it was an underground theater, because some actors from the Moscow Art Theatre were involved there. But we have an underground theatre. Not long ago in Leningrad there was a festival of such theaters. Students in my theatre seminar are very impressed by this theater. Boris Yukananov is their beloved director.

Q: How do you define underground?

A: There are some performances where there is no language, only visual art and music. They publish their own journals.

Q: Where do they perform?

A: In Moscow, Leningrad, . . . big towns. They perform in small rooms.

Q: Is this underground covered in *Pravda* or other papers?

A: *Pravda* used to feature a lot of material about experimental studios, but speaking of the underground theater, this doesn't mean that it is banned.

Q: Are you saying that the underground theater is your avant-garde theater?

A: To my mind, it's just a pure laboratory theater.

Q: When we saw the Squat Theatre in Budapest several years ago it was in a room at their home. No one could talk, no one could clap. If it had been found out that they were doing theater at their home, these people would have been put in jail. But this is not the same as your "underground"?

A: No . . . No.

Q: Is the theatrical underground in the Soviet Union the equivalent of *samizdat?*

A: No. If some underground such as this exists, I don't know of it. I've never heard of any underground theater that it was necessary to ban, though our official productions were banned very often.

Q: Did Russian theater artists know of the Squat Theatre when they were living in Budapest?

A: No. We lack information, and we are not well informed about Western theater or theater in those countries closer to us. We rarely travel.

Q: If you decide now that you want to see theater in Paris or New York, can you travel on your own, or do you need a festival invitation?

A: I can go to any festival if I get a special official invitation sent here, and only in that case.

Q: I have one more question about the underground theater. You mentioned that this theater uses images more than language. If you choose now, in the age of *perestroika*, to do a play by Vassily Aksyonov or Joseph Brodsky, will those plays be done in the underground, as you are calling it, or done by Sovremennik or Moscow Art Theatre or Taganka?

A: Now we've got theatrical experiments here, and these theaters are used to choosing plays for themselves. They are free to stage anything they want because they have nothing to do with the Ministry of Culture—a great victory for the time being in our theater. Before, any minor official from the ministry could ban a performance, not only Aksyonov or Brodsky but even Chekhov, if from his point of view he disliked it. You cannot even imagine the conditions under which our best artists lived here.

Q: We are told that Heiner Müller's GERMANIA DEATH IN BERLIN is going to be performed in Moscow.

A: There's a misunderstanding. A West German production of the play will be at the festival of German theater coming to Moscow in January [1989]. We expect Peter Stein, too. . . . I was in Omsk, in Siberia, and local theater people there asked me to find out about these performances. Foreign theater is of great interest. We haven't seen any productions by Brook, Mnouchkine, Strehler . . .

Q: It seems as if a much more avant-garde type of *mise-en-scène* has been possible outside Moscow and Leningrad. For example, at the State Theatre of Lithuania, where Eimuntas Nekrosius directs. Is that still true?

A: First of all, our Baltic republics have their own very good, very rich theatrical tradition, and during the period of stagnation they could do more than those in Moscow. At that time they staged Beckett, Pinter, Mrozek. Our theater suffers from a deep crisis, due to so much politicization. During the period of stagnation Efremov and Lyubimov used to give people some fresh air, and at the theater the audience had the chance to show their social attitude by reacting to this or that situation. Now such forms of work are no longer a surprise, and we haven't found anything new. Vasiliev said those directors were just a rehearsal, simply steps in which the future generation will pass. Maybe this time only a future generation can stage some aesthetic discoveries, but we're too weak and helpless now. You know, we have lost a lot of the culture of acting and the culture of directing. We need time.

Q: In the school where you studied, are constructivism and futurism taught? Will that tradition ever again be rediscovered?

A: There are many formal tendencies, not only in theater but in painting too. I saw a production in Omsk staged by Vasiliev's pupil there that was based on Dario Fo. It was an attempt at a new aesthetic formalism.

Q: Do you think that the path for the future will be played out as the choice between Stanislavsky or Meyerhold?

A: I think that the whole world of art is characterized now by postmodernism, that it just derives a lot of styles and tendencies. The future theater will take something from Stanislavsky, from Tairov, from Michael Chekhov, from Meyerhold. And only on this basis will something happen.

Q: Earlier you mentioned that people looked toward art as a kind of magic to restore the spirit. In your society during the period of stagnation, was it art and the artist that essentially kept a pre- or proto-*perestroika* underneath the culture? Was it a parallel culture underneath the official culture?

May I add one thing. . . . If you see when certain plays that are now performed were written, you will always find dates such as 1979, 1980. Many of these plays were written in the Brezhnev period, and some were even performed in the very late period of stagnation. So it seems that the way for *perestroika* was already prepared in the cultural field before it surfaced in the official political field.

A: You are quite right. It was during the period of stagnation that we had people who were not conformist at all. As a rule, their destiny was very tragic. Some emigrated to the Western world. But of course they had prepared *perestroika*. Not only the intelligentsia but the common people started to realize that it is impossible to live as they lived before. In particular, Lyubimov, with his productions at the Taganka Theatre, prepared this moment. And for this new consciousness Vysotsky's songs were extremely popular. Of course, it is our problem that Lyubimov is far away from our country and Vysotsky is dead.

(1989)

Berlin Theatertreffen, 1984

|||||||| For years the German theater has been looked upon as the enviable model of government-subsidized theater. Surely it has the biggest theater budgets in the world, and its productions display the most lavish use of technical and design effects, by any standards. American artists who have worked in German theater have often exclaimed that there is more money around than anyone knows what to do with. How to invest it? But the more troubling aspect of theater in Germany is the seeming impossibility of any renegade, nonestablishment theater. Instead, all activities are dependent upon, nourished and bolstered by the state treasury and central and local cultural policy. Perhaps at a later date the results may be promoted abroad through the programs and funding of the Goethe House. German theater can have no real rebellious aspect even when productions or plays try to be politically radical, as they often are. All theater that has a cultural impact still occurs in an establishment context, with all the trappings of Culture by a state that absorbs any attack on its structure, be it by Handke, Fassbinder, Hochhuth, Kroetz, Müller, or Peymann.

In this context, seeing Genet's *The Blacks* in a Schaubühne production directed by Peter Stein, known for his radical interpretations of old and new plays, was much less than provocative. Though not part of the Theatertreffen (a yearly festival of the ten best German productions), it was playing at the same time in Berlin. The whole ambience of going to the Schaubühne, now that it has moved from the working-class district of Kreuzberg to the center of Berlin, is like spending an evening at the local exemplar of a hotel chain rather than in a comfortable pension. There is something to the architecture of feeling.

The Blacks seemed absurd in this new Schaubühne home: black drummers entertaining a bourgeois audience before the start of a play by white actors playing blacks playing revolution; white audiences sipping from small coffee cups at intermission, perhaps glancing through the elaborate program, with its commentary on white colonialism, "negritude and humanism," and the attached pamphlet of economic statistics on African nations (contrasted with those on West Germany); the centerpiece of this foldout program, which would make an American dramaturg's mouth water, a large color map of Africa.

How is one to view Genet's subversive "ceremony"—it is not really a play, but a prologue to a future (revolutionary) play—about the enactment of social roles? The German context is ambiguous: unlike France, which inspired this drama, Germany never had an imperial empire, and even the obvious Turkish reference point doesn't easily equate itself to the situation. Stein's *Blacks* didn't really perform a "clown show," but rather a more serious tragedy in a post-Beckettian landscape. At the end of the play the actors walked into the deep space of the fully opened stage to confront a huge, lighted map of Africa, their backs to the audience. Subversive art in this theatrical jargon of authenticity seems awfully silly, even pretentious: it makes one wonder how serious, truthful theater, more than simply the representation of roles, can be done, should be done, in civic theaters. A theater that is only about pretending is not enough; it has to be more an act of criticism. If the contours of Genet's play have formally softened through age, rhetorically it is still shocking. It is a theater that does not belong in a playhouse except to show up that absurdity.

The dramatist who has taken Genet's rhetoric, and his form, further is Heiner Müller, who now appears to reside both in East and West Berlin. For him there is scarcely a difference between each city's illusions of the fourth wall. His DESPOILED SHORE MEDEAMATERIAL LANDSCAPE WITH ARGONAUTS was directed by Manfred Karge and Matthias Langhof, in a production that originated at the Schauspielhaus in Bochum, where Müller's work usually premieres in the West. Müller's vision that in one devastating stroke links myth and history in Jason's walk through the ruins of East Berlin is also, like Genet's, a theater of death.

The directors chose for the production a closed, boxlike environment papered in foil with a tin-can-covered floor; a ship, an airplane, and a sink the images in the post-Holocaust landscape. Here in this blood-red, metallic environment sat Jason and Medea (and occasionally her nurse) like expressionistic dummies struggling to come to life.

But the confined space of the production was too constricting for Müller's work, even antithetical to this theatrical idea of landscape, which is part of the ecology of his theater. His plays aren't square, they are horizontal; they need height and depth for the poetic field of words that flow from his characters like aged tears. Another Müller play, GUNDLING'S LIFE FREDERICK OF PRUSSIA LESSING'S SLEEP DREAM SCREAM, playing concurrently at the Schiller Theatre, though not as part of the Theatertreffen, was presented in the big, open space of the large state theater. Here Müller's use of classical forms to criticize the language of the classics was clear as a political and aesthetic strategy. (GUNDLING . . . was the basis for the Cologne section of Robert Wilson's the CIVIL wars, also seen at this festival.) In both cases, Müller's plays were acted too representationally, and the visual aspects were more de-sign than landscape; it seems that the German theater is not ready for Heiner Müller. His extraordinary dramatic vision overpowers conven-tions of theater through its sheer mythic implosion, and in this respect Wilson is his natural ally in the creation of a new stage language.

One of the attempts to break through the conventions of German theater is the work of the Bremer Tanztheater, under the direction of Reinhild Hoffman, whose aesthetics are linked stylistically to the work of Pina Bausch. In a series of eight vignettes, the company's piece Callas played with the idea of theatricality and quoted Callas's great roles. Much of Callas was genuinely witty and engaging, though the imagery was often too literary in that it didn't trust free-floating languages of the stage but instead felt compelled to present scenes with a linear, narra-tive obstinacy. It is important for German theater that Hoffman's work, and Bausch's too, helps expand the possibilities of theater and dance in the metamorphosis of German taste. But in the history of the perform-ing arts, after the Ridiculous theater, pop art, and the Judson Dance movements, Callas can best be viewed in a geopolitical perspective, culturally rooted.

Geopolitically is perhaps also the fairest way to view the Austrian writer Thomas Bernhard, represented in the Theatertreffen by Bochum's production of his *Appearances are Deceiving*. Bernhard's plays are about language and role-playing, specifically the social language of being a cultured German. In his most recent play, the virtually alternating monologues, at times duets, of two brothers, one a retired juggler and the other a former actor, create a universe of words out of their understanding of the meaning of life and art, on the occasion of a beloved woman's death.

Bernhard is a master of the short, ironic phrase that aphoristically articulates a history of German character in the history of a life. But clearly, he is a boulevard Beckett in this play—here are Beckett-type characters on the way to their years *in extremis*—a small play, overproduced and overdesigned in Claus Peymann's production, which apparently was meant as a vehicle for Minetti as the one-time juggler, also alluded to in the play in a double entendre.

In the final analysis, how does one measure the political economy of German theater? Even if growth rates are up, more people employed, and exports thriving, one has to deal with deficits that exist side by side with the conspicuous consumption if theater is to have more meaning than as a line item on a budget. That theater now subliminally senses its problematic status in contemporary culture is demonstrated by the fact that throughout the West it is taking theatricality, the very essence of social role-playing and its representation, as subject matter: now staging and writing situate themselves as acts of theater. For German artists it is no longer a question how to make a living in theater but how to make a life there. And for German audiences, as for those elsewhere, the question is how to experience that shared life.

(1984)

Isak Dinesen in Three Parts

Prologue

Dear Hanne,
On my desk sit a few stones I picked up on the beach across from Rung-
stedlund the last time I was in Denmark. Do you remember? Two years
ago I had only a passing interest in Isak Dinesen—Karen Blixen, to you
Danes—so I did not stop to see her home there, nor the beech tree that
shelters her grave. Now I must ask these stones to conjure her up for me—
the sound of the Sound, the whisk of the air, the restless water that slinks
back and forth from Denmark to Sweden. "Where does this water live?"
her Farah would have said. The stones are pastel like Danish evening
light, and only slightly harsh to the touch, like the softest grade of sand-
paper. I wonder if she once picked them up and rolled them around in her
hand, vowels that might have told a story. More likely, she told them one.

How does one tell a story of Isak Dinesen? For her the finest tale was
the silence of the blank page. I look at this white silent sky before me, I
try to read its transparency, to glimpse her image, elusive as a firefly that
sets off intermittent sparks in dark night. Like all writing one longs to live
in, the more comfortable it feels, the more quickly it vanishes, as if it were
an extraordinary sound in a landscape that leaves one helpless to search
out its source.

O Isak Dinesen, on which of these little pebbles, compelled to act the
part of runic stones, is your life written?

A Writer, A Story

One day in Africa, as she lay deathly ill from an accidental overdose of arsenic, Karen Blixen recalled a passage in Alexandre Dumas's *La Reine Margot* in which the king is cured from arsenic poisoning by a concoction of milk and egg whites. It was not the last time writing saved her life. Of course, the humor of this *opera buffa* would not have been lost on the distraught woman, who lay in bed, surrounded by her worried servant chorus.

European culture was always the ironic root of the African bush she inhabited, for although Blixen went to Kenya to escape the old Europe that had produced her, along with her china, silver, and hardwood furniture, she took its repository of texts, its myths, and her own itinerant mind, which was a remarkable center where paganism, Protestantism, and romanticism flourished in triangular splendor. It was a very special, come-and-gone life of modernism poised between two worlds—the overcultured and the underdeveloped—that Blixen would live between two wars. She was not merely a woman but a world.

The young lady who traveled to Africa in 1914 and married the Baron Bror von Blixen-Finicke, whom she did not love, had that Chekhovian blues characteristic of listless, longing womanhood dying of a nineteenth-century obsolescence in the best castles, manor houses, and mansions Denmark could offer. The three sisters were educated at home, and one of them, Karen, left Denmark and Europe: it would irrevocably change her life and make her the most celebrated Dane of letters in the twentieth century. She was liberated—by disease, violence, and the sheer struggle to survive—in the Ngong hills of Kenya. It is no small irony that when Hemingway received the Nobel prize for literature in 1954 he generously announced that it should have gone to the woman who was now known to the world as Isak Dinesen. She was, after all, a lion hunter. (Another woman whose writing Hemingway admired was Beryl Markham, who as a child ran barefoot in the African wild with young Masai warriors.) Bror Blixen became Hemingway's model for the title character in the "Short, Happy Life of Francis Macomber." These were no ordinary people, but the stuff of myth.

Baroness Blixen was a woman who could ride the open plains where no human had ever been, wearing a string of pearls; who could drink a toast from a crystal goblet to celebrate a lion hunt in terrain so unknown even water had not yet traveled there. She could play on her gramophone Stravinsky's *Petrouchka* outdoors of an afternoon and later that evening put on a silver brocade gown fashioned in Paris to watch an ancient Kikuyu ritual celebrating a simple song of harvest time. She could easily shoot a gun at a lion but not a film of one ("I do not like photography at all"). If, as Cioran observed, the human race has progressed from agriculture to paradox, then surely this scenario was played out on her African farm. Yes, God could have Paradise if she could have Ngong.

Isak Dinesen, for such is her name in the world of art, was of that generation of artists born in 1885 who straddled the dying Europe of the nineteenth century as if it were a horse they were riding all the way to the next century. And in her own switch from riding sidesaddle to spreading her legs apart luxuriously over the horse's back can be read the freedom she found in Africa. It was freedom and space to create a new self. (Curiously, Scandinavian women, real or fictive, have slipped in and out of the last hundred years of history to give the West its idea of the modern woman.)

Dinesen joined the romantic longing of an earlier age to a modernist sensibility that would organize itself around ideas of writing, performance, and God—the latter combining them in his capacity as the first storyteller, the first actor. For Dinesen, his earthly representative would be the dandy, a heroic aesthete. She herself was one, perhaps the last of the female dandies, along with Rachilde, Djuna Barnes, and Gertrude Stein. To be a dandy is to have a personal attitude toward performance, the greatest role being the construction of a persona. Already this is life in fictional time.

Yet Dinesen did not inhabit the world of literary fiction so much as she attached herself to a long line of storytellers that included, besides God, Scheherazade. There is a difference between storytelling and fiction. The pleasure of storytelling is the retelling of a past event, while the pleasure of fiction remains the organization of a new narrative world. The world of the storyteller resides in the imaginary or absent Other to whom the story is addressed: a longing for company is part of its feeling. Therefore, the story is friendlier, more desirous, more seductive, more theatrical. Storytelling embraces the idea, even more the necessity, of the human *voice* as presence, in the story itself. The voice, then, acts as a mask. Grounded in orality, that happy state of immediacy, its life as literature comes later.

When Blixen began to write down stories, first on the farm in Africa, she contrived a voice for herself as the voice/author in the story; and from 1931, at home in Denmark, she chose a new name—Isak Dinesen (the initials "I. D." relate to the provocative issue of identification)—and a new language, English, while she lived in her own country, Denmark. There are, of course, other writers who mastered a foreign language as a new literary field once they left their native country: Conrad, Nabokov, and Joseph Brodsky come quickly to mind. But to write in another language in your own country is an act that lifts writing into the realm of ontology. Dinesen wrote the long, liquid line of a woman filled with desire, loss. "The eloquence of grief is boundless and infinitely inventive," mused Kierkegaard, who taught Dinesen the meaning of *or* when *either* reaches its limits. Dinesen's writing is so sensual, so erotic, precisely because it is filled with whispered longing. Eroticism appears in a life that imagines absences. Where soft winds move restless seas under a moonmask. Dinesen was delighted with a good friend who observed that she was so sensual, but so little sexual, for she preferred Diana to Venus. Living opposite the Sound (Oresund), her own stories came to be dominated by rhythm, by sound (the irony of the English pun would not have been lost on her), which is to say, the voice. Surely it was the writing of a woman who loved music.

English had a special place in her imagination. Not only was it an international language in which to reach more readers but it was a language in which, in Africa, Dinesen learned the language of freedom. It was a striking gesture of rebellion to refuse Danish and its system of thought—the mother tongue and the mother with whom she had a lifelong struggle of conflicting values—Danish life itself, as provincial, simply not the cosmopolitan language of her new identity (I. D.) or refusal of identity (it can be read two ways). Her first book, *Seven Gothic Tales*, was published in America in 1934, before it was published in Denmark. Even now she is known in Denmark as Karen Blixen, still attached to the name of her former husband and his social status. In Denmark she was a baroness, but in America simply a writer. If Danish circumscribed her social language, English charted her imagination, and together they formed a dialectical view of conscience, the one answerable to society, the other to dreams. It was Marguerite Yourcenar who cautioned, "The world of sensual realities is hedged about with prohibitions, the most dangerous of which are perhaps linguistic." (Perhaps there is a parallel in the writing life of authors such as Yourcenar and Dinesen, who were raised by nineteenth-century-bred Romantic fathers they adored and whose inner life attracted them more than the socially restricted life of women in that age.) In her notebooks Dinesen wrote both in Danish and in English; it would be interesting to see which language embodied the important concepts and issues in her writing. Clearly, her choice of language was an attitude toward the social life of words, just as in her story "Sorrow-Acre" an uncle and his nephew slip in and out of French and Danish when they change topics of conversation.

Though her desire begins in the English language, it does not end there. Diction and genre were also to have a language. Dinesen wrote her African memoirs in a plainspoken, direct tone, unlike the winding, highly literary movement of the fiction. Furthermore, she never set any fiction in black Africa; the storytelling had a European setting, with a few Mohammedan exceptions. She separated the real and fictional in her personal geography and in her life: her characters must always know the difference between what is their real life and what is a fictionalized treatment of it. She would come to organize her writing around the quadrangle of sensibilities that included Denmark, Africa, Italy, and Persia, each land a distinct world of sensuality, of sociability. Dinesen's whole being was organized around her use and attitude toward language; her stories became stylized languages of feeling.

If Dinesen was careful to distinguish between kinds of writing, she also distinctly separated speech and writing. Even as an old woman she preferred the thrill of telling stories to an audience to the fate of "printed matter." Her conception of the story finds its elaboration in the Platonic preference for speech over writing, which is to say, memory over documentation: presence not absence. For storytelling preserves the historical link between people and ages, in the imagination of a word remembered. In the hierarchy of forms, a storyteller/narrator takes on the status of an omniscient, guiding spirit who knows the whole story before it is revealed in writing. If it is not always interested in human psychology, it does linger over perspective. Perhaps fiction is the more open, critical form, while storytelling accepts human destiny.

Dinesen was a precursor of the modernist storyteller, in the self-conscious line that leads to Borges and Calvino. She did not, as Calvino would at times, make of the text a game, though she was playful and observant of life's comedy of manners; but as he would later, she often put stories inside stories inside stories, set in a faraway past. Perhaps Dinesen is closer to the baroque spirit of Borges, which magically translates myth and ancient patterns of language and thought in a ravishing alchemy of the word. Coincidentally, she used her syphilis the way Borges used his blindness, as a symbology of disease that separated her from the circumstances of the external world, a purification of the senses, as it were. (So long ago, Nietzsche called for a physiology of aesthetics, and still little more has been contemplated than the crossovers between madness and art. The body of the author waits patiently to be noticed in the body of writing.)

Dinesen is a bridge from the oral tradition of ancient, anonymous authors to the modernist author of the twentieth century, the line that extends from epic to text. Paradoxically, no other self-conscious modern writer of stories was so steeped in the ancient beliefs, myth, symbolist fantasy, and aristocratic values. (Eliot combined modernism, royalism, and religion in less sensual ways.) Dinesen illumines the contemporary link between the impulses of symbolism (the sacred world of the sign) and anthropology (the world of primitive feeling) as a structure of images repudiating the material world in favor of mystery, spirit. The symbolist aspect of her work suggests a way to understand how the rhetoric of religion enters the world of letters, in the modern sense. Her religion, however, was one of Art. All things—objects, places, trees, even color—roamed in the world of spiritual values. She was drawn to the essences of things more than to the things themselves.

It was a natural move from the act of storytelling to a philosophy of literary form that would announce itself in the stories. What comes with grace and ease to the self-conscious writer is a taste for the ornate that exults in a study of style against the background of historical time. Dinesen's skill as a painter transferred to the stories in the attention to design, the line that merged with the word, the feeling for space, the voluptuous symmetries that act as echoes in her gorgeous, limpid prose. They contoured her pastoral worlds, their romance and special beauty. When *Ehrengard*'s Casanova comes upon his love bathing naked in a mountain lake one fragrant night, the scene is set in classical motifs. It might be Diana at her bath painted by Claude Lorrain. The Romantic mind loves the idea of ruins—physical, social, psychic. If, as Walter Benjamin noted, "allegories are, in the realm of thought, what ruins are in the realm of things," then her attraction to allegory is inseparable from her sense of aesthetics (which included, on occasion, adopting the mask of Lord Byron, that lover of ruins).

Perhaps there is not so wide an abyss between Romantic ruins and poststructuralist traces. The tales debate and suggest positions on all aspects of writing: politics and style, the real and the fictional, interpretation, authorship, reception, intertextuality. Dinesen even wrote some of the same characters into several of the stories, as if the world were a small one where they might meet. From another perspective, perhaps it was the joy of spending time in the company of good friends, a reflection of the great value she placed on friendship, now transferred to the story. Just as Dinesen turned to Dumas for help in her arsenic cure, she would look to other literary figures for spiritual guidance. Only a refined, confident mind could announce, "All my life I have held that you can class people according to how they may be imagined behaving to King Lear." The Danish king Frederick IX, who in the author's lifetime rode through the streets of Copenhagen in an open carriage, did not partake of the same tragic order of things, his own daughters lovingly at home in the palace to greet him on his return. Still, Dinesen preferred monarchs and artists to the bourgeoisie ("I cannot live with the middle class"), and it was in Lear, a man who would not listen to reason, that kingliness and the critique of illusion came together in the struggle to live amidst a crumbling world order. Lear, like Dinesen herself, tried to live in a modern society whose horizon lacked regal latitude. Was it madness?

Of course, Shakespeare was never far from her thoughts, for she lived between Amalienborg Palace and Hamlet's castle. For she who was to return home to Denmark, brought down from the heights of Africa to sea level, then to start a new life at the age of forty-six, cultured but untrained for anything but a sensible marriage (and even that she did not make), there was always the nagging question, If to be, how? ("It is really very difficult to see what if anything I could do in this world. . . . I have wondered whether I could learn to cook in Paris for a year or two, and then perhaps get a post in a restaurant or a hotel. . . . I have started to write a book.") She chose a life of writing.

The stories, worlds imagined by a woman of rococo dreams and starlit nights, had to account for themselves, just as she did, every moment of her life and theirs. One of the mottoes she lived by: "Je responderay." To respond is to bring thought to action.

"The literature of individuals, if we may call it so—is a noble art, a great, earnest and ambitious human product. But it is a human product. The divine art is the story. . . . A story . . . has a hero to it, and you will see him clearly, luminous, and as upon a higher plane. . . . But by the time when the new literature shall reign supreme, and you will have no more stories, you will have no more heroes."

"The Cardinal's First Tale"

How like you to have a cardinal give a lesson in writing. For you, realism was a sin; only in the heroic tale does one find grace. "I would like to be a Catholic priest," you once wrote. Only a life devoted to God or art frees one from the world of everyday things, free to pursue the real instead of reality.

"Who then . . . tells a finer tale than any of us? Silence does. And where does one read a deeper tale than upon the most perfectly printed page of the most precious book? Upon the blank page."

"The Blank Page"

In your sensual way, you compare the sheet of the bridal bed (in this story framed as a matter of honor by old Portuguese families) to a sheet of paper. Sexuality and writing— it isn't only the French who have thought of that. A sheet of paper and a bedsheet, each an unraked stage of dreams. The sheet unites nature and culture, being and becoming. What is interpretation but the wishful reading of stars in an endless sky? A kind of astronomy. The world of the symbol is part of the history of the world, quietly.

For the reader, the silence of the blank page is joy, imagination, mental space; for the writer there is no more harassing silence than this abyss where one goes to arrest passing thought. The Sound that flowed opposite your house spread out like a blank page on which you would write, and nature erase.

"In the beginning was the word. . . . It is still the principle of our world, its law of gravitation."

"Sorrow-Acre"

Do you know how often in the stories you use that phrase, "law of gravitation"? This law is beyond physics, beyond time: it partakes of cosmic infinitude in its recognition of an all-encompassing order, that is, rightness of things. It was Nietzsche who said, "We have not gotten rid of God because we still believe in grammar." Writing reaches the state of exhaustion—when adjectives, smells, feelings are lost—in a Godless world. Yours was all flowing words and colors.

" 'I will make a covenant between me and you. I, I will not measure you out any more distress than you need to write your books. . . . But you are to write the books,' said the Lord. 'For it is I who want them written.' "

"The Young Man with the Carnation"

Sooner or later the reader gets trapped between the psychic biography of the author and the life of a character. That is criticism's law of gravitation.

"At the moment when my Almighty Father first created me by His word, He demanded and expected from me that I should one day return to Him and bring Him back His word, as speech. That is the one task alotted to me, to fulfill during my time and my course on earth. From His divine Logos—the creative force, the beginning—I shall work out my human mythos . . . this mythos of mind shall remain after me on earth."

"Converse at Night in Copenhagen"

A Swedenborgian twist in the relationship of the writer to the heavenly symbolism: speech (mythos) is the earthly reflection of God-the-Word (Logos). Today, the only mythos a writer can aspire to is celebrity or intertextuality.

"The performer stopped his speech upon the arrival of the distinguished spectators, and brought them two armchairs to sit in near the stage, in front of the audience. Then he took up the thread where he had interrupted it. . . . The play which was being acted was the immortal *Revenge of Truth*, the most charming of marionette comedies. Everybody will remember how the plot is created."

"The Roads Round Pisa"

Remarkably, you worked on this play from adolescence to old age. Like a thread that never stopped unraveling, it followed you from Denmark to Africa and back to Denmark. You give it as a present to favored characters in one of your stories.

"He never read a printed book, but had his authors of the day copied by hand in ultramarine and scarlet letters."

"The Deluge at Norderney"

Once you wrote, "I have always thought that one might be as severely judged on the Day of Judgment for having juxtaposed the wrong colors as for having borne false witness against one's neighbor." Beauty, wit, modernity—each was a color. Perhaps the dandy, ever the painter of modern life, is God's brilliant fool.

Who is happier, the person who lives without God, or your lady Helena, who spent so much of her life searching the world for a particular blue?

"I have behaved to my reader . . . as the Lord behaves to Job. I know, none so well, none so well as I, how the Lord needs Job as a public and cannot do without him. Yes, it is even doubtful whether the Lord be not more dependent upon Job than Job upon the Lord."

"A Consolatory Tale"

Job is to God as the writer is to the public. But is it not the public who continually revises the definition of God?

" 'In a hundred years your works will be read much less than today. They will collect dust on the shelves.'

'I do not much mind,' said Lord Byron.

'But one book,' said Pipistrello, 'will be rewritten and reread, and will each year in a new edition be set upon the shelf.'

'Which book is that?' Lord Byron asked.

'The Life of Lord Byron,' said Pipistrello."

"Second Meeting"

The last works of artists are always fascinating. You return to Italy, the land of myth, to contemplate your reputation after death. How telling, the geography of the imagination. You slipped on your worn Byron mask and traveled to Italy to set the stage for your thoughts: here was your wise puppeteer, Pipistrello. You were prophetic: there is great interest in you, a recent biography. A film based on your life. Lady of Fashion, do you know safari clothes are in this year?

If Dinesen sent her stories to God as if they were prayers, still she didn't want to deliver them herself. Instead, this woman of supremely elegant mind sought out Lucifer as her subversive spirit. Paradise was calm, orderly, self-satisfied—like Denmark. Lucifer had the eye of a critic, a connoisseur; he struggled in the search for truth. His critical eye would balance the perfect eye of God, the artist. When Dinesen had her fall from the garden—Ngong—she struck a Faustian bargain with the devil to live completely in art. "I cannot *possibly* write anything of the slightest interest without breaking away from the Paradise and hurtling down to my own Kingdom." All of her life would be turned into stories. The great events in Dinesen's life did not remain for long in the sphere of the human, but were given mythological license.

Her wit was devilish, arrogant, stylish. It swirled around a sense of humor extraordinarily philosophical in nature, in that it was the foundation of the way she was in the world. If it was a lightheartedness, that was so only in the sense of Nietzsche's gay science or Kierkegaard's irony, or Pirandello's *umorismo*. All of them played brilliantly with appearance and its opposite, with eros and irony. (In Hebrew *Isak* means "the one who laughs.") For Dinesen, humor was the mastery of a moment, a fearless capacity to make fun of anything; the sublime vision connected to existential freedom, absolute thought. With God on her side as source of the Word and Lucifer as in-house critic, how could she lose?

But this complex woman whose ideas of God encompassed Norse sagas (the Scandinavians were the last of the European peoples to be Christianized), the Lord of the Old Testament, Nemesis, and Lucifer had a painter's sense of perspective. She believed in the Day of Judgment, but in a very special sense. It was the Day when God would judge one's life as art. It was the ultimate critique.

Woman with Landscape

The people on the farm said it was "she who first of all sees the New Moon." Dinesen loved the moon in all its phases. Perhaps it was the moon's longing for fullness that enchanted her. She read the heavens like a great book. When she left Kenya, she wondered if the moon would throw a shadow in the shape of her body over the gravel drive of her lost home. "What business had I ever to set my heart on Africa?"

But if she loved the moon, it is water whose destiny one can trace in the stories, for water came to be their overriding elemental force. Marvelously, the moon and the sea unite in a symmetry of perspective—above and below—as the two most narcissistic images in nature: the mask and the mirror. The Dinesen landscape shimmers between their separate reflections. This attraction is a special law of gravitation in the writing.

The sea is not merely a decorative or entertaining setting where a story unfolds, but the very essence of the story. Water flows through the stories she wrote in Africa and those she wrote in Denmark. It is a special event when water imagery comes to dominate a writer's work. In Africa most of the time there was little rain. By her own admission, Dinesen wrote during periods of drought to keep her mind off the farm. But the waited-for rain came into the stories anyway, like a flash flood that suddenly appears in a place, out of sheer psychic conjuring, it would seem. Now in Denmark, Dinesen lived alongside water. Here it was an ever-present reminder of her own floating existence, the immeasurable desire that made her live in other times, in other places. The Sound opposite Rungstedlund appeared like a fluttering blank page, and in the worst of winters, more tauntingly, a sheet of ice. Of all the elements it was the sea around which Dinesen organized her anecdotes of destiny. The sea is, finally, art itself: surface, depth, illusion, infinity, chameleon beauty.

And yet, Dinesen—for herself—loved air most of nature's pleasures. She mixed water and air and art in one of her last, charming stories, "Tempests." An actress sailing to Norway to play Ariel on stage in *The Tempest* is caught in a storm at sea, where she confuses that storm with the storm in the play. The creator of this "tempest" is one Herr Soerensen, whose philosophy might well have been Dinesen's: much of what is unworthy in life could be avoided if people would speak in verse. (All writers know that language is the larger part of being.) Living halfway between the cities of Kierkegaard and Hamlet, how could she not think of what it meant to be? If Dinesen wrote her own diary of a seducer, she also wrote prose worthy of Shakespeare's reading. Few writers of English in her century can equal the complexity and poetic dimension of Dinesen's intellect, nor her breathtaking prose style. But if Dinesen had had to choose between Prospero and Ariel, Ariel would surely have been the beloved one. For Ariel is air, breath. And what is air but the voice—the spirit—of the universe, its speech. Air is the storyteller who circles the globe, the ceaselessly speaking voice that tells the history of the world to the world. Water is its echo. And in that wondrous lightness of being lived a woman who thought she had a talent to amuse.

Dinesen's attachment to nature was so humble, so noble, her pantheism was bound to unite with art as the essence of narrative. She never chose her landscapes as mere settings. Her sense of space was epistemological, philosophical, historical. Landscape reflected the style of a country, the way its people thought about themselves, lived and died. One can trace an ecology in the writing as a measure of the way she interpreted aesthetic distance. The places that shaped her imagination were Denmark, Italy, Africa, Persia. Denmark always represented nature; Italy was the home of sensibility; Africa moved in the world of the real, never the fictional; Persia alluded to disguise, storytelling. All of the writing attaches itself to a particular landscape, a way of life: in this way writing is transformed into a longing for travel.

The stories set in Jutland cast their even, devout tones across the flat countryside where Denmark's highest point is a modest hill of no more than six hundred feet. Here one finds in old churchyards runic stones that mark the exploits of a heroic Viking past; here and there are the castles and manor houses of Dinesen's lords and ladies—here she herself learned to detest the pietistic world of women and to envy the unasked-for freedom of men, here a Rosencrantz still lives at Rosenholm. Jutland is Danish history, the continuity of its people and customs and countryside. In Jutland the dark joy of Carl Dreyer and Isak Dinesen meet in the vast, clean loneliness of cornfields.

There was always a contrast between country life and its social perquisites and the gay abandon of the city, represented by Copenhagen. Here was the center of romance, intrigue, witty conversation, erotic life; when characters dress up as Pierrot and Arlecchino for an opera carnival, of course it takes place in Copenhagen. When a poet and a king exchange roles and talk about the three kinds of perfect happiness, it happens in Copenhagen. Here even the copper roofs of its old buildings have given themselves leave to wear green masks.

If one can imagine Dinesen strolling grandly through the old streets and squares and beside the fine canals of this wonderfully civilized city, watched over by the innocent sculpture of a little mermaid sitting in its eastern harbor, just as serenely can one picture her in the spring at the Deer Park looking at the hawthorns in bloom. She loved the linden blossoms that line the allées of palaces and country estates (even smell has its class distinctions). She loved peonies, which she tried to introduce into an Africa that rejected their cold temperament. Nature with its flowery eroticism was a world inside a world for Dinesen, as it was for Colette, entering the writing of these women in ornamental sentences. Dinesen knew that the nightingale returned to Denmark around the eighth of May. She gloried in the stars, the birds, the sea, the long summer northern light, when the Danish sky turns blue in the middle of the night, unable to withhold the gift of its color until morning. She was a woman of the world, in the most luxuriant sense of worldliness: her example tells why one cannot live a full life if it does not include nature.

If Denmark played in her imagination as a simple chain of beauty topped by its crowns of trees, Italy was the land of sensual thought, refinement, *commedia* pleasures. Dinesen couldn't help bringing herself personally into "The Roads Round Pisa" to compare Danish and Italian civilization:

> The youth rested his left arm on the table, and Augustus, looking at it, thought how plainly one must realize, in meeting people of this country, that they had been living in marble palaces and writing about philosophy while his own ancestors in the large forests had been making themselves weapons of stone and had dressed in the furs of the bears whose warm blood they drank. To form a hand and wrist like these, must surely take a thousand years, he reflected. In Denmark everybody has thick ankles and wrists, and the higher up you go, the thicker they are.

Denmark was nature, Italy culture.

Africa was something else altogether, beyond nature and culture. It was a land and a truth unto itself, beyond fiction. "When you know what things are really like, you can make no poems about them," explains a wise man in one of her tales. Time before time. Here when the natives on the farm would listen to Dinesen make up verses—they had no verse form in Swahili—they begged to hear more. "Speak like rain," they said; language was to them beloved water. That way of thinking about words became as natural to her as Kamante's manner of naming the food he cooked for her after one of the day's events, such as "the sauce of the lightning that struck the tree." In Africa words still retained their magical properties: they too were part of the landscape. In Africa Dinesen learned a new language of space, both personal and topographic, at the same time that she had revealed to her the vast poetic resources in a language whose adjectives were still tied to nature. This luxury only underdeveloped countries can afford.

To the Scandinavian, the European, the African, was added a fourth world, the Mohammedan. Dinesen often turned toward the East when she wanted to give a lesson in illusion. Two figures presided over this realm, her great storyteller Mira Jama and the Caliph Haroun of Baghdad, who would travel through his kingdom in disguise. *Tales from the Thousand and One Nights* was a book she read with the Bible and the Icelandic sagas, tales inside of tales. Together they would provide all the lessons about the performance of one's life. They would encompass cosmic time and fictional time, which filled her narrative lives.

Theatrical Moments

When it was clear at last that the baroness would have to give up the farm, and she spent the last days preparing to go home to Denmark, her Somali servant Farah began to dress more and more elaborately. He put on his best silk robes, his embroidered vests and bright turbans, his gold rings. In the great, bare paneled rooms, which acted now like sounding boards, echoing the stories that once had decorated them, Farah presided over the domain staked out by packing crates, which were, at the end, the only furniture.

That Farah costumed himself this way for her was a magnificent act, so knowledgeably theatrical and pure, a profound understanding of life in the authentic gesture. This act partook of an ethics of performance, that is, a self-consciousness of human action that was fantastical in its glorious, thoughtful presentness. A performance act that unfolded in the world of spirit more than spectacle, it was first ontological, then social. In this scene one can speak of performance values.

Farah became a sign by which human beings exalt their humanness. This is the deeper significance of performance in that it makes of one's life art, a symbol. Which is to say, both the thing itself and a representation of it. Dinesen, who loved a consciousness that was theatrical, would have understood this idea of the mask. It partook of a realness beyond dreams. Alas, sometimes the mask has a way of framing the more essential truths that play on the surface of things.

There are other times, of course, when truth lies in the collision of illusion and reality. The stories have that ability to move with finesse between the fictional and the real, as if either one were enough to justify existence. Characters are frequently called upon, as if being tested, to separate what is real and natural to them from what they are aware of enacting. That is the nature of the immortal story. They swing so easily toward the theatrical as a way to confront the world of illusion. And through playing with the nature of appearance, even assuming the disguise of someone else, characters gain knowledge of new dimensions of experience. Dissembling offers a great opportunity for self-knowledge, of selves beyond a limited one. "All people in the world ought to be, each of them, more than one. . . . Is it not strange that no philosopher has thought of this, and that I should hit upon it?" asks Pellegrina Leoni, the opera singer of so many lives, in so many tales. How disingenuous of her.

Dinesen herself played many roles. She was Karen, Tania, Tanne, the baroness, Osceola, Isak Dinesen, Pierre Andrezel, Scheherazade, to name a few. Sometimes the roles would require new languages: she and her sister Ellen as adults conversed in "Pirogets," their private childhood language. Sometimes the roles sought new masks: an older Dinesen would sign letters as Lord Byron to her long-time friend Ellen Wanscher's Lady Arabella. With the young poet Thorkild Bjornvig, who made his extraordinary pact with her and then, under her spell, moved into Rungstedlund, Dinesen would converse through the literary masks of letters, stories, and poems sent as missives from her end of the house to his. (One remarkable incident: Dinesen claimed that during World War II she began to dream of her African servants, an occurrence that was unusual, since she never dreamed of human beings. An occupied Denmark apparently induced the role reversal between master and servant in her dreambook.)

The concept of the mask was extended most curiously in the idea of the double, which lingered in Dinesen's life and work: in characters divided into opposite sides of the same person; in the many names by which she was known; in the double, even multiple lives and disguises of characters; in the patterned, reflecting stories inside of stories; in the glass, the sea, the mirror imagery. One extraordinary irony is that she married Bror Blixen, the double—the twin brother, that is—of Hans Blixen, who was really the one she loved.

The psychic and actual doubling she played with was another measure of her feeling for abstraction and critical perspective and, not least, theatricality. Doubling made identity a question of form. A self could view (it)self as subject and object, from the first or the third person. This device allowed the possibility to experience oneself at various times as an event, a stylized self, a social type, and, more gloriously, a mythology. It was simply another kind of aesthetic distance—comedic, dialectical, philosophical—that could turn one into art.

The crisis of identity taken to aesthetic extremes must sooner or later confront the philosophy of the mask and, in turn, the marionette, for they are what make a life ironically lived. It was not the deception of the mask that defined Dinesen's attraction to it, but the aloofness. The mask served her as mediator of destiny. Naturally, she believed God thought so too. In the life he led in her stories, the aristocratic spirit of comedy dominated human affairs. As the eccentric Miss Malin explains, "Truth is for tailors and shoemakers. . . . I, on the contrary, have always held that the Lord has a penchant for masquerades." The Day of Judgment was, of course, the day when God would let his mask fall. He was Arbiter in life's great show of puppets.

Dinesen used kohl on her eyelids and white powder on her face. She deliberately made herself masklike, as if she were a character in a drama. Even her speech style was theatrical in an archaic way, as it recalled "old Copenhagen" of generations ago in the long, drawn-out performances of the vowels. In later years the effects of illness joined with her aesthetics to give her face the sculptural quality of a mask, like a fine chiseled stone one might read. And when Dinesen slipped on her Pierrot costume, she entered into the world of two formidable symbolist lovers: the mask and the moon. If Dinesen reveled in the *commedia* spirit of modernism, she also partook of the natural fantasy life of a country that produced Hans Christian Andersen and the pantomime theaters of Tivoli and where even the socialists love the monarchy, history's oldest.

For her the theatrical became a way of life and thought in a cherished, existential sense. She carried her roles, and those of her characters, to archetypal heights that resounded in biblical themes, in ancient sagas, in art, in myth. "A group of my young friends has determined that I am three thousand years old," she proclaimed. Dinesen imagined that her life extended from a history that preceded the written word, a history founded in speech.

Toward the end of her life, when she was preparing an English translation of the one text she worked on all her life, *The Revenge of Truth*, a marionette comedy that reverses the logic of the universe, she wrote in the stage direction where the witch appears: "Amiane, in costume and mask as like Isak Dinesen as possible." In her first book this play entered one of the stories. Now she entered the play. Marvelously, she had herself become a character, but in a drama whose truths become lies, and illusion reality. There was no longer any separation between the life and the art.

In the beginning was the Word. If the Word was made flesh, it would show itself in the body of writing that is the body of the writer, its double. By the time of her death, in 1962, Isak Dinesen, who at seventy-seven already had lived longer than even pain expects of one, was subsisting on oysters, grapes, champagne. This diet light as air virtually transformed her into pure spirit. Perhaps it was the food of gods in an affluent age.

She had a farm in Africa . . .

(1988)

The Virtual Theater of Herbert Blau

Thirty years ago Herbert Blau wrote *The Impossible Theater* to talk up a revolution, setting his provocative analysis against the background of American theater in the cold war era and the psychic problematic of the search for identity then. His vision was attached to the modernist dream of uniting socialism and surrealism. In the years since its publication, domestic and global cultural politics have conspired to make the body politic as much a part of Blau's latest thinking as at the beginning of his career. If his attention to performance settled formerly on the suggestive metaphor of the Iron Curtain, now the shift is to the more transparent scene of contemporary culture.

In our postutopian age Blau has relinquished his vision of a decentralized popular theater culture capable of spawning a new civic culture in which theater is a validation of public life; or, in Hannah Arendt's way of thinking, theatergoing as a form of citizenship. An engaged life in the theater is now largely an impossible American dream, but over a period of four decades Blau tried as much as anyone in the country to join aesthetics to politics in the gesture of political commitment. Blau (and Jules Irving) started the Actor's Workshop in San Francisco in 1952, then moved on together a dozen years later to head the Vivian Beaumont at Lincoln Center. When, after only a few short seasons, that artistic directorship was no longer tenable, Blau became involved in founding the controversial California Institute of the Arts as provost and dean of the School of Theatre. By 1971 he had departed, this time for Oberlin College, where he organized his own theater collective, KRAKEN. In the last decade Blau, who teaches at the University of Wisconsin—Milwaukee, has turned his redoubtable intellectual energy more and more to writing on theater, consumed by the same issues that informed his earlier practical work. The cumulative effect of his several books is to outline an ontology of theater.

In his new book, *To All Appearances: Ideology and Performance*, Blau links the two subjects conceptually as bodies of knowledge, implicated especially in the elaboration of illusion, and what contemporary thinkers like to call the "imaginary." His attention is drawn to that transcendent moment in which theater, or any other practice, changes, as ideology itself does, into something other than what it appeared to be. Both ideology and performance, dependent as they are on disguise and yet committed to demystification, affirm the difficulty in resolving theory and praxis. It is this theater of illusion, or what Engels called "false consciousness," that Blau addresses, admittedly having rethought and rewritten much of his book after the collapse of the communist world.

But aside from the acknowledgment of Brecht as initiator of the discourse on ideology in performance and references to Meyerhold's new technology of the body or an occasional mention of the Berlin Wall, Blau doesn't really concern himself with the social experiments of Eastern Europe or the (former) Soviet Union. Even the writings on politics and theater by the playwright-statesman Václav Havel don't figure much in his book beyond their quotation. The topography of his thematics is French. Likewise, if Blau was influenced by Marxism, with its theatrical notion of "phantoms in the brain," the theorizing of Derrida, Deleuze, Guattari, Lacan, and Foucault have more prominently laid the foundation for the poststructuralist understanding of what he defines as the phantasmaphysics of postmodern performance, its "epidermic play of perversity" having turned the body itself into a theater, and society into spectacle. Though he has been deeply influenced by French schizoanalysis, Blau is more Freudian than Lacanian, and I doubt if he would truly prefer one of Deleuze and Guattari's cherished rhizomes to a taproot of the classics. What he has joined to an abiding infatuation with the performing body, now considered in light of its inscriptions of ideology and power, is a belief in the unconscious as the originary mise-enscène. In a larger sense, Blau is interested in the relationship of repression and acting out and the drama's heritage of paranoia, in addition to its recurring taboo of watching. From this psychological vantage point there is no difficulty in agreeing with Blau that theater has an uneasy accommodation with appearance, and so do audiences.

A certain part of Blau revels in an antiscopic, antitheatrical mentality, the latter bias having more problematic ramifications in contemporary performance than Duchamp's anti-retinal stance could effect in the visual arts. Perhaps that is why Blau can so assuredly define the audience, in his recent book of the same name, as a "body of thought and desire," in his view a figure of speech articulating for itself the relation between seeing and understanding, which is central to Western metaphysics. "The audience is what *happens* when, performing the signs and passwords of a play, something postulates itself and unfolds in response," he writes. The palpable reality of the stage gives way to Blau's virtual theater in the mind, the thing seen disappearing before consciousness. The audience itself acts as a subversive presence, constructing its own dialectic out of subjectivity and the historical process. In the early history of modernism, Duchamp had already acknowledged the spectator's completion of the work of art.

If Blau is attracted to the opacity of experience, he is never one to pass up a slippery signifier. His writing uncoils in extended cerebration, not on the thing itself but on the way it affects him. Like Henry James, whose sentences are elaborate wanderings of thought, or Gertrude Stein, whose theater amplifies the same technique of deferral, Blau seems to welcome the denial of the appearance of a subject in favor of its mere allusion or coding. He concedes "a rather high modernist disposition to difficulty and even obscurity." Even his admirers don't disagree.

The circularity of Blau's thought generates a playful style in which he will argue numerous positions, refusing any single focal point or centeredness. He uses the rhetoric of Marxism, postmodernism, and feminism, all the while declaring that he is neither a Marxist nor a postmodernist nor a feminist, only a subverter of ideologies. Nor does he wish to be considered a critic, but that stance is understandable, since his writings can be more expansively considered philosophical meditations. Blau is a lapsed modernist at heart.

In some sense he is a master of cross-dressing. Even as his essays draw into their frame of reference and intricate circuitry all manner of people and places—a single page might include mention of Barthes, Brecht,

Wilson, Bunraku, Müller, Aragon, Glass, Paris, and the new Germany in a veritable planetization of critical writing—Blau himself refuses to be framed, or to be known. All his appropriation of isms and their sub-version are like so many acoustic masks. At times the obsessive inclu-sivity tends to equalize all art and artists without offering a clear enough sense of which work or artist is more important than another, though, to be fair, more often than not he is outspoken in his judgments. The "threshold" of experience, to which he refers over and over again, is the time when an event becomes something other than what it had been, a liminal state that emphasizes his own slippage. Perhaps it is this mo-ment Heidegger describes as the moment when "reflection transports the man of the future into that 'between' in which he belongs to Being and yet remains a stranger amid that which is." There is something rab-binical in Blau's relentless, global heuristic drive, his reverence for the Word, his absolute focus on identity. Surely, for the theater world he is a model of the critic as wandering Jew.

Brecht has always been one of Blau's guides. The Actor's Work-shop helped introduce his work and that of Pirandello, Genet, Beckett, Pinter, and others to the provincial American theater culture of the fifties and sixties. Notwithstanding, it is remarkable to discover a Brecht-ian dramaturgy at work in Blau's recent stagings of himself. As his writ-ing demonstrates, Blau does not inhabit any single point of view but acts as if he were an observer of a given ideological position. His strategy unfolds as *Gestus*: writing conscious of itself as performance, and his-toricized consciousness. Moreover, the Brecht-Diderot Enlightenment project is at the heart of Blau's deeply philosophical theatrical think-ing, however much an attack on the Enlightenment informs the French theories that delight him. Their abstract, sociolinguistic orientation is inadequate when tested by the body in real time and space. The very nature of dramatic literature and theatrical performance demands that they play out their own theory/praxis dialectic. The word *theatron* de-rives from theory, and Aristotle placed theater between philosophy and history. Brecht's own contribution to the empathy/estrangement issue is theater history's best example of ideology deliberately interacting with performance, even being defeated by it, and demystified. When all is said and done, one lives a life, not a theory, even as an actor. The act-ing out of ideology and psychology in the social body of each performer creates theater's profound cultural significance. Try as he might, Brecht could not free his own theater of its psychological impact, which was often at odds with his ideological intentions.

If Brecht's science now appears outdated, Blau, who was trained as a chemical engineer, is more tuned to contemporary thinking in the sciences, drawing frequently upon catastrophe and chaos theory, plate tectonics, and biology for his metaphors. In an all too brief passage in *To All Appearances*, he notes in passing that at the time of the Revolution the study of ideology was first considered by some French thinkers as a branch of zoology. Given the attention to the biological in his book and the return of this subject to contemporary discourse, Blau might have gone on to explore the linkage of ideology and zoology by Destutt de Tracy, who, at the end of the eighteenth century, attempted to enlarge upon the sensationalist approach to knowledge. In recent years the empirical body has become central to the idea of performance, as issues of race, gender, class, and spectatorship have replaced aesthetic ones, and solo performance especially is regarded as a form of social activism. Blau ignores the opportunity to address the implications for the study of performance and audience reception of joining ideology and the natural sciences, even though he himself characterizes ideology as "a body of thought to which we give our bodies."

To pursue this theme one step further, it may be important to point out that Gregory Bateson has called epistemology a branch of natural history, urging that the life process be viewed in a systemic context. He speculates further that the ecology of ideas (thoughts, perceptions of self, affects) might be synonymous with aesthetic sensibility. Through my own attempts to develop an "ecology of theater" I have come to believe that the nature-culture antinomy can be set in a new frame by thinking of performance as a life science and linking science and art in any study of it. Performance then is understood as an epistemology, and ideology as an ecology. In recent decades no artist has more profoundly united ideology, ecology, and performance than Joseph Beuys, in his utopian conception of the social organism as a work of art and the shaping of society itself as Social Sculpture.

Since the drama of knowing and perceiving is the organizing principle of Blau's theatrical consciousness, more urgently as each book appears, it is not surprising that so much of *To All Appearances* centers on the notion of the body as epistemological site. In the essay entitled (after Sartre) "The Surpassing Body," which is the heart of the book, Blau writes with passion and eloquence of the body and performance, bringing together physiology, psychology, and technology. His far-ranging reflections encompass numerous subjects: the feminist body, the AIDS body, body politics, the Jewish body, cyborgs, the historical body, language as body. Today especially, the critique of theater, which is a critique of representation, has forced what Blau calls a "postmodern Platonism." Much contemporary performance (and critical theory) cannot decide whether the body is really there or merely a signifier. The issue of performance is finally an ontological one.

But Blau can go only so far with the "desiring machines" of the postmodern body or with the current infatuation, inspired by the French, for Artaud's "body without organs" before admitting to a preference for the *essential* body. For this humanist at heart the body is still a center of enlightenment whose timeless subject is appearance. The body may be an ideological home, but it is a living, breathing organism that he chooses over its supposed function as a sign, likewise preferring the biological system to the linguistic system. Around the body Blau constructs a history of ideas that outlines new ways of looking at performance. In one provocative passage he juxtaposes the violent body art of the avant-garde and the ancient theater of the Greeks, suggesting that the discourse of violence might begin with Prometheus. Elsewhere he criticizes the retrograde quality in the dramaturgy of much performance art when compared with sections of Pinter and Beckett that seem models of solo performance. Insights like these can inspire theatrical form itself, having as they do much larger potential than mere commentary. They also offer a subversive, healthy corrective to the more extravagant claims of the avant-garde, which ignore the achievement of the theatrical past. One of Blau's most valuable contributions has been to reread and rethink the classics and theatrical canon in relation to contemporary practice and to avoid dismissing drama in favor of performance, which contemporary thinking exalts. Today painting is frequently subjected to the same dismissal for its emphasis on the private relationship between the spectator and the work of art, while the more public interventions of installations, body art, and video are encouraged. Postmodernists and political correctionists have their own hierarchies.

Though Blau himself is interested in systems—his writing is a kind of systems analysis—in *To All Appearances* he proves that in profound ways he himself is a philosopher without a system. That is why even though he shows much sympathy for the Continental effusions in critical discourse, he has no compunction in upholding the necessity of the theatrical canon or in pointing out that realism, now fashionably in disgrace as a "reactionary" form, evolved as critique. Nor does he avoid taking up the subject of emotion within his heavily materialist approach. In an earlier book, *The Eye of Prey*, Blau, who volunteers his dubious belief in the valorization of *communitas* in the theatrical experience, wrote of his preference for the solitary quality of the performer, his or her "essential aloneness." Nonetheless, he quite rightly links the much vaunted Method acting that dominates theater and film to the contemporary culture of narcissism. If he celebrates the contemplative life of the spectator, Blau offers no apologies for disregarding the presumed benefits of audience participation. In this disdain for blurring the boundaries of spectacle and audience, he parts company with one of the tenets of postmodernism. A central issue for Blau, which he identifies as struggling through the profusion of cries for liberation, is the return of the repressed in contemporary theory and practice. Anyone tracing the interplay of the American sixties and contemporary French culture quickly discovers that Norman O. Brown has been repositioned on the thousand plateaus of Deleuze and Guattari and reinvested in Baudrillard's libidinal economy. But how far can the body go in its gratification of desire? Into what political space? Blau wonders. Ultimately, for his ethos of performance, of the artists who have most completely (and oppositely) provided the philosophical theatrical options of the twentieth century he chooses Brecht rather than Artaud, the social text over the defeat of language.

Blau regards ideological struggle as that over the future of illusion. In this context he chides Foucault for missing in his writings the sense of illusion upholding power. For his own worldview he prefers Gramsci's "organic ideology," with its traces of prior systems of thought and recognition of the place of illusions, or Althusser's description of the problem of self-deceit in spontaneously lived ideology. Enormous political transformations of the last few years highlight the important question before contemporary society: What shape will illusion take now that certain utopias of the twentieth century have been discredited? Blau doesn't address it with any sense of prediction; rather he declares that ideas should be subject to a statute of limitations. Theater, a form whose very aim is to imagine new worlds, has deeply utopian tendencies, which is why it plays such a significant role in totalitarian societies. No wonder theater, in the broadest cultural sense, has become *the* political/art form of the century, increasingly as private worlds are played out in public space.

There are times when the scent of elegant thought sweeps ravishingly across the pages of Blau's writings. At other times too willingly it is overwhelmed by his weighty, curtained prose. He shifts constantly between the positions of ironist and moralist, a man who chooses to present himself as the hemorrhaging image in the mirror, cloaked in the motley fashions of contemporary discourse. Is it that the good life is now simply the theoretical life?

In this book whose subject is ideology, Blau shows the real blind spot of the left in focusing its energies on "late bourgeois capitalism," while ignoring the corruption of illusion that drives totalitarian societies. If, as he asserts, performance is the "delirious symptom of the postmodern condition," the indiscriminate possibilities it offers for both liberation and oppression in the construction of social roles, depending on political conditions, should be acknowledged. Foucault has left us his magnificent obsessions on the power discourse of the West, but the postcommunist world has only begun to deconstruct the power virus that created a fourth wall in front of the scenes played in its societies.

Certainly, there are wise words in Blau when he speaks of the actor's power, more phenomenology than ideology, in the final analysis. Nowhere is he more lyrical than at the end of the chapter "The Struggle to Appear." Here, in what amounts to a little parable, Blau describes the awesome ghosting effect the theater has on him as he confronts the wisdom of the actor: that residue of light, what the actor knows without realizing it and no one else does. This is one of the threshold moments of the unconscious that turn experience into something transformative and mysterious. It is Blau's sublime.

The subtle ruminations that grace the pages of *To All Appearances* only serve to bring an almost sad quality to the experience of reading it. How else is one to contemplate that an intellectual such as Blau could have headed Lincoln Center as recently as 1965–67? That is inconceivable now, in the mediocre theater culture that is spreading across America like Wal-Mart. The marginality of theater in American intellectual life is compounded by the fact that important contemporary works and the writings of theater intellectuals are not better known in literary circles. Nor is the literary world's knowledge of contemporary dramaturgy or performance issues very sophisticated in matters of form, having ended for the most part with Miller or Williams or perhaps Albee, for a very small few with Sam Shepard or David Mamet. The work of Robert Wilson is virtually unknown to the literary intelligentsia, the exact inverse of his reputation in Europe. Here fiction is at the center of intellectual life, and even when widely admired novelists such as Thomas Bernhard or Marguerite Yourcenar or Milan Kundera or Max Frisch have had their dramatic works published, they were not individually written about. In his *New York Intellect* Thomas Bender remarks on the schism between literary intellectuals and the visual and performing arts. It will be interesting to see what attention is given to the recent publication of the first play [*Alice in Bed*] by Susan Sontag, who, it should be noted, is one of the few intellectuals in this country whose writings over the years reflect serious interest in theater, opera, film, and painting, in addition to literature. Finally, nearly all the general theoretical books, uncovering whatever new *ist* conspiracy, ignore theatrical performance even as they applaud the performance gesture in every realm of culture, all over the globe. Indeed, at the end of the twentieth century it is clear that the idea of theatricality is inseparable from an understanding of modernity, their collusion acting as its organizing principle.

Blau himself seems to have exhausted his subject. His essays are exploding out of their frame, now bracketed into titled sections on specific themes. Where these fractal essays will lead is difficult to predict, except to believe that Blau will continue to appear as a pristine consciousness mapping performance at its transformation into culture.

(1994)

Originally published as a review of Herbert Blau's *To All Appearances: Ideology and Performance*.

Acts of Criticism

IIIIIIII   I am sorry the first recipient of the George Jean Nathan Award, Harold Clurman, who was one of my teachers, isn't here tonight. If wherever he is there's a St. Mark's Bookshop and he is looking through my book, he might be amused to find how much my work has changed from a dozen years ago, when he told me it wasn't personal enough. Then I mistakenly believed that criticism was an objective form, whereas now I see that it is the most subjective kind of writing. Perhaps he is looking kindly on me, remembering his own fervent years. Though I never had the opportunity to study with either of them, first as a reader, then as a publisher I have come to know Eric Bentley and Stanley Kauffmann. I have always valued their commitment to a life in the theater, and I hope my own will have such generous proportions.

When I first learned that I was to receive this award, I naturally went to my drama shelves to see which of Nathan's books were there. I immediately put my hand on his book with a Latin title, *Materia Critica*. It is ironic because at the end of the sixties I was in college preparing for a career as a Latin teacher.

I thought that since today is April 15, I might speak of the taxonomy of criticism and in particular what it is I think I'm doing and why I'm doing it. One of the reasons I do what I do, that is, write, is that it is all I have ever done or wanted to do as a way of being in the theater. I think of it less and less as criticism and more and more as, simply, writing, and perhaps that is why I called my book *Theatrewritings*. In the Anglo-Saxon tradition there is too much distinction between what is called

286

criticism and what is called writing. I look forward to seeing those borders abolished in a new cosmopolitanism of the pen. With the same
stroke, I look forward to seeing advances in the social sciences incorporated into the humanities for a richer, more pluralistic account of the
contemporary world and all of its artifacts. Anthropology and literary
criticism are beginning to have the same texture of desire.

What is wonderful about writing is its ability to reimagine worlds
in endless possibilities, and what is more remarkable, even dangerous, about theater is its ability to demonstrate the potentiality of future
worlds in their very possibility of being acted by human beings living
now. Increasingly, what intrigues me is to read the future in works of
the past and to read the past in works of the present—simply, to find
a way to make writing live in historical and aesthetic time. In Edward
Said's graceful phrasing the world, the text, and the critic form an in-
eluctable trilogy that shapes being in the state of writing. That state also
has a politics that is, finally, a matter of taste.

The question before us now is not so much how to make a living in
the theater, but how to make a life in the theater. Where does theater,
with its obvious identity crisis, fit in the culture at this time of crisis in
contemporary life? Even more to the point, what will theater do now
that life itself is experienced more and more according to a theatrical
paradigm? What is it that will make being in the theater important to
us today?

I just returned last month from ten weeks of teaching at the University of California in San Diego. During that time I lived near the
Pacific Ocean and spent many hours walking along the beach, thinking about these questions. The ocean in front of me was like an endless
blank page that my thoughts could never fill up. Consequently, all the
writing that I did in this period was in invisible ink. I was only writing
in the landscape. Italo Calvino once wrote, "There is no better place to
keep a secret than in an unfinished novel." I believe the same can be
said of the essay.

Among the ecologies of theater, I began to think of the promise of
culture as horticulture and myself as a naturalist, so to speak. Theater
appeared as an endangered species. This way of thinking seemed to me
to point to an all-encompassing humanism that would embrace biological, social, ecological, and political issues in the study of an art form

in relation to its environment, its culture, in other words, its livingness. In this context, critical writing is not merely an activity but a way of life, an attitude toward living. It is the same verb, *to cultivate*, that gives definition both to cultivation of the land and of the human body. And sometimes in history knowledge grows on trees.

It is the promise of worldliness that makes writing so powerful a way of being. I love the idea of "worldliness." That is what attracts me to beloved writers such as Anton Chekhov, Marguerite Yourcenar, and Hannah Arendt. In fact, it was Arendt who wrote, "Art works clearly are superior to all other things; since they stay longer in the world than anything else, they are the worldliest of things." I used this sentiment as the inscription for my book. Each of these exquisite writers honors the world in all its objecthood, in all that space and time between its past and its futureness. In their deep and abiding humanism they love the thingness of the world, in all its incomprehensible splendor. At times I feel that they exist to help me understand how to live in the world and how to live the life of the world, and perhaps how to write it, or to know it cannot be written.

To live life fully is to live it as an act of criticism. Writing is thinking and thought is language, and to choose words is to imagine worlds. One reason to live is to have the luxury to know writing. If all this is beginning to sound a bit mystical, perhaps there is something to that. It was Nietzsche who said, "We have not gotten rid of God because we still believe in grammar."

The language of the stage is only one of the many kinds of writing. There is so much work to be done in the field of theater writing, especially in these glorious days when scholarship at its best is so open to what Bakhtin brilliantly articulated as "the dialogic imagination." Very early on he discovered that there were languages within languages, worlds within words. Later it was Roland Barthes who seduced us with the pleasure of the text. These are good days for criticism and for theater, as intellectual pursuits. If once all the arts were said to aspire to music, now it seems that art—and psychoanalysis and politics and sociology and literary theory, not to mention painting and dance—have been drawn to the notion of the theatrical as a way of understanding human activity.

Of all new languages it is the theatrical vocabulary that has most revitalized American scholarship in the last two decades. But too few theater people have contributed to the grammar of this startling event. Those of us who write should write more often, and more fervently. Not only for ourselves but also to leave new species of writing for those who come after us. Writers are a little like gardeners. They are drawn to the activity of hybridization as a way of generating new forms. They are cultivators of their own and other people's backyards.

Just as we here tonight have fed on the good books of our time, perhaps future generations will be as fortunate to discover the pleasures of worldliness in simple acts of language.

(1985)

Speech delivered on the occasion of receiving the 1983–84 George Jean Nathan Award for Dramatic Criticism for *Theatrewritings*, April 1985.

Library of Congress Cataloging-in-Publication Data

Marranca, Bonnie.
Ecologies of theater : essays at the Century Turning / Bonnie Marranca.
    p.   cm. — (PAJ books)
Essays previously published in various magazines except a few selections.
    ISBN 0-8018-5272-2 (acid-free paper). — ISBN 0-8018-5273-0 (pbk. :
acid-free paper)
    1. Drama — 20th century — History and criticism.   2. Theater.   I. Title.
II. Series.
PN1861.M36   1996
809.2'04 — dc20   95-38937